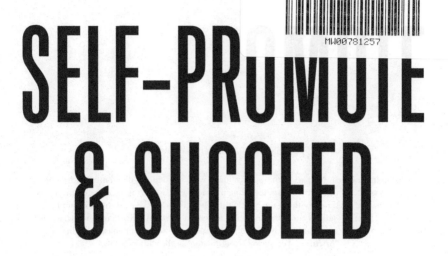

SELF-PRoMUTE
& SUCCEED

Stick Horse Publishing
10845 Griffith Peak Dr. #2
Las Vegas, NV 89135

ISBN: 978-1-7360315-1-3
ISBN: 978-1-7360315-2-0
ISBN: 978-1-7360315-3-7

Ordering Information:
Special discounts are available on quantity purchases by corporations, associations, and others. For details, visit juliebroad.com, email team@booklaunchers.com, or call 1-877-207-7666 x1.

SELF-PROMOTE & SUCCEED

& SUCCEED

The 'No Boring Books' Way to Build Your Brand, Attract Your Audience, and Market Your Non-Fiction Book

JULIE BROAD

THANK YOU FOR READING THIS BOOK!

Marketing a book is a journey, not a destination. As with any journey, it can be a lot more fun and rewarding when you have a map, the right tools, and the right people around you!

To support your book marketing journey, we've put together a special resource page for you at https://selfpromoteandsucceed.com

You'll find email templates to help in your book promotion outreach, sample launch calendars, the launch strategy menu (in detail), videos to support your marketing, and more.

And, if you'd like to have a team to surround you and support you in your journey, we have courses as well as hands-on services to help you. Visit www.booklaunchers.com to learn more or send us an email at team@booklaunchers.com.

Thank you,
Julie & the Book Launchers team

CONTENTS

A PEEK BENEATH THE COVER OF BOOK MARKETING

MANY GOOD BOOKS DON'T SELL.

This isn't meant to discourage you. It's meant to inform and motivate you.

Writing a book is a wonderful accomplishment, but it's not the finish line. It's really where the work begins.

Publishers know this. For them, a book's success is clearly defined, and it's about making money from each book. Because of this, they strategically plan to make money from every book they publish, and that plan begins well before the book is complete.

When most authors choose to self-publish, money would be nice, but there are often other objectives in play, like brand recognition and business growth. What happens then is that the author often writes the book and *then* figures out how to market and sell it.

In other words, everything that should have been done to set the book up for better sales and marketing hasn't been done. Maybe the author has written a good book, but unless they are lucky, it's not positioned to attract readers. And once the book is on the market, there's a limited number of things you can do to improve the book's positioning and sales.

An even bigger issue for many nonfiction authors is that book sales are one metric of success, and often the easiest to measure, but they are not the true objective. The power of publishing a book is that it can lead to something much grander and more lucrative than book sales. For you, that may be achieving:

- audience impact,
- differentiation from competitors,
- increased personal-brand value,
- lead generation,
- thought leadership,
- paid speaking engagements,
- workshop or course sales, and so much more.

These goals must be carefully considered at every stage in the process of researching, writing, editing, designing, and distributing a book so that you're set up for success.

Self-Publish and Succeed: The #NoBoringBooks Way to Write a Non-Fiction Book that Sells addresses a lot of the early-stage requirements to plan and write a book that will achieve your goals and get copies into readers' hands, but it didn't dive into the strategic decisions and tactical moves you need to make once you are involved in book marketing.[1] That's what's in store for you in the pages ahead.

---

1 Julie Broad, *Self-Publish and Succeed: The #NoBoringBooks Way to Write a Non-Fiction Book That Sells* (Los Angeles: Stick Horse Publishing, 2021).

This isn't about how to send mass press releases or print stylish bookmarks to attract an audience. It's also not all about how to use AI to succeed as an author, although AI has quickly become a wonderful way to shortcut some of the research and content creation you'll want to do. What you're about to uncover are high-level marketing strategies to plan your own book launch.

You'll also receive expert guidance on the tactical execution of those strategies, along with some innovative ideas, because book marketing is one part tried-and-true methods and one part experimentation to find what will work for you, your book, and your audience.

There are no guarantees when it comes to book marketing, and looking for them sets you up for scams and disappointment. I don't want that to happen to you! I've witnessed too many companies publish books without proper editing or make big promises, like guaranteeing bestseller status or fake awards. It makes them money, but it's a major disservice to their authors.

After self-publishing three of my own books (now four!), including a title that hit #1 on Amazon overall for print books, winning 15 different awards for my books, and helping more than 400 other authors write, publish, and promote their nonfiction books with my company, Book Launchers, I've learned an incredible amount about the hidden pitfalls, as well as where the greatest opportunities lie.

Book marketing is full of rewards and fun—but only if you have the right mindset, strategy, and tactics. By the end of the book, you will have all that and a little more.

If you ever have questions, head to **https://selfpromoteandsucceed.com** and download the bonuses we have for you to supplement this book. You can also find my contact information so you can reach out. Feel free to say hello by posting comments on any of my videos at www.booklaunchers. tv—I promise I always read and respond.

CHAPTER 1

BOOK MARKETING DOESN'T SELL BOOKS—SO WHY DOES IT MATTER?

YOU WANT YOUR BOOK TO BE A BESTSELLER, RIGHT?

Now, what "bestseller" means to you might be different from the next author. For some, it's getting that little orange flag from Amazon. For others, only major bestseller lists like the *New York Times* or *Wall Street Journal* will do.

Regardless, the path to success is the same. Topping a list requires connecting to an established audience of eager readers or exciting a new audience enough to buy your book.

If you can do that, you're going to sell books. And if you can get enough people to act and make their purchases on the same day or during the same week, you're going to top lists. It's that simple—and that difficult.

My first book, *More than Cashflow*, topped Amazon charts for print books because of my newsletter list and the lists of a few key influencers who simultaneously promoted my book.[2] Together, we sold roughly 3,500 books in a three-day period on Amazon.ca. The book continued to sell well past that period and stayed in the top 100 print books for 45 days. I'll share exactly how I did it later, but the majority of those sales were due to newsletter lists (mine and those of influencers).

Beyond how to become a bestseller, the bigger question you need to ask yourself is, "Do I need to be a bestseller?" Be aware that there are a lot of people in the book publishing and marketing business ready to make a lot of money from your *not* asking yourself that question.

When you honestly ask yourself how much your book needs to be a bestseller for you to achieve your goals, you'll realize you're better off spending $5,000 on proven marketing methods to cultivate long-term success than using a gimmick to get a bestseller flag from Amazon. Book marketing isn't overnight magic. It's planting seeds today that you can fertilize, water, and watch grow over months and years.

But we're not there yet. First, we need to cover what is actually going to sell books—and what isn't. Then we have to talk about the fact that book sales may not be the most important target for you as an author.

Sales and Marketing Are Not the Same Thing

For a successful book launch and long-term gains, you need both. And for your mental sanity, you also need to understand the results that are reasonable to expect from your efforts.

Marketing is about strategy. It's about creating awareness. You need marketing, especially if your ultimate goal is to become an industry thought leader, grow your brand, and build your business. Book sales are a metric that can help you understand how well your marketing (and advertising,

---

2   Julie Broad, *More than Cashflow: The Real Risks & Rewards of Profitable Real Estate Investing* (Los Angeles: Stick Horse Publishing, 2013).

publicity, and promotion) works. However, they do not help you accurately understand what is effective in helping you achieve your bigger goals.

Marketing is eyeballs (and hopefully, attention) on you and your book, while sales are credit cards and contact information.

Now you might think, "Okay, I want book sales, and book marketing will get me those book sales." That is true … sort of.

It is true that the more marketing you do, the more sales you *should* see. However, the correlation isn't that simple.

Let's take PR as an example. If you have an earned media feature (what it's called when you haven't paid for an interview or appearance) on a popular outlet like TechCrunch or *Good Morning America*, you may or may not wind up selling that many books.

However, you likely will have gained some exposure and credibility as an expert in your space.

If you leverage this wisely (and I'll show you how), you can often gain other opportunities, build your brand even more, and increase the size of your platform. That's when you'll start to see a difference and sell more books.

What You Measure Matters Most

Many authors long for that major media appearance. It looks and feels so good to say you were featured on a national show, whether you post it on social media or include it in your bio (or both). But it may not necessarily lead to book sales. Does that matter? Maybe, maybe not. It depends on your goals.

A friend once introduced me to an author to see if I could help market his book. It had been out for four years, and he'd sold 12,000 copies, mostly at speaking engagements. Those are pretty good results for a first-time author, but he was disappointed. He made money because the book was built into his contract and increased his fees for speaking engagements, but he didn't receive more bookings, which was his primary goal.

That told me that all the marketing in the world wasn't going to help. Instead, he had a positioning issue with his book in terms of what companies would hire him to speak about. If you've sold 12,000 copies without a larger tangible payoff, there's a disconnect somewhere.

You see, book sales are great, but they aren't everything.

It's essential to measure and monitor other factors besides sales to understand whether a book works for the bigger-picture plans and goals that drove you to become an author. You could look at:

- book reviews (number, overall ratings, prestige of the review source),
- bulk-sale inquiries,
- leads generated from your book that result in new clients or product sales,
- opt-ins to your email newsletter,
- speaking engagements,
- unexpected opportunities (invitations to discuss partnership opportunities, awards for achievements or other recognition),
- website traffic, or
- your rates for consulting, speaking, and services.

Most authors measure book sales against an arbitrary number and feel disappointed if they don't meet it. Before you set out on this marketing journey, figure out what is most important to you. In other words, what is the best way to measure your book's success against your ultimate target? When you know that, you can focus on what will get the results most important to you.

Self-Publish and Succeed hasn't even sold half the copies that *More than Cashflow* did in the same period. But I still believe it's a success because:

- A speaking engagement in front of my ideal client group for Book Launchers landed in my lap as a direct result of an event organizer getting a copy of the book.

- Additionally, it's led to forums, panels, awards judging, and many other event invites, including being a featured expert workshop speaker at the American Library Association's national learning event. During that talk I was able to feature a bunch of our authors and promote self-published books as credible and worthy of librarians' attention.

- When we turned marketing off for Book Launchers for four months due to a company restructuring, my organized content on BookLaunchers.tv generated new authors, but the consistent sources of new authors for us were referrals and people who had read the book. Often, they were the same! You see, it is much easier for a friend to refer someone to a book resource than to a company sometimes.

- The book has won 13 awards and received very prominent recognition from people in the independent-author world, including a glowing review from Jim Barnes of the *Independent Publisher*. They review 5,000 books a year, and he gave the book an absolutely glowing review: "This book is loaded with helpful information, and I highly recommend it to anyone involved in or considering self-publishing. The Book Broad really knows what she's talking about, and *Self-Publish & Succeed* is truly *not* a boring book!"[3]

- Many of the authors who chose to work with us in the last couple of years have done so entirely because they read the book and knew self-publishing was for them.

---

3   Jim Barnes, "Self-Publish & Succeed," *Independent Publisher*, March 2021, https://www.independentpublisher.com/article.php?page=2474.

- I've received dozens of messages from authors who've written and published a book they are proud of and that is doing well solely because they followed advice in the book!

For me, my book is a success because it's doing what I wanted it to do, and more. Of course, I would love more book sales, but it's not as important to me as the fact that it helped achieve these other goals.

Morning Media Means More Coffee Is Needed

When *More than Cashflow* came out, I was a featured real estate expert on morning news shows in cities all over Canada. I often had to be in a green room before 6 a.m. and ready to sound intelligent half an hour later.

The pictures of me in the broadcast studio were really popular on social media, and the television exposure lent credibility to my real estate training and education company at the time. The producers were great and always made sure to put my book on the table when I was interviewed or have it shown at least once during the show. **That marketing was very valuable, but it didn't sell many books—at least not directly.** I never saw a lift in sales after a television appearance.

TV appearances led to more TV appearances, then more referrals and more speaking engagements. Those engagements often came with a table at the back to sell books or give books to audience members. In other words, the media appearances likely led to book sales, but it was not a direct path.

More important, it led to the growth of both of my businesses at the time. I attracted more investors and many more coaching clients for my businesses. It was a lot of fun for a while, and I only began referring producers to other experts when I wanted to focus on other things (and get a little more sleep!).

We've seen the same thing with our authors at Book Launchers with only one real exception, a true-crime book that came out at the same time the criminal in the story was in court and making major national news headlines. That author's 20/20 appearance and other national news channel appearances definitely contributed to a lot of book sales as well as a movie producer wanting to buy the rights to his book. In the end the author didn't want all the attention and faded into the background, but in that one case, the media attention did lead to major sales. But that was the exception, not the rule.

One of the marketing and PR contractors on our team told me a story about how she landed an author client on the *Dr. Phil* show. She was pumped up because she thought this was going to rocket her client to the top of the sales charts. It didn't. But the instant credibility lent by *Dr. Phil* made it much easier to land other major media appearances and higher-paying speaking engagements for her client.

Understanding this is important because we don't want to discuss tactics until you are clear on strategy and goals. You can spend a lot of time, money, and energy on book marketing and book promotion, so let's make sure that you get the results you want from your investments.

If Book Marketing Doesn't Sell Books, Why Bother?

Marketing is important because it builds awareness. You've likely heard the old statistic that it takes seven touch points to get a sale.[4] Rarely will anyone buy something the first time they hear about it.

Effective marketing reaches the same person repeatedly until they engage with you.

The kind of marketing you must do largely depends on your primary and secondary goals for your book project. We'll get into the specific strategies

---

4   Michael Cohn, "Seven Touches: A Basic Marketing Principle in Action," Social Media Today, November 27, 2013, https://www.socialmediatoday.com/content/seven-touches-basic-marketing-principle-action.

that make sense for these goals in a moment, but for now, know that book marketing is necessary. It just looks a bit different for each author.

For most nonfiction authors, book marketing tremendously benefits your business because it creates a *know*, *like*, and *trust* feeling that is invaluable. You're top of mind when someone asks for a referral. And your personal brand has greater value, which can translate into higher consulting fees, more clients, and just a lot more ease in your business life.

Marketing can open the door for large speaking engagements, where you can sell books to the organizer or at the back of the room. Your email newsletter list and business will also grow as a result of the right marketing. As you expand your audience, you can find partnerships and spread the word about your book so more people buy it. The value of your book goes well beyond its actual sticker price.

Your first step is to get clear on what is important to you.

Your Marketing Mindset

Many authors think they should copy the marketing techniques of successful people in their space. But they don't take into account the years prior to publication when those authors dug deep to build an audience or held event after event where nobody showed up until they finally found a formula that worked.

It's great to get ideas from others and then use a curious mind to move forward with your own marketing. Ask yourself, "What if …?" and "I wonder if …?" Don't expect an overnight solution to anything. The majority of "overnight" bestsellers result from authors building audiences for many years before publication.

Book marketing is a long journey, not a one-time event like a book launch. The good news is that even if your launch is a bust, it's not the end of your book. Visit author forums or groups and ask if anyone had a slow launch but found success later. It happens all the time. In traditional publishing, if a book doesn't succeed within the first three months, they turn their resources and attention to other books. But that doesn't mean *you* have to stop putting in effort.

Go into your marketing journey with the mindset that you're going to create success and make decisions for the end goals you've set for yourself. Remember, **marketing gets the word out for your book**. It's the act of getting in front of other people's audiences through things like podcast interviews, speaking opportunities, and newsletters while connecting with your own audience.

Promotion is when you discount your price or create an incentive to buy your book, as I do with my books. If you visit https://selfpublish andsucceed.com, you'll see incentives to get your copy of *Self-Publish and Succeed*. These incentives can include an e-book sale, a 2-for-1 deal, or bundling it with other offerings for a limited period of time.

Advertising is when you pay money for promotions and listings. This could be paying for media placement, running Amazon Ads, social media ads, or banners on websites your audience frequents, taking print space in newspapers or magazines, and more. Advertising is when you pay to get your book in front of your target consumer, bookseller, or organization.

Publicity is when you get other people talking about you, your book, and your message. Publicity can take on many forms these days, from podcast appearances and traditional media to blog tours, live streaming, or influencer platforms. Publicity is great for thought leadership and brand awareness. It's often the first thing people think about when they consider marketing, but it is only one piece of a bigger strategy.

Each strategy is designed to achieve a specific goal. If you combine them without considering your overall plan, you might not get the outcomes you desire.

For instance, most *marketing* doesn't result in book sales at first. It's essential in the long term but usually yields minimal results in the short term.

Book *promotion*, however, should yield book sales. You might run a 99-cent deal, or maybe you sell several books packaged together. I've done promotions at live events where people could buy my book and get another book free. That's a promotion, and the goal is book sales.

In my opinion, there are only three reasons authors should pay for *advertising*:

1. Attract book reviewers

2. Build an email database and author platform

3. Sell books

All three of those goals are essential and well worth paying for. They also give you valuable information that you can use going forward (more on that later).

The key is to understand that you need to get behind your book over the long term. Be prepared to invest time, energy, and money into your marketing, promotion, and advertising efforts, but also be clear on your goal so you can set realistic expectations and get the results you want.

Let's look at some common book-marketing goals and how promotion, advertising, or publicity can build toward that goal.

GOAL	TACTIC(S)	MEASURE OF SUCCESS
Book sales	Promotions—99 cent e-book sales, BookBub features, 2-for-1 offers, incentives for purchase Advertising—Amazon ads, banner ads, social media ads, Goodreads ads, BookBub ads	Number of books sold per $ spent

GOAL	TACTIC(S)	MEASURE OF SUCCESS
Platform growth	Advertising—Promote your book as a lead magnet, or sell it for the cost of shipping only Publicity—Use the book to land PR and then drive people to connect with you	The size of your audience (email list is best but this could also be social media, phone numbers, addresses, your network)
Business growth	Publicity—Use the book to put you in front of the right audiences so you attract sales, leads, clients, or speaking engagements	Measure the leads and the sales

- If your primary goal is book sales, then promotions and advertising are key. *Promotions* could involve partnering with other authors to do 2-for-1 offers or running e-book sales. There are a ton of e-book websites that will run 99-cent deals on your e-book. You can also run promotions through programs like BookBub. *Advertising* will get your book in front of eyeballs, and if you do it on the right channels, ideally those eyeballs are your target readers'. You may find select book catalogs in which to buy ads, or you might pay to place a banner ad in someone else's newsletter. Or you can leverage the power of paid ads on social media, BookBub, Goodreads, or other places your reader may hang out. Your measure of success is simple—*the number of books sold for every dollar spent.*

- If your goal is to *build your platform* (your platform is anyone in your audience but likely measured by the number of newsletter subscribers, social media followers, or subscribers on a platform like YouTube), *advertising and publicity will likely be the best way to get results.* You have to offer an incentive for someone to sign up for your newsletter or promise some amazing content that provides added value if they follow you or subscribe to your content. Your goal is to use your book to open the door to a larger audience for other products, services, or books. (More on how to do that later.)

- If your goal is to *grow your business or get on big stages as a speaker*, getting books into the hands of the right people and getting your name known as an expert in a specific space will be really important. This is harder to measure because it can be hard to identify the "right" people. That said, *publicity* is a key piece to achieving this goal. The more media attention you receive, the more potential buyers may see you as an authority on your subject, leading to results you can quantify.

We have a lot more to cover. Before you go too deep into the rest of the book, take a moment to think about your goals and what success looks like so you know what type of marketing to focus on.

How Many Books Do I Have to Sell to Break Even?

Are you scared you'll lose money on it or just break even? I have many, *many* thoughts about this, and the first one is that this is actually the wrong question to ask.

Goodbye, break even.

Hello, incredible returns.

When we really get down to the nitty-gritty of whether a book is a success, it's rarely about units sold but instead what that book does for you and for your business.

My favorite story about this comes from one of my podcast interviews. The host said, "You know what? I didn't sell many copies of my book, but one guy read it, decided he wanted to buy my business, and he paid me $6 million. So, I consider that book a success."[5]

---

5 John Bowen, "Navigate the Waters of Book Publishing on a Budget with Julie Broad," in *AES Nation*, podcast, transcript, 1-15, https://www.aesnation.com/wp-content/uploads/AESNation199_Julie_Broad_Transcript.pdf.

I think I probably would too. That was a conversation with John J. Bowen, who has authored more than 20 books. **He said every single book has been a success, but not all have sold very well.**

Some turned into great lead magnets, generating seven figures in sales. Others sold thousands of copies at events or led to big speaking engagements. And that one copy led to the sale of his business.

Many authors try to figure out how many copies they have to sell to pay back the cost of writing, publishing, and promoting their book. Most authors of nonfiction books who invest in creating a high-quality product have to sell around 1,500 to 2,000 copies to break even. A better question than how you can break even is how you can multiply your investment by 10.

Of course, this depends on your goals and your business. For you, it may look like 10 speaking gigs, a TV or movie deal, 20 new clients, a strategic partnership, or brand extensions, like swag, courses, retreats, or workshops. The point is to turn your book into a massive profit-producing product.

If all you do is figure out how to break even, you're probably always going to break even—but you're limiting yourself by not thinking bigger. What is it that you really want your book to do for you?

How can your book be a tool and a vehicle to help you get there? Focus and work toward that!

Five Things That Won't Help Your Book Marketing

In the upcoming chapters of this book, you're going to get an enormous list of things you can do to set yourself up for successful book marketing, publicity, sales, and promotion. Much of what we'll cover is going to help you become a thought leader, build a brand, or grow a business around your book in addition to book sales.

You'll learn about building an author platform, ads, e-book sales, the wide array of distribution channels, corporate partnerships, library events, launch events, virtual events, bestseller strategies, media pitches, and so much more. It's going to be a lot. **You don't need to do it all, but you need to do a lot in order to achieve your goals.** Before we get to everything you should consider doing, let's start by telling you what you should *not* do.

1. **Don't ask your friends and family to buy and review your book on Amazon.**

You need reviews on Amazon, Goodreads, and wherever books are sold. That said, you really don't want reviews, or even a lot of sales, from people who are not your ideal readers. This is especially true when it comes to Amazon.

This isn't just because Amazon expressly prohibits reviews from your friends and family, but also because Amazon is an algorithm machine. You need to teach the Amazon algorithm to identify your ideal reader. If a bunch of people who would normally buy gardening books buy your book on software strategy because they want to support you, Amazon might show your software strategy book to the gardening community for a long time. That's going to hurt your sales, not help them.

Your friends and family can help you in other ways (like asking the local library to get your book), but when it comes to buying your book and getting reviews, let's focus on getting that to happen from people who are your ideal readers.

2. **Don't spam groups online looking for reviews or book sales.**

Add value to the groups you're in. Answer questions. Cheer people on. This takes time and effort. Over time, by supporting others, you will uncover opportunities to pitch your book as something that brings them value. Or someone will ask you about your book, and you can share. Until then, you're in that group to help.

Spam groups, and you will lose your network along with any book sales.

3. Don't treat your book like a hobby.

Even if your book is a side gig or a passion project, being an author means you have a business to run. You have to invest in the success of your book. You will have revenue. You'll have things that you can write off for tax purposes. You'll have things you need to buy, and you'll have business decisions to make around your book.

We'll talk about business considerations later. For now, invest money where it makes sense. Protect your assets. And, most important, plan for your success.

4. Don't look for "easy" wins.

Occasionally, a book hits big because it covers the right topic at the right time, but that is incredibly rare. More likely, you're going to work for years after your book is out.

An investment of $150,000 might buy you a spot on a bestseller list (on top of the costs incurred to create your book and brand), but you better have a big way to capitalize on that to make up for your expenditures. Buying a list doesn't buy people who actually read your book—so if your results need to come from readers, you're out of luck.

The vast majority of authors have to find success the hard way, which takes consistent effort over time.

Know that if you haven't already built the audience for your book before it comes out, you're going to be building it afterward, when it's harder to generate the momentum of a launch. If you do something every day, you'll find success in the long term.

5. Don't try to do all the things.

There's a lot to cover in this book. Please don't freak out that you'll never be able to dance on TikTok *and* stand out on Instagram *while* building an email list *and* growing a speaking business *and* building a course *and* selling your services all at once. Tackle one thing at a time. You don't even have to do all of these things. (You will never find me on TikTok, for example.) Find the tactics you like and that are getting results, then double down on them and add to them.

Let me say that again for you to really let it sink in: **There are hundreds of things you could be doing, but you don't need to do them all.**

There are also things that you should stop doing. Stop assuming someone will say no before you even ask them. Stop trying to do everything yourself. Book marketing is a team sport. You need help, even if it's recruiting your son or your daughter to help you. And for goodness' sake, stop trying to sell your book to everyone. Everyone is not your market. You get the picture, right?

Okay, now that we've covered some things you don't need to do (and shouldn't do), let's get into what you should consider doing—and when!

Chapter Summary

1. Book marketing doesn't always lead to book sales, and it often takes a lot more time. Set your expectations and plan the right tactics for your specific goals.

2. Big media features and appearances have benefits beyond book sales, which is good because you often won't see an immediate increase in sales.

3. Promotions should sell books.

4. Advertising can support book sales, audience growth, business development, and other bigger-picture objectives, but paid ads should have a clear, measurable objective.

5. Most important, make sure you match your big-picture objective to day-to-day tactics and measurable goals.

CHAPTER 2

THE MARKETING LAYERS YOU NEED TO SUCCEED

THE MOST COMMON EMAIL I GET FROM STRANGERS READS, "MY BOOK IS on Amazon, and now I need your help to market it."

Here's the bad news: It's very hard to get a book to sell after you've published it on Amazon, and nothing has happened for a while. It's like a house that sits on the market too long.

Here's the good news: I did not use the words "impossible" or "never" or "can't." It's possible to get this book to sell, but it usually takes a cover redesign, content improvements, better keywords, and a renewed sales and marketing effort behind the book.

Now, here's the best news: It's much more effective and efficient to lay a foundation for marketing by layering it into your book writing, editing, and design.

Layering in Marketing

What does that mean, "layering in marketing?" It all begins with knowing what your ultimate goal is for writing the book. Once you know that, then you need what I call "the five layers:"

One: A connection to and understanding of your audience

Two: A clear brand that communicates your message to your ideal reader, so they care

Three: A juicy reason why that audience *needs* to read your book (the "hook")

Four: Invitations that ask readers to form a relationship with you beyond the book

Five: SEO (search engine optimization) using metadata that positions your title, cover, and book copy for marketing success

What do you offer your reader that they're not getting elsewhere? What problem do you solve in a unique way, even if it's only a little more unique than others? And does your book improve your reader's life? This is true even if you're writing a memoir. If you're trying to write something that gives readers hope, how do you address their fears and aspirations?

Notice that I didn't ask you about demographics.

Knowing your audience and what you want to offer them has little to do with age, gender, education, or economic status. It's about hopes, dreams, worries, and challenges.

This was covered extensively in *Self-Publish and Succeed*, so if you followed our #NoBoringBooks process, you likely have baked yourself a deliciously marketable book cake.

Let's look at an example of how the first three layers work together:

Michael Brenner had a career as a consultant for marketers at big organizations. The challenge he kept bumping into was that people were unhappy in their jobs because of the tendency for company leadership to try to get things accomplished by being "mean."

To help these organizations achieve better employee engagement and customer connections, he wanted to confront middle managers about their leadership style. Just writing a book telling them to be nicer wouldn't work. The people who most needed to hear his message were not likely to listen.

Instead, he positioned his book *against* mean people. *Mean People Suck* became his book title and his mantra. He advocated using empathy as a leadership style to create better teams, bigger profits, and a better overall life.[6]

For this message to work, he had to:

- identify a specific audience (middle managers at big companies),
- understand what their challenge might be (growing and succeeding as leaders), and
- demonstrate how empathy could get them the results they wanted.

He also had to watch out for the trap that so many authors fall into, which is thinking the hook of their book is a message of hope or inspiration that can apply to anyone. You can easily believe the audience is everyone, because who doesn't want that message? *But if you try to write a book for everyone, it will be important to no one.*

Not only that, but it will prove impossible to market. Even brands with the biggest marketing budgets like Coca-Cola, Tide, or Samsung aren't marketing to everyone. They know that some people will use their products and some people won't.

---

6   Michael Brenner, *Mean People Suck: How Empathy Leads to Bigger Profits and a Better Life* (Marketing Insider Group, 2019).

Even more important, while it might be true that your book is going to motivate, inspire, or give hope to the reader, *those desires are not marketing hooks*. Let's take the example of hope.

The concept of hope could be applied to anyone. But if we get clear on our audience, we could say a book gives hope to single people looking for long-lasting love without using an app. Or it gives hope to cancer patients that they can be in control of their treatments and enjoy long and meaningful lives. Or for people who have lost loved ones, it gives hope that there is light amid darkness and lessons in grieving. The more specific, the better.

Book Launchers client Dr. Leslie Kernisan is a practicing geriatrician and founder of the popular website and podcast *Better Health While Aging*. While aging is an issue we all will encounter, Leslie wanted to specifically target adults with parents showing signs of declining health. Specific, right? By homing in on her audience, she was able to write a book that addresses their specific challenges and questions. She even calls out her audience in the title: *When Your Aging Parent Needs Help*.[7]

To succeed in your mission, you have to get into details and connect with a specific reader. If you can't do that, you need to spend more time figuring out who your reader is and how your book will benefit their life.

Layer One: Ideal Reader Intimacy

The greatest sales letter of all time is one that sold more than two billion dollars of subscriptions to the *Wall Street Journal*.[8] Here's how it began:

---

7   Leslie Kernisan, *When Your Aging Parent Needs Help: A Geriatrician's Step-by-Step Guide to Memory Loss, Resistance, Safety Worries & More* (Better Health While Aging LLC, 2021).

8   Steven Fitz, "The Best Sales Letter Ever Written and Why It's So Great," Digital Domination, March 20, 2019, https://digitaldomination.com.au/best-sales-letter-ever-written/.

Dear Reader:

On a beautiful late spring afternoon, 25 years ago, two young men graduated from the same college. They were very much alike, these two young men. Both had been better than average students, both were personable, and both—as young college graduates are—were filled with ambitious dreams for the future.

Recently, these two men returned to college for their 25th reunion.

They were still very much alike. Both were happily married. Both had three children. And both, it turned out, had gone to work for the same Midwestern manufacturing company after graduation, and were still there.

But there was a difference. One of the men was manager of a small department of that company. The other was its president.

It starts with a story that most *Wall Street Journal* readers can relate to—the tale of two college graduates with shared traits and credentials entering the workforce. But then there's a twist. And the letter eventually leads readers to believe that subscribing to the *Wall Street Journal* will put you on the path of the more successful of the two graduates. Read us, and you'll win at business, the letter suggests.

It's great copy because it connects to the aspirations—and fears—of the publication's ideal readers immediately.

I'll often post a YouTube video to BookLaunchers.tv, and someone will comment that they felt as if the video was made just for them. That kind of connected feeling arises from intimate knowledge of my audience and industry. I read every comment, I speak to authors every single day, and I'm an author too. *I also write down the exact words people use when they describe their frustrations, when they ask questions, and when they explain what helped.* Paying attention to specific details creates the connections you need to get attention for your book.

If you're not as intimately connected to your reader right now, try lurking around online forums, Facebook groups, LinkedIn groups, influencers' social media platforms, YouTube channels, or anywhere your ideal reader is hanging out. Read the questions, contributions, and answers. Also read reviewers' comments on Goodreads for books in your category.

Other websites can be useful, like Reddit, Answer the Public, and Quora. Search your topic and see what people ask and how they answer questions. Find communities or topics related to your book subject. Attend live events that attract your ideal reader so you can meet them and learn what is on their mind.

You'll know you have a good grasp on your reader when you can do this exercise easily:

Imagine telling someone why you wrote your book and how you know it's for them.

Complete this sentence:

Hey, I know you're worried about this [insert specifically what this is]. And you're probably wondering if there is a way to do this without hitting [insert the common fear, common obstacle, or the biggest objection].

I wrote this book so you can [insert the desired outcome of your book for the reader].

Let me show you:

Hey, I know you're overwhelmed with all the things you have to do to write a book, but you're also pretty worried nobody will even care you wrote a book, let alone buy it. And I know you're afraid you're wasting time and money on this project.

Book marketing is a huge subject, and there's a lot you can do. I wrote this book to help you know what you need to do to market your book to achieve your specific goal—whether that's book sales, a bigger audience, a known brand, or paid speaking engagements!

When you've nailed a specific problem and how you solve it in a specific way that works where people failed before, you will have their attention—and the sale. Promotional partners will step forward, too, because they will see how you can help their audience and make them look good too!

Layer Two: Author Brand—Your Pitch-Perfect Appeal to Your Reader

I've dedicated an entire chapter to this subject in chapter 3, so let's move on to the next layer.

Layer Three: Your Book's Hook

Your book's hook is that "outcome of an outcome" that we discussed earlier. This is the piece that makes your book irresistible, and without a strong hook, no amount of marketing will ever boost your book sales!

One of my favorite examples of a hook is in the title of *Tactical Lock Picking: A Systemized Approach to Responding to Locked Obstacles in Emergencies.*[9] What's the outcome? The reader will be able to pick a lock. What's the outcome of the outcome? By knowing how to pick a lock, the reader may be able to save lives and reduce property damage when responding to an emergency. It's a powerful skill, especially for firefighters and first responders.

Brandi Olson also has a powerful hook with her book, *Real Flow: Break the Burnout Cycle and Unlock High Performance in the New World of Work.*[10] The first outcome she's promising organization leaders of high-complexity

---

9   Pat Watson, *Tactical Lock Picking: A Systemized Approach to Responding to Locked Obstacles in Emergencies* (Uncensored Tactical, 2020).
10 Brandi Olson, *Real Flow: Break the Burnout Cycle and Unlock High Performance in the New World of Work* (Star Blazers Press, 2022).

teams is to handle burnout. The outcome of the outcome is that readers can create happy, healthy, and engaged employees and achieve a high level of performance.

Layer Four: Creating a Deeper Out-of-Book Connection with Your Reader

Research from Kindlepreneur indicates that including a simple line at the end of your book description telling the reader to buy your book increases sales by 3.7%.[11]

That speaks to the need to explicitly tell people what action you want them to take. In your book description, you may tell them to buy the book now. Inside your book, you need to tell them what to do too! If you want your reader to join your community, let them know with invitations telling them explicitly what website to go to, what to do when they get there (i.e., enter your email address), and what they will receive when they do that. If you want them to write a review, you need to tell them where to write the review and post it.

This is something to consider before you publish your book because you can create plenty of opportunities for readers to build a relationship with you throughout the book. Of course, sharing your personal story helps a reader feel connected to you, but then you want them to take the next step to strengthen the relationship.

Social media connections are okay, but you don't control them. Platforms come and go, and digital algorithms suppress or shut down users.

It's far superior to get an email address from your reader. To make invitations effective, however, consider how to add value and continually serve your reader. It's why you will see different places in this book where I in-

---

11 Jason Hamilton, "How to Write a Book Description: The Ultimate Guide to a Best-Selling Book Blurb," Kindlepreneur, last updated June 29, 2022, https://kindlepreneur.com/write-a-book-description/.

vite you to go to www.selfpromoteandsucceed.com for various resources. Sometimes a video, a link to a service, or a downloadable checklist or tool is a much better way to serve you, and it's a great way for us to connect beyond the book.

Layer Five: Metadata and Market Research for Book Marketing

Chapter 9 addresses this topic in depth, but let me share some information here to whet your appetite. You can access a lot of ways to do metadata research, and more tools will likely emerge over time. We use two primary tools at Book Launchers—KDSPY and Publisher Rocket. There's also K-lytics, which is a fabulous tool for fiction authors and, with limitations, nonfiction authors.

In Publisher Rocket, you can search keywords, categories, competitors, and more. For the purpose of understanding where you'll fit in the market, and how that should be layered into your book positioning as you write, edit, and design your book, I recommend you find the category in which you want to compete. Then, head to the page of each of the top 10 books in that category and read the reviews. What do you offer that is different from those books? Is there a gap that you can fill?

Pay special attention to comments like "This was a great book for a beginner, but I was hoping for advanced strategies," or "This book did a great job of tactical tips, but the emotional aspects of this were ignored." If your book addresses the things that are missing from other books, use that in your marketing—put those things in your description or other promotional materials!

Identify common elements in that category and aim to have some common elements while using your specific title, brand, and hook to position yourself to stand out.

You'll also want to consider common keywords in Publisher Rocket, KD-SPY, and even Google because your title and subtitle offer high-value space that can make it much easier for readers to discover your book. Your title also needs to sell your book, so it's an important part of the marketing cake you're baking.

Your book title is an important layer of the cake that is tough to change after publication, so keep those keywords in mind. Like leaving out sugar or eggs, a cake may come out of the oven, but it won't necessarily be appealing. A book missing one of the layers won't appeal to your reader the way you hope either.

In the next chapter, we'll get into layer two: your author brand. Who you are is just as important to your success as knowing who your reader is.

Chapter Summary

The Big Five Book-Marketing Magic Moments from this chapter:

1. The best book-marketing plans begin *before* you start writing your book.

2. Your readers aren't numbers or demographics. They are people with specific challenges, fears, aspirations, or circumstances that you can help or support in particular ways.

3. Hope and inspiration are not enough to sell your book—even if your story is powerful.

4. Book marketing should be layered into your book. You need to develop an intimate understanding of your readers, your brand positioning (why *you* are the person they need), the hook, invitations to build deeper connections, and metadata that makes your book easily discoverable by readers.

5. Your book is not for everyone, and if you try to make it for everyone, it will be important to no one.

CHAPTER 3

YOUR AUTHOR BRAND

"I GREW UP IN AND OUT OF FOSTER HOMES, LIVING ON THE STREETS IN between, and being part of a gang to survive." This guy went on to tell me how he built—and then lost—a multimillion-dollar business and was now a few years into a pretty great career in sales.

His ability to understand people and truly connect was next level because he'd experienced so many things in his life. He didn't judge anyone—he looked beyond circumstances to find the heart of the person.

In our 30-minute book-strategy call, I could see how he'd be great at sales and even better as an author and speaker. But then he said something that crushed me. He said he wasn't ready to write his book. The reason?

"My story doesn't have the perfect ending yet," he said.

Nothing I could say would persuade him otherwise. He'd come back to me when he had a perfect ending.

Perfect endings are for fairy tales. In fact, many fairy tales don't even have a perfectly happy ending! Did you read "The Little Mermaid"? She died with a broken heart. "The Red Shoes"? I mean, she gets her legs chopped off and is left alone.

Here was this man with an incredible personal brand—he just didn't know it yet. He believed he had to be more, do more, and have a perfect ending to write a book. In fact, he just needed to write.

You don't need a perfect ending to write a book either. *But you do need to figure out who you want to be*—in other words, your author brand.

Most of us resist who we really are. We worry we won't be liked, and that fear holds us back. But if you try to hide who you really are and what you think, you'll struggle to sell your book. So much of book marketing is actually *author marketing*. If you pursue media appearances, they want to speak to you about your personal story as much as your expertise. **The very thing that is going to make your book stand out and be amazing is you.**

Most interviewers want me to talk about my publishing rejections, my struggles with immigrating to the United States, or the challenges I've faced in real estate and business well before they want to dive into the details of any of my books. That's typical. The media doesn't want to promote your book as much as share news, expertise, and powerful stories that entertain and inform their audiences.

When we exhausted outlets that wanted to talk about war-related stories for Jill Phillips's memoir, *Lamlash Street*, we found even-greater exposure for her book when we focused on selling her personal story about how she came to write it.[12] Her book is the center of the conversation, but her story is the reason people want to hear from her.

---

12 J.M. Phillips, *Lamlash Street: A Portrait of 1960's Post-War London Through One Family's Story* (Red Damask Publishing, 2020).

Building Your Brand from Your Book

People will define you if you don't define yourself first. What do you want to be known for?

If you want to have an impact on others, you must be noticed. You may also be judged, and that can be terrifying. I promise people *will* say mean, critical, and absolutely unfair things to you when you stand out.

Instead of fearing that negative feedback, prepare to celebrate it. You now stand out enough that someone is trying to knock you down!

Take BookLaunchers.tv as an example. I get people criticizing my hair, my clothes, my voice, how much coffee I drink, and occasionally what I've said. Here's what you need to know: I stand out, my videos are not boring, and I take a stand and say some unpopular things, and that is okay. The channel is growing, it helps a lot of people, and I'm human.

My brand is friendly, supportive, real, and encouraging.

I'm not perfectly polished or perfectly anything. When you meet me in person, I am the same person you've seen online. My brand is authentic.

Also, just a side note, most people *do* want to support you and see you succeed. The people who judge and criticize you unfairly are not typically successful (or happy) themselves.

If you're new to building your brand, let's walk through how to approach it.

Step **One** in building your brand is to find your voice and use it.

Your book is going to be sitting beside some heavy hitters. *What do you offer that will appeal to your ideal audience?* This is ideally an evergreen message rooted in your personal story that you can promote for years to come. If your book isn't done, what is a concept, method, or approach you hang your hat on and can lean into a long time? (Think about the attention-grabbing example *Mean People Suck.*)

Step Two is to use your book to define your brand.

One of the things we work on with our clients is figuring out how to brand them. I call myself "Julie, the Book Broad" as a branding activity. How do you want to be known in your marketplace? How will you be memorable? Your book is a tremendous opportunity to define yourself. More than a cute label, your brand is what you stand for, what you believe, and how you leave people feeling. What is that for you?

It may feel silly the first time you say you are "Chemo-Crusher Carrie" or "Save-the-Sale Gale," but when people start remembering you by your brand, you'll be glad you did. We see many authors hold back the good stuff of who they are out of fear. That makes brand building difficult because the very thing that makes you memorable is *you*.

Take a moment to pull out a piece of paper and write the answers to these statements:

- "Wouldn't it be nice if I were [insert answer]?"
- "If I had a magic wand and could wave it today, I would want to be known tomorrow for/as [insert answer]."
- "I'm on stage about to do a keynote address. Who is in the audience, and what am I delivering that they can get only from me?"
- "When people describe me and my brand, what words would they use?"

How you want to be defined can be a great starting point for determining your brand. Most important, you need that "thing you hang your hat on" for your brand, which is the foundation of your book marketing.

For Book Launchers, #NoBoringBooks is our mantra (what our hat hangs on). We think about book marketing the minute someone says they want to write their book, and part of that is writing a book people actually *want* to read (as well as knowing who those people are and why they need that person's message).

Step **Three** is to make your brand visual.

The first two steps are the foundation of your brand messaging. *That* is your brand, not the logo or colors. Still, you need a visual representation of your brand for consistency and to build recognition. Consider visual aspects of your brand, such as:

- color palette,
- fonts,
- imagery, like photos or other branding elements (even specific pieces of clothing),
- personal logo, and
- tone.

What emotional tone should you and your brand strike in the world?

We have #NoBoringBooks swag we give away at BookLaunchers.tv—tying our hashtag into swag with our logo is a powerful way to brand and be remembered.

I'm a member of the Entrepreneurs' Organization, and we start every meeting with a one-word emotion—for instance, excited, exhausted, stressed, content, irritated, or worried. It's a word that lets the other people in our forum know our emotional temperature at the moment. We close out meetings with another word to show how it's changed.

Your brand tone is similar in that it should be largely one primary word, or a couple of single words, that connote something positive or generally upbeat. It can be words like any of the following:

- Authoritative
- Caring
- Cheery
- Encouraging
- Enthusiastic
- Frank
- Friendly
- Humorous

- Informative
- Irreverent
- Nostalgic
- Passionate
- Reassuring
- Supportive
- Sympathetic
- Witty

Choose a word or couple of words that will shape the tone of your brand, and then build on them.

Step **Four** is to create the messaging for your brand.

Now that you have the technical elements in hand, let's go back to the messaging. This needs to come through all of the copy created around your marketing.

This is the *who, how, why,* and *what* of your book:

- Who are you serving?
- How do you serve them?
- Why do you serve them?
- What do you do that makes an impact?

Think about the feeling you want to be known for—and even the one word you most want people to use in describing you.

Your answers become your messaging pillars, the content that holds up your brand. It will be used on your website, in the content you create, and in the book and whatever else you build, including courses, speaking engagements, or consulting sessions. Knowing these pillars gives you a great running start to becoming established as an authority.

Step **Five** is to develop your brand origin story.

What part of your story sparked the brand? What happened to you that led to this goal? This becomes part of your messaging and brand identity.

My first book experience is the origin of Book Launchers. After being asked by an acquisitions editor at Wiley to write a proposal for a book idea they wanted me to write, and working on that with them for three months, they rejected me. They told me I couldn't sell enough books to make a deal worthwhile.

After I recovered from that rejection, I decided to write an idea I was passionate about (and they'd told me was too generic) and to self-publish it.

My former belief that I needed to be chosen for a book deal to be a legitimate author was replaced by my belief that the only person who truly mattered was the reader. I decided to write a book that my ideal reader needed to read. I was also going to make sure my ideal reader knew the book existed by shouting it from the rooftops.

The whole experience was a challenge because there weren't self-publishing services like Book Launchers. Editors think about style guides and proper grammar, but their changes would impact my marketing. How do you title a book so it will sell? I discovered that even book cover designers aren't thinking about your book from the perspective of your ideal reader. They seek your approval, so it's up to you to know what is most likely to sell.

I became passionate about writing books and setting them up to sell and achieve goals from the start.

That rejection was a gift. I was forced to self-publish and now think it was the best path for me. I own my rights, keep all my royalties, and believe most entrepreneurs and subject matter experts will be better off doing it that way too! Publishers need authors *far more* than authors need publishers—and the better we get at distribution, book marketing, and book sales, the more that will become obvious as well as true. Book Launchers has been built upon this belief, and my brand has blossomed through it all.

Your brand at a high level is about how you make people feel, what you are known for, and how your brand came to be. It's important to know your origin story, share it as part of your brand building, and work that into the development of your author platform.

What Is an Author Platform?

Author platform is really a fancy way of saying "audience."

It's everything you do and create that connects you to other people. It's not just social media and websites, although those certainly factor in. Your platform develops from speaking engagements, your newsletter, social media accounts, videos, blogs, podcasts, and any other ways you reach people.

The right people or organizations can catapult your book to the top of the charts. Your network, community, and association memberships are part of your platform if you're visible and involved. For some authors, their client base or the company they work for can also be a big part of their platform.

No Platform? No Problem (Just Set Your Expectations Accordingly)

The big, splashy, successful launches are almost always the result of years of author platform building. If you've been head down building a company or climbing the corporate ladder, you likely haven't built much of a platform. Without a big platform, you need to mentally prepare yourself for a longer, steadier promotional push to get your book in front of your readers. You may not sell thousands of copies on launch, but you can still achieve great things with your book.

All the things you do to build your platform and attract readers are the same things authors with a platform do. If you're starting with no platform or a small platform, your goal should be to gain momentum and continually share your message so you're constantly talking to new people.

Most platforms don't appear overnight. It takes consistency. You can use your book to build your platform and invite your readers to connect with you (remember the fourth layer of your book cake).

The best day to start building your platform was yesterday, which means you need to start today. We're going to dive deep into what that means in the next chapter, but the first thing I would recommend is setting up a simple landing page with an awesome invitation to join your newsletter list.

You can see an example of a simple opt-in page at https://booklaunchers .com/7steps or https://booklaunchers.com/businessbook.

These pages look simple, but don't let that fool you: They convert more than 40% of their visitors—four out of 10 people—into newsletter subscribers. People subscribe to the email list so they can get a download, which is something of value to them. We call that a "reader magnet" or a "lead magnet."

No Free Chapters, Please

When you offer something to encourage people to sign up to your newsletter, please don't offer a free chapter of your book. *If you want to use a chapter to entice readers, look at what that chapter is going to do for them.* For example, if I were to give this chapter away, I would say, "Download a complete guide to building an author brand that sells books, builds your business, and leads to thought leadership."

When someone gets the download, I wouldn't even tell them it was a chapter from this book until the last page. That's where I would let them know there's more amazing content like this coming soon (or if the book is out, where they can buy it). Nobody really wants the chapter from the book, but they sure do want insights that lead to book sales and thought leadership, right?

Once you have that page set up, you can start writing articles for popular websites or online magazines. Include a short call to action at the end of each article for followers to connect with you and get your awesome download.

Now you're ready to learn more about using your author brand to build your author platform. My perspective on social media might surprise you.

Smile for the Camera—Author Photo Essentials

You're going to need a great author photo for many purposes, including your Amazon author page, "About the Author" page, the inside of your book or the back cover, PR kit, podcast or speaker one sheet, Goodreads page, podcast bookings, your social media profiles, and so much more.

Because you're going to use it over and over while marketing your book, let's make sure you get the best one possible. Make sure you:

1. Hire a professional. Ask for:

   - at least three different, edited shots,

   - several changes of clothes, and

   - at least two types of backgrounds (including solid white or black).

   Some photographers may give you all your digital images but allow you to choose three to five to be edited. That's ideal because the unedited ones can be great for your social media or website content. It allows you to have images with different poses while maintaining the same look for your brand. If you insist on doing it yourself, make sure you've got great lighting and a good background. Don't do it in direct sun with your eyes squinting or in your dimly lit living room.

2. Ask the photographer to send you different sizes or cropped images, or make sure you have the ability to do it yourself. For example, your Goodreads author profile is 400 by 400 pixels, so you need a square.[13] Many social media accounts will require a tightly cropped square of your face, but a poster or other book-related promotional materials may require images showing more of your upper body. Remember, digital images can often be used with lower resolution than printed images, so make sure you get a variety.

3. Find your best side. Usually, a pro will have you experiment with different expressions and positions. With digital photography, you can do a whole bunch of looks and find a good one. Bring someone with whom you enjoy talking to your shoot to help you get more relaxed photos that really capture your personality.

4. Dress the part. Consider your brand and what you want people to feel or think about when they see you. My friend Scott Sylvan Bell wears these amazing Hawaiian shirts for all his videos. It's impossible to see a Hawaiian shirt and not think of him. He also loves Hawaii and goes multiple times a year, so it's a fit for his brand. I've seen people consistently rock a specific color or always wear a hat. When choosing your outfit, keep your background in mind. If you want a black background, don't wear black. Same thing for white. It's also why I like to plan for a few changes of clothes when I do a shoot.

---

13 "Strike a Pose: Optimizing Your Goodreads Author Profile Picture," Goodreads, February 10, 2018, https://www.goodreads.com/blog/show/1177-strike-a-pose-optimizing-your-goodreads-author-profile-picture.

5. Plan your styling in advance. Whether it's haircuts or color, cosmetics, waxing, nails, or styling elements before you get your photos, make sure you schedule well in advance of your photo shoot. It's also worth asking if your photographer has an assistant who can handle powdering your face or tend to flyaway hairs, especially if you're going to be photographed under bright studio lights. (Outside light on a cloudy day can be ideal for photos, while standing by a window can give you optimal partial light.)

Chapter Summary

1. Find your voice and use it. What's your equivalent of the *Mean People Suck* evergreen message that you want to stand out for?

2. Use your book to define your brand. What's your version of "Julie, the Book Broad"?

3. Make your brand visual. What word defines your brand, and how do you convey that visually for your audience to see, recognize, and remember?

4. Craft messaging pillars for your brand, so you are always thinking about your target audience, how your book helps them, and what they need to hear from you.

5. Tell your brand origin story to build connection and establish your credibility and authority.

CHAPTER 4

SOCIAL MEDIA DOESN'T SELL (MUCH), BUT RELATIONSHIPS DO

I BRACED MYSELF AS A MAN SPRINTED UP TO THE BOOK LAUNCHERS event booth while reaching into his backpack. I was about to be book bombed.

"You clearly love books," he shouted, without greeting me or introducing himself. "Let me give you *my* book!"

He didn't wait for me to respond. "After you read it, can you please write a review on Amazon? You know how important those are, so I am sure you do a lot of reviews, right?" he said, opening the front cover to his book. "Right here is my card so you can subscribe to my newsletter too. I'm trying to grow my platform. My publicist told me to get my book in as many hands as I can. You launch books, so you probably help with that, too, right?"

At this point, I still hadn't said anything. Not a word.

I looked down at the book and couldn't actually figure out what it was about. The title was abstract, it had no subtitle, and the cover art was vague and didn't give me any information about the content inside.

"Who did your cover?" I asked in an even tone.

"Oh—you like that? It's great, right? My daughter's in design school and did that for me," he replied. He pointed out a couple of details on the cover he loved, and as soon as he saw someone he knew, he said goodbye and was off.

I stared at his book and wondered if he considered our conversation (if you could call it that) a win. Did he think he had achieved what the publicist requested? Was he going to be wondering why he gave out 100 books at the event for free, and not a single person wrote a review or signed up for his newsletter?

My message to you: Don't be that guy. And to make sure that never happens, let's take a look at the right way to build your platform.

Author Website Essentials

In the early days of Book Launchers, we pitched one of our clients for an article in a major magazine. The magazine responded with interest, but when they found out the author did not have a website, we lost the opportunity. They said the author lacked credibility.

If you are hoping to land big media, speaking engagements, or other business opportunities from your book, at the very least you need a website. Or if you have a business website already, you need a page dedicated to your book and your credentials as its author.

This is not an optional part of your marketing plan. The good news, though, is that website designers are everywhere, and it's easier than ever to create professional book sites.

I'll give you a few examples of sites we've built so you can see they don't have to be fancy, but they do need to be effective. You'll also see that they all have some core common elements, including these:

1. Author bio (hint: that's you)

2. Book (or books) you've written, where to buy them, and any awards or reviews

3. Contact information

4. Easy navigation

5. Newsletter opt-in (something of value offered in exchange for the email address)

First: Your Newsletter Opt-In Offer (We Call This a Reader Magnet)

The first element? Front and center, above the fold (which means before you have to scroll down) there is **an offer to get something of value in exchange for an email address**. This is your reader magnet, and you sell it with an outcome-focused offer.

Consider offers like these:

- Do you have enough to retire? Grab this workbook to calculate how much money you need to retire without a lifestyle change.

- Download the *Spicy Relationship Checklist* to spark the love you once had.

- Is your team following your lead? Take the leadership quiz to find out if your team respects you—or not.

Avoid doing these offers:

- Join my newsletter list for the latest updates.

- Get a free chapter from my book.

- Be the first to know when my new book is out—get my newsletter.

I'm sure you're surprised that the subscriber offer is first on the website. Why aren't you promoting the book first, right?

A book buyer is nice, but an email subscriber can become a long-term relationship, so they buy *all* of your books, products, services, and recommended resources—and tell their friends too.

When I launched Book Launchers in 2017, I was not known as a publishing expert. I was a real estate–investing expert who had published two books. When I was ready to launch, I emailed my real estate list about the new business venture and told them I was looking for beta authors. The first 10 Book Launchers clients came from that list, and many others from that list have since published books.

It might be hard to see the value in email addresses when you start out. But if you invest in each and every person who trusted you with their contact information, it could be financially profitable and personally fulfilling for years and years to come.

Second: Book(s) Page

The second must-have on your author website is a **section dedicated to your book(s)**.

If you've only published one book, you can showcase it using additional information about your brand to build out the page. If you're like our prolific client Carol Sanford, you're showcasing a long list of books on your website.[14] Just be sure to shine the spotlight on your latest release.

For each book, make sure you include:

- cover image,

---

14 "Books," Carol Sanford, accessed March 15, 2023, https://carolsanford.com/books/.

- description,
- how-to-buy links (or even better, a universal book link that takes you to a page where the buyer can choose what to buy, like this: https://books2read.com/ap/RDOjGr/Julie-Broad), and
- reviews, accolades, media articles, or endorsements.

If you offer bulk sales (large orders), you should also include that information here.

💡 **TIP:** Universal links are free to create, and they're a powerful selling tool. Readers can buy a book from their favorite site without your needing to include 20 different retail logos on your site. You can get yours at https://books2read.com or https://booklinker.com.

Third: Author Bio (You)

The third author website must-have is your **author bio**. For many books, it's important to share your background (i.e., education, occupation, expertise) and why your message is important to you. Include your **professional author photo** and other photos of you that relate to your topic, if appropriate.

Some author websites have a link where media can download a digital media kit or additional images that can be used when they feature you and your book.

It's not mandatory to include content like a blog, podcast, or videos, but having some content that showcases your personality, expertise, and message can go a long way to opening the door to more opportunities. It lets visitors get to know more about you, and it's also good for SEO over time.

If you are a speaker or you want to do more speaking, your speaker reel video or pictures of you at a speaking engagement can also be included here. It could also be on your website as a separate tab titled "Speaking" or "Work with Me."

Fourth: Contact Information

The fourth essential element on your author website is your **contact information**. If at all possible, include a phone number and email address instead of a blank form. Some people prefer to directly contact you. You don't want to miss out on opportunities like speaking engagements because it was too hard to reach you.

Fifth: Navigational Tools

Make the site **easy to navigate** and **mobile friendly**, and provide easy ways for folks to **connect with you on social media**. Most of the author sites we build are fewer than six main pages ("Home page," "Book," "About," "Contact," and "Blog").

Tobin Lehman[15] adopted a single-page website but hit all the important points. While he did offer free chapters as part of a lead magnet, he also included three other downloadable resources that tied in with his approach to marketing. These sites make it easy for a target reader to get content, buy a book, and join an email-marketing list.

Shaun Hayes[16] created a website and wrote a book to build his speaking career. You'll see his speaking topics and videos are positioned on the website as prominently as his book. You also can't miss the fact that he is an incredibly successful entrepreneur *and* a felon. Imagine having him speak to a corporation about ethics!

If you don't know where to start, try looking at author websites to get your creative juices going. Better yet, look at authors who share your target audience, and view that information through the lens of your author brand and your goals. Your website is the home base for your brand and all the things you do, including your book.

---

15 https://ridethetornado.com
16 https://shaunhayes.com

Email Marketing Is So Old School

In 2006, I flew to Florida to take an email-marketing course from a company called Early to Rise. I promptly launched my first email newsletter, which two years later evolved into my first online business.

I know that an almost-two-decades-old practice might seem out of touch today compared to the hottest social media platform. But when it comes to marketing your book, email newsletters are still high value.

An email that pops directly into the inbox of your target audience creates a much better opportunity for connection. It also builds a foundation for a long-lasting relationship that can help you achieve bigger goals. And it can't be emphasized enough that it's a list that you control.

An email newsletter is your own media, and you own your content channel and strategy. With this content, you build more than a transactional relationship. You're providing value to your own community while gaining value in data that helps you market your book, build your brand, and provide better services.

Where do you start with your newsletter? The first step is to figure out the right opt-in to connect your audience with your brand. Basically, what do you promise to provide them in exchange for their email address?

This is your reader magnet, a kind of quid pro quo. Visit https://booklaunchers.com/businessbook to see an example of an opt-in with a value-add offering that works.

The Making of a Great Reader Magnet

What problem do you intend to solve with your content? That's the key to developing your reader magnet.

Think of something you can offer related to your book topic that will give someone a quick win. When I was in real estate, I offered a quick cash flow calculator spreadsheet that I knew would help potential investors analyze deals and would be hard to pass up.

How about a little sex talk to liven things up? Sex and relationship coach Dr. Lanae St. John[17] aims to help adults in three different ways. She coaches:

- couples on how to regain their sexual spark,
- parents on how to talk to their children about sex in healthy and positive ways, and
- women on how to explore their own sexuality and confidence.

On her website, three lead magnets address each audience and allow visitors to choose their own adventure. They can download one or all three.

The bonus here for Lanae is that she can see which of her lead magnets gets the most attention and downloads. Identifying popular content gives her an advantage because she can tweak weak messaging to expand her audience.

Presentation expert Dan Fraser, author of *Kickass Presentations*, helps presenters deliver dynamic presentations.[18] His lead magnet is a six-page guide to the impact of color on presentations.[19] It's super useful and packs mega value for anyone who has to create presentations on a regular basis, and all they have to do is join his email newsletter list.

Whatever you create, make sure you get it professionally designed so it's aesthetically pleasing and cohesive. It should represent you and your brand, with your chosen fonts, colors, logos, and a call back to your book and website. It should fit seamlessly into your brand and how you service your target reader.

---

17 https://themamasutra.com
18 Dan Fraser, *Kickass Presentations: Wow Audiences with PowerPoint Slides That Click, Humor That's Quick, and Messages That Stick* (Spirit Bear Book, 2022).
19 https://kickasspresentationsbook.com

You can find talented and affordable designers on Upwork, Guru, or Fiverr. Your reader magnet may be the first impression someone has of your brand, and it's worth your time and investment to make it look good and increase your odds of building a long-term relationship.

Email Newsletter Setup: Quick Tips

You can find great guides on how to set up an email newsletter from a technical standpoint, so I'm going to focus more on developing strategy.

In terms of service providers, we like ConvertKit and Mailchimp. A quick search will help you determine the features that are most important to you. Various options include cost, deliverability, ease of setup, simple design, integration to websites, opt-in page templates, and more.

My advice is to keep it simple. My best-performing opt-in pages (after sending hundreds of thousands of visitors to different pages) are always the ones that have a simple image of the reader magnet with a compelling headline and a name and email form to complete. Simple sells!

Your newsletter doesn't need to be really fancy either. What matters most is that your newsletter gets delivered to the inbox of your readers, matches your brand, and adds value to their lives.

Don't Give Your Readers the Silent Treatment

As soon as a new subscriber signs up, make sure they are immediately greeted with some type of content. Set up an automated sequence so that they receive a welcome email. Provide the promised reader magnet as part of that welcome, and get readers excited about what's coming next.

Decide how often to send your newsletter and the type of content to include, and let subscribers know—then stick to it. Ideally, send your newsletter at least once a month. Biweekly or weekly is better, so you can build a connection and people remember who you are.

Craft subject lines to catch subscribers' attention right away and convince them that your newsletter content is worth their time. You're going to fast-track yourself to trash bins if you write dull titles like "Monthly Tips Newsletter" or "Julie's Update."

Headline your email the same way you would title a chapter. (You did write compelling chapter titles, right?) Write something that creates curiosity, adds value, or sells a benefit.

Social Media Doesn't Sell Books (for Most Authors)

Building an audience on social media benefits your author platform. It can help you get speaking gigs, podcast interviews, and other promotional opportunities. Being active on social media is also one of the criteria that international publishers look at when considering an author for a foreign rights deal, according to the team at DropCap.[20] The folks at Underground Jam, who help turn books into screenplays, also indicated that building a presence on social media helps your book become something for a screen too.[21]

In other words, social media can be a powerful piece of your author brand, helping you build an audience and establish yourself as an authority in your area of expertise. If you have an audience on social media already, it also will likely help you sell some books.

If you're an author who is starting from scratch, expecting social media to sell books is going to be a long, painful road, though. If you have started a social media channel and watched your audience grow by single digits for months at a time, you know what I mean. Even if you've been at it for a

---

20 Shared live at the IBPA University Event on May 5, 2023.
21 Book Launchers, "How to Turn Your Book into a Movie or Adapt It for TV," June 16, 2020, YouTube video, https://www.youtube.com/watch?v=HirXaRmOpwM.

few years and have thousands of followers, you're still not going to see a lot of book sales from that general audience.

In other words, if your overall goal is book sales, and you don't already have an audience, investing time, energy, and money into social media is a mismatch of tactic and goal.

To emphasize this, let's do some math with a hypothetical example.

Assume you already have 10,000 followers on a given social media platform. Look at how many people engage with your content by way of likes or comments or shares. That tells you who is actively involved in your content enough that they might be interested in taking advantage of a book offer.

Certain platforms let you view analytics by clicks and clicks-per-post views. You can also use a service like Bitly or Pretty Links (a WordPress plug-in) to track your links for a month. This ought to shake loose your dreams of selling thousands of books on social media.

If you are doing really well, about 10%–20% of your followers or connections see your content. Of those, unless you're posting something really juicy, less than 5% are going to click on your link. That click rate is closer to 1%–2% for the content I post, but let's use 5% because you are probably doing a better job on social media than I am.

How many of those people are going to buy your book? That really depends on a lot of factors, but I'm guessing anything more than a 10% conversion of those clicks is extremely rare. Based on this hypothetical scenario, here's the math:

TOTAL OF 10,000 FOLLOWERS
20% view content = 2,000 people
5% of 2,000 click on link = 100 people
10% of 100 buy your book = 10 people

The more realistic scenario—what most authors actually experience—is half that number.

Of course, this is one post, and it doesn't consider the impact of other people sharing the post, and you'll most certainly be sharing about your book more than one time. (I've kept it simple to illustrate my point, which is simply that most people grossly overestimate the power of social media for direct book sales.)

It's also worth noting there are always exceptions. One of our clients had fewer than 20,000 Twitter followers, but his audience was full of influential people who were so engaged that it led to thousands of book sales.

We also had another author with an audience of about 100,000 people on Instagram outperform expectations. He sold more than 1,000 copies on launch, and it was almost entirely from that one social media platform, which included influencers who amplified his message. But these examples are the exception, not the rule.

If it's not likely to sell that many books, why bother?

As noted above, if your bigger-picture goal is something well beyond book sales, like speaking, thought leadership, international rights deals, or movie moments, social media is an important tactic to reach your bigger-picture goal.

Social media can also offer high-value links back to your website, and it provides places where you can engage and connect with your audience. You can also connect with influencers to develop partnerships to get exposure and gain more opportunities.

Plus, when speaking or media opportunities come up, you have an advantage over other experts if you have a larger following. Promotion is a two-way street.

Social media takes a lot of energy and effort, so if you aren't interested or excited about it, focus on finding people who have an audience with whom you can connect. There are plenty of other things to do to help make your book a success, and we'll get into them soon!

Social Media Tips for Savvy Authors

Let's say you *are* interested and excited about connecting with your readers on social media. That's great. There are going to be plenty of experts to support you with specific platforms, so here are some general tips to help you use social media to accomplish your overall author goals:

1. **Pick one platform.** Just because you can be on every form of social media does not mean you should be. What platform do *you* enjoy? Do you find more like-minded people on LinkedIn than Facebook? Each platform has its unique features and users. *Find your audience*, and if you use their favorite particular platform on a regular basis, create great content for them.

2. **Play to your strengths.** If you love photography, you'll probably have a blast on Instagram or even Pinterest. If you like dancing and being creative, TikTok could be fun. If you're into deep thoughts and professional insights that spark conversation, LinkedIn might be your place. You'll find me most active on BookLaunchers.tv on YouTube. I love creating content, responding to comments, and meeting other YouTubers, so I focus my attention there.

3. **Uncover the hook for your social media.** Consider your author branding. What do you offer your audience? What do you hang your hat on? What are the consistent messages you want to put into the world? Follow the 80/20 rule: 80% of your content could be audience-centric focused on offering value, and 20% might be brand-centric with calls to action, like subscribe or buy.

Audience-centric content provides value with material that offers your audience appreciation, entertainment, or education. That means tips, quotes, steps, excerpts from your book or high-value content. Brand-centric content, on the other hand, asks for a sale, a subscription, a donation, a review, or anything focused on your brand.

When you've provided content that's valuable to your audience, they're more receptive to invitations such as "Buy my book," "Schedule a consultation," and "Write a review."

4. **Get familiar with hashtags.** You probably know what a hashtag is, but just in case, hashtags are words or phrases preceded by a number sign (#) and used to link a message with a particular topic, like #NoBoringBooks. Hashtags are useful because they make your posts more searchable. Kindlepreneur has even created a hashtag generator for authors.[22] (We love it!)

Including too many hashtags or hashtags that are too general or too obscure won't accomplish much of anything. A report from Sprout Social found that engagement drops when more than one hashtag is used on Twitter and Facebook.[23]

5. **Be consistent.** Success on social media takes a long time. Focus on creating a strong, engaged community with consistent, valuable content. Really, truly care about the people with whom you're connecting. To generate engagement, you need to engage first, and do so at regular intervals. With YouTube, I have found that a predictable content-creation schedule and a commitment to replying to the majority of comments builds a strong community. If you can, reply to every person's comment, then head on over

---

22 Dave Chesson, "Hashtags for Writers: Free Generator Tool," Kindlepreneur, accessed August 23, 2023, https://kindlepreneur.com/hashtags-for-writers/.

23 Chloe West, "The Complete Guide to Hashtag Analytics," Sprout Social, June 14, 2021, https://sproutsocial.com/insights/hashtag-analytics/.

to their pages and comment on their content too. A retweet or repost is okay, but personalized comments are far more valuable and appreciated.

Just because social media won't usually fuel book sales doesn't mean you shouldn't use it if it fits with your bigger-picture goals. Remember, it can be an asset if you want to build credibility and be known as an influencer. But the most important piece of your author platform is your email newsletter. To help you build your newsletter and create a content calendar (which we'll talk about shortly), head over to www.selfpromoteandsucceed .com where we've got some wonderful resources to help you. Plus, you can download a sample author–content calendar to get you started.

Developing a Content Calendar to Keep You from Going Crazy

It's easy to go days or even weeks without posting content, which is why spending time planning (and even using a scheduling software system to set up your posts in advance) will help you immensely.

Planning your content is as simple as filling a jar with rocks, pebbles, and sand. If you fill your jar with all your sand and pebbles first, you won't have any room left for your rocks. To get everything to fit in the jar, insert your big rocks first, then your pebbles, and then pour in the sand. Everything will fit and work together.

Think about your content calendar as your jar. Put your big ideas, events, or news in place first, and then build out the rest of your content. When you start big and then work smaller, smaller, smaller, you'll have a much better idea of the type of content that you need to create from a brand perspective.

Instead of freaking out, rushing around, and stressing while you try to figure out what to post every day, you'll know exactly what to post on a daily basis. And you'll have planned content that aligns with your brand's latest developments, events, or news and your vision for your brand's future.

Start with the current year and break it into quarters (every three months). For each quarter, think about your big rocks. They could be:

- Book release or book release anniversary.
- Course launch or a live workshop or training.
- Major theme, season, or event that you plan to promote around (This could be Breast Cancer Awareness Month, Earth Day, Valentine's Day, or Father's Day—it's something that people will be celebrating or talking about.)
- Sales or special promotions for your book or your business.
- Significant dates for your business, brand, or book, like the day you launched the business, the day your book hit #1 on a list, or even your birthday. What dates are significant to you and your business? These milestones are great promotional opportunities.

After you plot out your quarters with your big rocks, break your calendar down month by month. What kinds of content do you need to create in that month to align with your big rocks?

Beth Cavanaugh builds promotions around Nursing Week, which makes sense since she is the author of *Some Light at the End: Your Bedside Guide for Peaceful Palliative and Hospice Care*[24] and *The Power & Pain of Nursing: Self-Care Practices to Protect and Replenish Compassion*.[25] That's a big rock for her calendar. Around that, she'll have pebbles for 99-cent promotions, content from her book specific to Nursing Week, and maybe some give-

24 Beth Cavanaugh, *Some Light at the End: Your Bedside Guide for Peaceful Palliative and Hospice Care* (Chatham: Bowker, 2019).
25 Beth Cavanaugh, *The Power & Pain of Nursing: Self-Care Practices to Protect and Replenish Compassion* (Los Angeles: Sun and Moon Press, 2022).

aways. Her sand will surround the stones, filling in empty spaces, with tips, pictures, and personal content.

November is Adoption Awareness Month, a great time for author Trisha Campbell to focus on promoting her memoir *Eight Was Enough*.[26] Similarly, *Don't Ask a Blind Man for Directions* by John Samuel is the perfect book to promote during October's National Disability Employment Awareness Month.[27]

Doing outreach to influencers, associations, and media when there is an awareness month or a holiday that is a good fit for that group can be really effective. They are likely looking for time-sensitive content related to those topics, and you have expertise to share!

Remember, your entire strategy should have a clear purpose, and that purpose isn't promotion. Think about your ideal reader and the audience with whom you want to connect. What can you offer that's going to be of value and of consequence to them?

Your reader research tools are useful for coming up with ideas for content, but you can also use your book. There's a whole lot of content in those pages, and there's no rule that says you can't recycle it into your email or social media strategy. Pull out your tips, resources, quotes, and stories!

Pick a chapter that pairs well with your big rocks or that month's theme. That chapter can become a blog post. From there, you can pull out specific tips from the blog to turn into social media posts. Take another piece of the chapter for a LinkedIn post. And then use a segment for an Instagram Live or for that week's email newsletter.

---

26 Trisha Campbell, *Eight Was Enough: A God-Led Adventure with Adopted & Special Needs Kids* (Pro Zoe Publishing, 2021).

27 John Samuel, *Don't Ask a Blind Man for Directions: A 30,000-Mile Journey for Love, Confidence, and a Sense of Belonging* (Baron Publishing, 2022).

You don't have to come up with entirely new content to build out your entire strategy. When you repurpose your content and cross-promote it, you're guaranteeing that your content aligns with your overall brand and captures your messaging as a whole.

For added inspiration, look at your industry. If you're in real estate, check when housing reports or interest-rate notices come out, and plan content accordingly.

Also consider messages that relate to the time of year. If you're a tax specialist, you certainly know when people are thinking about taxes. If you're in health and fitness, pay attention to cyclical trends and hot topics, and prepare to be a trusted voice on these subjects.

You're an expert, so your audience will want your perspective. Providing insight on relevant topics can be a really great way to deepen your connection with followers, highlight your authority, and build trust and credibility, all while tying it back into your brand.

Notice book bombing hasn't come up once as a tactic. Of course, we're not done platform building just yet. Next, we're going to cover the pieces of my platform that sold thousands of books and boosted it to #1—my real-life connections and incentives to buy the book now! We'll also cover speaking engagements, LinkedIn, and partnerships before we get into the book sales and promotional tactics ahead.

Chapter Summary

1. Social media isn't usually the best method of selling books, so it's best to have realistic expectations and use your time and energy wisely.

2. Old school strategies like email marketing play an important role in helping you sell books, offer your services and products, and build deep relationships with your readers.

3. A chapter in your book is only a good reader magnet if you position it to solve a problem for your ideal reader. (Never offer a "free chapter.")

4. You don't need to be on every platform, or any at all, if other tactics are a better fit for your goals. Focus on what you need to deliver to align with your author goals.

5. Use a content calendar to get organized around your communications and keep your readers engaged.

CHAPTER 5

BEYOND THE BUSINESS CARD—PLATFORM BUILDING LIKE A PRO

BUSINESS CARDS CAN MAKE PEOPLE LAZY. AFTER SEVERAL CONFER-ences where I was added to a dozen newsletters without opting in, it seemed to me that some people's platform-building strategy was to just get email addresses.

The real goal of building a platform is to build relationships—not build out a list. There are effective ways to do this and quick ways to be marked as spam. Focus on what's going to work best for your bigger-picture goal, which is always quality and connection first.

The Power of the Right Words

Whether your goal is to use your book to establish yourself as an industry authority or to generate business leads, words can be powerful when it comes to achieving your end goal.

When I launched the first online course for my real estate training and education company, I hired a junior copywriter to write the sales page. He charged $2,700. At the time, I was stunned that copy could cost so much, especially from someone fresh out of copywriting training at American Writers and Artists Institute. A senior copywriter said he would charge me 10 times that amount.

What I didn't realize is that **the right words count for everything when it comes to converting a visitor to a subscriber and a subscriber to a customer.** There's an art and a science to writing copy that connects with readers in a way that motivates them to act. There are rules to writing copy that sells or copy that gets someone to take a desired action.

AI systems are skilled at writing effective copy because it contains formulaic elements. But you still need to understand those elements to refine the language and ensure that you're building relationships with your readers and selling books.

A great book engages the reader, but great marketing copy gets the reader to act. Read that again.

Everything from your book description to your opt-in page must be written to appeal to your reader by selling a benefit or generating enough interest or curiosity for them to take the next step.

Take a look at your opt-in copy. Does it read, "Join my newsletter for updates"? Or do you say, "Download the game plan to sell 1,000 books by spending less than $100," with a note that readers who complete the download also receive biweekly tips and tools? The difference is clear.

Copywriting is a skill and a talent, and it takes time to develop. That said, AI really has made copywriting so much easier. If you haven't played around with AI tools like ChatGPT for help with copy, you're unnecessarily struggling through this. But, even with AI you need to understand some simple strategies to help you craft and improve copy that will build your platform.

Focus on your reader with everything you write. Instead of saying, "My new book is out, grab your copy today," say something like "You are about to uncover the #NoBoringBooks way to write a book that will have impact and make you income. Ready to start writing that great book today? Great, click here."

Perhaps you're thinking, "I'm telling a story about myself to create connection, so it has to be about me."

That's true—you should share some of your personal beliefs, experiences, and stories. You can still do it in a way that brings your reader into your story. An opener with a sense of mystery or intrigue can work well too.

Here's an example:

"Have you ever met someone who was the center of a murder investigation before they were even born?"

Compare that to "I was the center of an investigation of murder before I was even born."

The first example is more intriguing because it draws the reader in. That's not my story, by the way. It's the incredible story of Nelson Tressler, who wrote *Unlucky Sperm Club*.[28] Ultimately, the more you present copy with a focus on readers, the more engaging it is to them.

Create a single call to action. When you have a single call to action, it simplifies expectations and makes it easier for someone to do whatever you've asked. Think about the end of a podcast interview when the interviewer says, "Where can our listeners connect with you?" Many authors reply with their website, all their social media handles, and where their book can be purchased. That's generally too much for one reader to absorb.

---

28 Nelson L. Tressler, *The Unlucky Sperm Club: You Are Not a Victim of Your Circumstances but a Product of Your Choices* (T48 Publishing, 2020).

Be specific: "Go to https://booklaunchers.com/gameplan, and you can download our guide to sell 1,000 books without paying for any ads. That will get you my email and all the links to connect with me too!" Simple. Clear. And it will achieve the goal of building your platform. You'll sell books to the people who subscribe to your newsletter and listen to your interview much more efficiently and quickly than if you had given them 100 places to find you.

In general, you have to tell people what to do, whether it's in emails or on social media. A single call to action makes it simpler for the person on your website or reading your newsletter to know what action they're supposed to take. You want to give them a direct path to your door, not a convoluted map with dozens of possible routes.

> **NOTE:** Some authors live in fear of being seen as selling anything. But the only thing worse than too many calls to action is none at all. Your platform won't grow with luck. Books rarely sell without effort. *Your momentum grows with intention.*

The job of writing copy is to get your reader to take some sort of action, and that action should align with your bigger-picture goal for your book. If you want speaking engagements, tell the podcast interviewer. Focus on the purpose of your book marketing, and you'll find it begins to work out over time!

Draw attention with the first line of a post, the title of your video, your email subject lines, and article headlines. Try to create curiosity or offer a benefit. What does your ideal reader get from consuming this content? Sell them on consuming the content.

Open loops that you'll close in the future. Your favorite show does this all the time with cliff-hangers. They have a giant car crash just before the episode ends, or your favorite character gets shot, and you don't know what has happened to them until a full episode later. Hook your reader in with a similar strategy by teasing future content or tools that won't arrive until your next post or email.

If you tease your readers with messages like "That's a pretty cool strategy, but I've got an even better one for you tomorrow," you can make someone eager to hear from you again. Or you could say, "PS—Watch for my next email in five days because I've got a checklist for you to get massive results using what you just learned. This checklist increases your success rate by 35%, so you'll want to keep an eye out for it."

Writing great copy takes practice, and it definitely takes intention. But if you remember these five tips, you'll have more success building an author platform for an audience that's going to pay attention to what you have to say.

Newsletter (or Audience) Swaps

Sometimes, you just need a little help from your friends to get ahead in the publishing game. Swaps are a simple type of mutual marketing that can work for just about any bigger-picture goal. Essentially, you're presenting an offer or great content with a call to action to someone else's audience, and then you reciprocate.

If your goal is platform building, this is a great tactic to try. It can work for selling books if there is really good alignment between your friend's audience and your book's hook. It's also good for establishing your credibility, especially if your swap is with a known authority in the space. But it's best for platform growth.

All this strategy takes is a newsletter (or some other platform like a podcast or a YouTube channel) and a willingness to promote other authors in exchange for their promoting you. To put it simply, you pair up with another author and agree to include some content and a link to whatever you want to promote in their next newsletter.

Depending on the goals for the swap, you should each include the book's cover image along with blurbs and ideally a mini author bio. You should also include a really clear call to action so that readers can learn more about you and your book. Newsletter swaps are most effective if you have at least a few hundred subscribers. The more subscribers you have, the more swapping opportunities are available to you. But having a small subscriber base shouldn't scare you away from engaging with other authors to initiate a swap.

Swaps are free, so you're not risking anything. The worst thing you might experience is a little rejection, which might sting, but you'll go on.

The hardest part might be finding people with whom to swap. If you already have an author network, start by asking those with similar books if they would be interested.

Getting involved in your industry events can also help. FinCon has an author table where authors can sell their books. Many of those authors have similar audiences that could lead to effective swaps. At the Entrepreneurs' Organization (EO), we have a MYEO Author and Speakers group where authors can connect to create mutually beneficial offers and opportunities like swaps.

Going to networking events like 20Booksto50k® is a great place to meet other authors. Another place to find newsletter friends is social media, especially on professional groups like LinkedIn or Facebook. You can even check out Goodreads or Reddit to see if any like-minded authors would like to swap. Of course, it's key that the authors you choose for a swap have something of value or interest to your audience and vice versa.

If you are writing for parents, and you're swapping with a business author, you won't get the results you want, and neither will they. Even with newsletter swaps, you want to offer value by providing a benefit or solution to a problem. Line up with authors who share your target reader. It's collaboration, not competition.

You can also turn to sites made specifically for this type of networking, like StoryOrigin and BookFunnel. They do the hard work when it comes to connecting you with the right author for your swap. StoryOrigin offers a ton of useful features for an author looking to up their newsletter game, and it allows you to connect with other authors to swap mentions in upcoming newsletters and group promos. This is where you can team up with multiple authors to promote your books on a single landing page.

BookFunnel is similar to StoryOrigin. It provides a toolbox of custom landing pages, e-book and audiobook delivery, and direct email integration. The difference is that BookFunnel is a paid subscription plan. But even their most basic plan gets you one-to-one author-swap organization assistance, along with group promos and a ton of other pretty sweet features. Once you find an author for a swap, simply exchange the information you both need, including a link, image, and reader magnet.

When sending links to authors to promote your work in their newsletters, put consideration into what exactly you want to share. Be sure to include a brief blurb about your book and a short author bio too. If you have accolades like awards, be sure to include those. Or if you have a positive editorial review or an endorsement, you can highlight a line or two.

Most important, before you send your materials to your newfound swap friend, check to make sure that your links work.

You have one chance to make an impression on subscribers. Make it count. You also want to make it as easy as possible for someone to promote you.

Plan the timing of your newsletter swap, and make sure you include everything you've agreed upon. And of course, I think this goes without saying, but let's say it anyway just in case: follow through on your side of the swap with enthusiasm and goodwill.

Finally, don't get disheartened if you gain and lose some subscribers while participating in a swap. Sometimes readers may not enjoy your work. You won't please everyone. Continue networking and building that platform.

Consistency, creativity, and continually trying new strategies work in the long run for platform building. Ten years from now, people will see your gigantic audience and ask you for the magic bullet to build a platform like yours.

Content Marketing

Building your platform is a long game. It's all about staying in the market and consistently doing things to find your audience day after day.

You'll have days when it feels as if nobody is listening. Worse, sometimes you'll get a troll who says something nasty. You'll feel like quitting. Keep going. Trolls are just a sign your content is reaching people who aren't already supporting you.

If you're reading this and wondering what content marketing is, here's a quick explanation: *It's any content of value you create that has a long life.*

This can be images, text, videos, in-person content, or audio content. Every nonfiction author should do some form of content marketing because it can:

- build a loyal audience,
- drive traffic organically,
- establish credibility,
- foster business growth,
- generate book sales,
- lead to speaking engagements and PR opportunities, and
- reduce advertising costs.

If you're starting completely from scratch, my suggestion would be to tap in to places that have an existing audience as opposed to starting a blog on your website and having to drive traffic to that blog. Websites like Medium, *Forbes*, *Cosmopolitan*, *Reader's Digest*, and the *Huffington Post*, among others, are major sites that accept article submissions. A few even pay a small fee if you are selected.

Building your newsletter and content marketing are constantly evolving responsibilities. So rather than give you a giant to-do list, my suggestion is to pick one task that appeals to you, even a little. Imagine someone said that you can create only one type of content for a year. What would that be for you?

For me, it's video. Amani Roberts, author of *DJs Mean Business*, has found a great platform on Twitch and live streaming video.[29] Nick Kennedy, author of *The Good Entrepreneur*, reluctantly entered the TikTok realm and has grown a nice following there.[30] And Peter Carayiannis, author of *Corporate Counsel*, does a wonderful job on LinkedIn with engagement and content.[31]

There's no pressure to be everywhere doing everything—just do something.

Meanwhile, remember—*with every piece of content you create, make sure you have a call to action that ideally sends people back to your reader magnet to opt in.* The #1 priority of content marketing is to build your audience so that you have people who are excited to read your book, post reviews, hire you, buy your course, and share your message.

If you're getting the feeling that content marketing is work, it is. There are no magical book-marketing solutions. AI offers opportunities for speeding up content creation if you're willing to learn how to use it. Personally I'm loving the ability to use a service like ContentFries or vidyo.ai to take long-form video content (like a live stream) and turn it into all kinds of bite-size

---

29 Amani Roberts, *DJs Mean Business: One Night Behind the Turntables Can Spin Your Company's Success* (Woodside Media Group, 2020).

30 Nick Kennedy, *The Good Entrepreneur: An Insider's Guide to Building a Principled Business and a Powerful Personal Legacy* (Sleeping Giant, 2022).

31 Peter Carayiannis, *Corporate Counsel: Expert Advice on Becoming a Successful In-House Lawyer* (Old Town Press, 2022).

content for shorts, reels, and more short-form content. That space and the tools in it are evolving so fast I'm not even going to go into this. Just know that content creation is getting easier and less costly every day.

You can also hire help with different aspects of content marketing, but one action will rarely lead to thousands of sales. Sometimes, you create something that really connects with people, and spreads, but results most often arise from consistent effort over time. That's why you should pick at least one form you enjoy and stick with it.

LinkedIn—The Professional Person's Social Media Platform

Many nonfiction authors have built a really strong following on LinkedIn, and it can be the perfect place to find your audience if you're in the business or professional space.

Notice that I did not say LinkedIn is the ultimate book-selling platform. If you want that, maximize your Amazon sales page, and run Amazon Ads. (More to come on that.) However, LinkedIn is a great place to be discovered as an expert and to connect with your potential readers. If you've decided your book should serve as a calling card for your expertise, LinkedIn could be one of the most promising platforms for you to use.

The best part of LinkedIn is, small adjustments can yield big results.

Before you do anything else, make sure you've recently updated your profile. (Or create one if you don't have it!) I generally recommend you use your legal name, but if your name is taken, you can go with your author branding. I don't recommend you use your book title, because you and your brand are much more than one book.

Your banner is a good place to invite people to join your email list (with your fabulous lead magnet) or advertise your book in a way that showcases the benefit to your ideal reader. When you create your banner, pay special attention to where the circular author photo goes. You don't want it to hide any text.

Next up, let's update your LinkedIn headline, and this should be short and clear and focused on your ideal audience (and what you offer them). Using keywords really helps, too, because you will be found in searches on LinkedIn when someone looks for an expert in a specific area. The optimization of your profile is all about what's going to generate more profile views, in addition to creating content that gets engagement from other LinkedIn users.

Remember, your profile might be about you, but it's not *for you*. Complete the "About" section to clearly explain:

- who you are,
- how you can help, and
- whom you can help.

You want someone interested in your product, services, expertise, or book to get all that in a few short sentences.

It's also useful to use this section to tell someone how you want them to contact you—by email, website, telephone, or snail mail—although most LinkedIn users are likely to message you right there on the platform.

Now comes the best part for any author: adding your featured items. Here's where you can highlight big media features, important things you've written, or awards you've won. And of course, your book.

You can add as many links as you want, including an Amazon link to buy your book, but only two are shown on your front page. Users need to scroll to the right to see any other links. Take time to figure out exactly what you want your ideal connections to see.

Once your profile is up and looks good, there are a lot of fabulous ways to use LinkedIn. Remember this is professional networking, so leave pictures of your kids off this platform unless there's a very clear connection to your work or messaging.

My friend Devin Karpes runs a successful international digital ad agency (and is founder of TooCool, a group focused on promoting the benefits of cold plunging and cold showers). Devin featured a story about his daughter. His post was all about how she learned the value of entrepreneurship when she earned $100 in a few hours at her lemonade stand. She realized it was going to take her 10 weeks to earn the same amount with her weekly allowance! That's the kind of post about your kids that's appropriate for LinkedIn.

You can post book-related content, such as advice or images from your book. Or try infographics, social media posts, or shares that highlight a quote. You can share interviews and media that featured you and highlight quotes or advice you shared in those features. This is not about promotion. It's about adding value.

You can also create a LinkedIn newsletter or write articles on the platform. This can be easier to gain traction than if you only post content to your own website because many people are on LinkedIn searching for content, commenting, and sharing cool ideas or interesting information. For example, Phil McKinney, a retired Hewlett-Packard executive, author, and podcast host, has written and maintains a popular LinkedIn newsletter, *Finding Ideas*.[32] That's a great way to build your position as a thought leader, create content that is easy for people to share, and as a result, grow your audience and stay in front of them.

You can also create video content on the platform. Linking to other video platforms doesn't work as well as posting natively to their platform because

---

32 Phil McKinney, *Finding Ideas*, LinkedIn newsletter, accessed June 20, 2023, https://www.linkedin.com/newsletters/finding-ideas-6877610204809228288/.

they don't want people to leave their platform. Often external video links will be suppressed in the feeds.

Now it's time to start looking for connections. Who shares your target audience? Check them out, reach out, and connect. Maybe there's a way you can help each other. Find relevant LinkedIn groups, and start adding value to the conversations there. People will see your comments and check out your profile.

Please don't post promotional content in these groups—add value. People want to connect with you only when you've added value to a conversation. And there's a lot more opportunity on LinkedIn if you decide to use it, but this will get you started!

Celebrity Status with YouTube

"I wonder how many people know we have a celebrity here?" said a man, who smiled as he walked up to my booth at a National Speakers Association (NSA) conference. "We have Julie, 'the Book Broad' in the house!!"

It turns out that he watched a bunch of my videos while he wrote his book and that led him to buy my book, which helped him even more. He came over to say thank you. It was a cool moment, and it happens more and more often, which is really rewarding.

It's also further evidence that YouTube is a powerful platform for being discovered and connecting with potential book readers, clients, influencers, and more.

Even if the idea of being on camera freaks you out a bit, the reality is the world is only moving more and more toward video. Plus, YouTube is owned by Google, so being prominent on the video platform gets you to the top of Google searches. It's also a place where people go to solve problems. People are searching on YouTube for the problem you can solve. If you're not there, they won't find you.

Plus, YouTube is totally fine with your selling your book and getting people to opt in to your newsletter or even buy your product and service. On top of that, when you get 1,000 subscribers, you can enable monetization, so every view makes you a little money. You can also promote other people's stuff with affiliate links, which can be pretty lucrative if you have a message-to-market match. Finally, you can get sponsorships and connect with potential clients for your business, podcast, or blog.

> **TIP:** If you are an introvert like me, video helps folks recognize you in real life. And being recognizable makes life as an introvert easier. You don't have to work so hard to meet people—they will come to you at conferences and networking events because they feel as if they know you already. You're welcome.

Now, I'm not going to give you a technical step-by-step guide on how to start a YouTube channel because there are plenty of fabulous resources online to help with that. But let's talk strategy.

How to Get Started with Your YouTube Channel

When your book goes to the editor, it's a great time to get your author website, newsletter, and YouTube channel all set up and ready to go. Even if your book is already out, it's not too late. It's never too late to start, but the sooner you do it, the better.

Here are a few quick tips specific to authors:

Title your channel something broader than your book. Name it after your business or your name, so you can build a community and use it to promote whatever you do beyond the book. *Kathy Loves Physics* is a great example. While Kathy Joseph wrote her book, she also created her YouTube channel (and built it big too—go, Kathy!!). Her first book was *The Lightning Tamers: True Stories of the Dreamers and Schemers Who Harnessed*

Electricity and Transformed Our World.[33] On her channel, she has series specific to this book, and when she moves her attention to a new book, she creates a series specific to that one. Her channel has a big enough umbrella to cover many books.

Use your book for content. When you feel stuck trying to plan your content—remember your book! Longtime viewers of BookLaunchers.tv have certainly picked up on the fact that much of this book started as video content. But the reverse works well too. Turn different sections of your book into short videos up to 12 minutes. You can also use a subject from your book as a live stream discussion topic! Potential content derived from your book could become a video about "The Single Most Important Tip to Get Top Results" or "Five Things You Don't Know About [insert your subject] but Should." Or maybe you can try something like "Three Myths About [insert your subject]." Numbered videos tend to perform really well for a lot of content creators—including BookLaunchers.tv.

Don't hold back trying to sell your book. You can realistically give one strategy or idea in depth or a handful of quick tips in one video. Let's say in your book you have a list of 10 things to say to a woman so she feels beautiful. Share the most surprising three things from that list, and then add this to the video: "Want to know the other seven? They're in my book! Pick up a copy, right here." Heck, you could even create one video for each tip and still have people who buy your book because they want it in that format.

Let's say your book has 18 chapters. You can easily shoot 20 videos and not even give away half of its good content.

People will still buy your book, even if they're already familiar with a lot of your content. Besides, even your biggest fan probably doesn't watch every single one of your videos. I mean, I think Shaun Hayes and Efren Delgado (two of my YouTube besties) are getting close to watching all of my vid-

---

33 Kathy Joseph, *The Lightning Tamers: True Stories of the Dreamers and Schemers Who Harnessed Electricity and Transformed the World* (Smart Science Press, 2022).

eos, but I bet they are also reading this book right now. Most people will probably watch only a handful of your videos or read only some of your content. But if they love it, they just might buy your book or even check out your website to see if you have a product or service that will help them even more than your video or book.

Remember the overall goal of your book marketing. Was it to sell books? Okay, then your call to action in every video should be to buy your book. If your overall goal was to create speaking opportunities, giving all your book content away on your channel makes complete sense because the goal isn't an $18 book sale. It's an $18,000 speaking gig!

Whenever you really question whether you should put your best tip out there, look at the movies and what they put in previews. If they didn't put some of the best scenes in that movie trailer, you might never go see the movie. They know they have to show you some of the best stuff to get you in the door. Worry more about what's going to interest people the most, *then* consider what might give too much away.

Some authors worry that if they put their best stuff in the book, people won't buy their course. Here's an example from my life:

Pitch Anything by Oren Klaff was one of my favorite books when I raised capital for my real estate investments.[34] When he came out with an online course, I happily bought it! Even though the course consisted largely of content from his book, I didn't mind because it was a different format. It also expanded on some of the concepts in the book just enough, and it included worksheets and tools. I was a huge fan, and I wanted to learn every single nugget of information he had to give, so it was worth it to me. If he'd come to my city or a city near me with an in-person event at the time, I would have paid for that too!

---

34 Oren Klaff, *Pitch Anything: An Innovative Method for Presenting, Persuading, and Winning the Deal* (New York: McGraw-Hill, 2011).

Bottom line—if you have great content, your fans are going to want to consume it, so show them how awesome you are, and don't hold back. Believe that you have enough greatness and amazing content to go around and make them want more.

Now that you know that you need to start churning out video content, and why it's important to post it consistently, let's turn our attention in the next chapter to getting out there through speaking engagements.

The Mindset for Platform Building Like a Boss

Imagine you're a singer. Your popularity is growing. You're not really famous yet, but people are starting to recognize you. You're scheduled to perform a free concert for about 500 people. You've traveled quite a distance for this concert, and you're excited to have such a great audience.

A few hours before the show, as you're setting up, a massive snowstorm rolls through. The snow piles up so fast that most people can't get out of their houses, let alone drive anywhere.

Instead of 500 people, there are 10 people in the audience.

Your opening act goes on stage but puts on a half-hearted performance. They probably feel as if it's a waste to expend a lot of energy playing for free for just a few people.

What do you do? It would be so easy to think, "Forget it. Why go on? What's the point of playing for 10 people?"

That's not what happened, though. This is actually a true story.

The performer stepped on stage and said to the audience, "Well, I am disappointed that there's so few of you here, but I want to thank *you* for being here. I have a new song I want to play for you. I hope you like it." He proceeded to belt out "What's New Pussycat?" as if he had a full stadium. That singer was Tom Jones.

I heard that story more than a decade ago when I interviewed Jim Randel, author of *Confessions of a Real Estate Entrepreneur.*[35]

Jim was in that audience of 10.

I think about it all the time, especially when new authors get hung up on the fact that they only have 100 people reading their newsletters or 20 people at their book launch. The truth is, it doesn't matter if there is one person or hundreds of thousands of people reading what you write or hearing what you say. It's a privilege to have an audience at all. Everyone, even Tom Jones and Tony Robbins, started small and worked their way up.

That's a big part of thinking your way to success: It's not about *you*. It's about your audience (or your client). It's the challenge and fun of being an author and working on the long game of getting paid for your expertise. It would be nice if you launched a book and made money the next day, but it rarely works that way, unless you've spent a decade building your audience before your book comes out.

What if you're an introvert, and the idea of building an audience and networking to develop connections freaks you out? My friend, the next chapter is written especially for you.

Chapter Summary

1. Become a better copywriter. Remember to focus on your reader and include one call to action per email. Write a compelling subject line, so your email gets opened. Also, open loops in that email that you'll close in the next email to encourage readers to keep looking forward to forthcoming communications.

2. Swap audiences with other authors to achieve your goals.

---

35 James A. Randel, *Confessions of a Real Estate Entrepreneur: What It Takes to Win in High-Stakes Commercial Real Estate,* (New York: McGraw-Hill, 2006).

3.   Create compelling content focused on the reader and what they need to learn for you to generate new subscribers, increase book sales, and enhance your authority.

4.   You don't need to be everywhere doing everything. Just be somewhere consistently.

5.   It's a privilege to have an audience, no matter the size.

6.   YouTube is a great platform (owned by Google) to leverage the content of your book into video for an audience that knows, likes, and trusts you and thinks of you as a celebrity in your niche.

CHAPTER 6

NETWORKING FOR INTROVERTS

MASSIVE, BESTSELLING BOOK CAMPAIGNS ARE ALMOST ALWAYS THE RE-sult of *the people* with whom authors surround themselves. Look at Tim Ferriss and how he broke into bestselling status—he'd made connections with bloggers by attending a lot of events and networking like a machine for years before the *4-Hour Workweek*[36] launched.

Sometimes surrounding yourself with successful people is about learning from their success. Other times, it's having friends who promote the book on your behalf to their big audiences. *More than Cashflow* topped Amazon because of my network (and the book being a great match for them to promote to their audiences).

When you see a nonfiction author topping the charts at launch, and they aren't a celebrity, look to see who supports that author. Chances are, there are celebrity influencers helping to peddle that book.

---

36 Tim Ferriss, *The 4-Hour Workweek: Escape 9-5, Live Anywhere, and Join the New Rich*, (New York: Harmony, 2009).

Authors who sell a lot of books in bulk (we're coming to that soon) do most of those sales because of relationships that connect them to people who buy books in bulk. On her podcast, *Book Marketing Mentors*,[37] Susan Friedmann said she sold 500,000 copies of her book to one company with whom she'd worked as a consultant.

From a strategic-goal perspective, you can already see how networking helps with every bigger-picture goal you might have. If you want to sell books, you may uncover big bulk-sale opportunities or the ability to reach a lot of other people through someone else's audience.

For the goal of becoming an authority, the more people know who you are and respect your expertise, the more credibility you gain. If your book goal is to generate leads or grow your platform, other people's audiences or the right connections can be all you need to reach that result.

You might be thinking, "Where can I meet some new people? My friends aren't cutting the mustard as far as the goals I have for my book and my business."

IRL Always Wins

You need to be face-to-face to build relationships. I attended six virtual conferences during the pandemic and didn't make any connections, despite having a virtual booth at four of them. I had plenty of conversations, but there just weren't connections. There is a big difference. I went to one event last month, and my friend introduced me to someone she knew I'd connect with. She was right! Three days later we were working together.

We had already been connected online twice before, but it wasn't until we met in person that we actually bonded and developed synergy for a business relationship.

---

37 https://bookmarketingmentors.com

Where do you find events so you can network with people who share your interests? Finding local events is a great place to start. If you're into real estate, look for investor groups. If you're into health-related subjects, find groups with similar interests—maybe running groups or cycling clubs. Check out Eventbrite or Meetup.com. If you have a business, joining a local chamber of commerce could be really valuable. Unless you're in a very small locale, you should be able to find people with common interests.

Next, I recommend finding educational or training courses you can attend in person. People who go to courses in person are a tiny, tiny percentage of the population, but they are the kind of people who take the time to show up and are generally enthusiastic about what they do.

Choose courses with topics that you need to grow your business. Look for industry-specific conferences as well. If you're a podcaster, check out events like She Podcasts, Podfest, and Podcast Movement that provide amazing educational and networking opportunities. Financial experts might enjoy FinCon. Speakers should definitely join NSA. Just start asking around, and you'll uncover some great options.

Prep Your Networking

If you are naturally extroverted and meet people easily, you can probably skip this part. This is more for the people who are wallflowers like me!

If I go to an event without a plan, then I leave without having met many people, unless an extrovert somehow befriends me. Many events have apps where you can start to network in advance. Other events have speed net-working, which is also fantastic to get some fast one-on-one connections. Either works well because you'll want to set meetings before you arrive so you are guaranteed some valuable conversations.

If it's Meetup, you can also see in advance who else is attending. Review the participant list to find people you want to talk to—and even plan *what* you might talk to them about. This is where I say to be strategic. It's okay to be a social media stalker. Maybe you went to the same school or have a common friend—having something in common can really help with breaking the ice. You may even be able to reach out to them on the platform's app and set a time to say hello.

If you have a common friend, you might ask for an introduction leading into the event, so you have a connection waiting for you there.

This is also where it's really useful if you have a highly extroverted or connected friend you can lean on for introductions. My friend Deb Cole is an extreme extrovert and knows everyone at most events. I can meet tons of people just by being her sidekick. Dale Roberts of *Self-Publishing with Dale*[38] networks like a boss and almost always knows people with whom I want to connect. He's kind and generous in making introductions, so I have come to rely on him to meet someone if I want to avoid a cold outreach.

Years ago, I taught people how to raise money for real estate investing. After I shared my advice about networking, an attendee came up to me afterward and said, "I'm not good at these things. What do I say to people?"

I shared my personal secret: *Put the spotlight on the other person.*

Often I will say something simple, like "What brought you to this event?" or "Have you been to this city before?" Then, after listening to their answer (rather than waiting for my turn to speak), I ask follow-up questions, like "What's been your favorite session?" or "What's been your favorite takeaway so far?"

Generally speaking, if you're smiling, having fun, laughing, listening to people when they talk, and asking a few good questions, you'll be miles ahead of a lot of the people who are at these events.

---

38 https://selfpublishingwithdale.com

And never eat a meal alone. Find a buddy. That's how my friend Deb Cole and I became friends in the first place—she challenged the audience at an event where she was a speaker to not eat alone, so I invited her to lunch.

Invite other people who are alone to have a meal or drink with you, so you can make new connections. Building relationships with other authors, influencers, or experts in your industry can be the single biggest thing you do to sell a lot of books as an author.

The Speaker's Edge

The second time I'd ever given a talk to an audience was at The Toronto Investor Forum in front of 600 people. My first talk took place before a dozen people in a small room at a community center—so it was a big change in experience.

Before I went on stage at the Investor Forum, I was shaking so badly that I was worried I wouldn't be able to walk on stage. My memories of being on stage are limited, but it must have gone well because I wound up speaking at nine more forum events over the next few years. In fact, I became one of their featured speakers.

This experience also unlocked what I found to be the most powerful advantage an introvert could ask for, and that is *the ease of connecting with others when you're a speaker*. People know who you are and come to you!

Networking also can be easier as a speaker. If you're speaking at an event, you can often ask for a connection to other speakers through the event organizer. And if they won't connect you, being a fellow speaker can go a long way toward initiating a conversation.

The other upside of being a speaker is that you can build your newsletter, sell books, and have a captive audience to talk about your subject and share your expertise.

Speaking supercharges your networking. This isn't a book about building a speaking business, but many people write a book for that reason. For many others, the goal of their book is more frequent or higher-paid engagements. The two go so beautifully together. If you are a speaker without a book, you're leaving money on the table. And if you've written a book, not giving some talks about your book subject is also leaving money on the table!

It can seem daunting, but if you add one thing to your platform-building efforts, I recommend honing your skills as a speaker and saying *yes* to any opportunities to get in front of your ideal audience—whether it's paid or free. When you're the speaker at an event, your name is automatically in front of attendees, organizers, and other speakers. You can walk up to just about anyone and say hello with ease, but the odds are, you'll be approached first. Your network expands, as does your authority.

What Is an Influencer?

We used to ask Book Launchers clients to give us their dream influencer list, so we could help them prepare for outreach to boost their book launch and promotion.

The lists we got typically included:

- Brené Brown,
- Dave Ramsey,
- Elon Musk,
- Jordan Peterson,
- Joe Rogan,
- Oprah,
- Reese Witherspoon,
- Tony Robbins, or
- Will Smith.

That wasn't working, so we got a researcher on our team to do the work. Sure, these celebrities are influencers with megapower, but the challenge of focusing on a list like this is that you can rarely get past the gatekeepers. You can spend years trying to get in front of these superstars and not have anything happen. It's easier to build momentum with people who are celebrities in small spaces and grow from there.

Cold outreach is one of my least favorite things, so I understand any author's resistance to influencer outreach—whether it's asking for endorsements, reviews, or promotional support. That is why I rarely do it without doing some groundwork.

First, I usually try to find a connection point—even if it's weak. That's where a more strategic influencer list makes more sense. It's far easier to tap friends of friends compared to someone who is seven degrees of separation away from you.

Ideally, it's best to build relationships before you need them, so you can call in favors for your book launch. At some point, however, you'll need to do some influencer outreach and make some asks.

To understand what that entails, let's discuss influencers and what matters for you, the nonfiction author.

Influencers have always been a significant sales tool, whether they were actually called that or not. If your goal is solely book sales, influencers should be one of your biggest points of focus beyond ads. *A powerful influencer helps you sell your book, but they are also a wonderful way to grow your leads and your platform.*

Influencers are notable people, thought leaders, media personalities, or celebrities. They have invested years and thousands of hours building an audience and establishing some kind of authority. Some influencers aim to be at the forefront of fashion and other industry trends. They help by lending you and your book their credibility.

A note in their newsletter, a smartly crafted blurb, or an opportunity to share a stage is the difference between selling a hundred copies and selling thousands of copies. But not every influencer is the influencer who matters for you and your book marketing. You need someone respected who has a platform to share your message with an audience of your target readers.

Just because you connect with someone who is on TV, for example, doesn't mean they're the best person to promote your book. Will your reader know who they are? Will your ideal reader trust what they say? Does their audience act on their recommendations?

It's much better to find people who are well known for their work in your industry or a similar industry. You may not know who Canadian athlete Patrick Vellner is if you aren't into CrossFit, but if you wrote a book on improving your athletic recovery time, I can almost guarantee getting Uncle Pat to endorse your book would be a huge commercial boost. Judging by the volume of his paid product endorsements, a lot of companies appreciate his influence with the CrossFit community.

If your book ties your business concepts back to Texas Hold'em poker, then getting a shout-out from professional poker players Phil Hellmuth or Jennifer Harman could be a game changer. Not everyone knows who they are, but what matters is whether your ideal reader does or not. It's much easier to connect to folks who are niche famous than people who are world famous, and the value will be just as high (or even higher) if they are the right influencers for your book.

Making the Ask—Mind Your Mindset First

Instead of feeling needy or self-conscious when approaching an influencer, do it knowing that your reader needs you to take this important step to help them find your book.

You've written the book to have an impact, and it will only do that if you find readers.

Additionally, if you can make any outreach part of **a relationship-building goal versus a transactional goal**, you'll likely feel better about it. And, most likely, your results will reflect that.

So, how to begin?

Do something that might get an influencer's attention in a natural way. Your inclination might be to send an email, and you can. But it's worth brainstorming other ways that are more organic.

I'm far from a big-time influencer, but I do have a robust and enthusiastic community of #YouTubeBesties. I value comments and engagement tremendously, so when someone comments on every single video, they get my attention, and I remember who they are. Steven Seril has commented on my YouTube videos for quite some time, so when he connected with me on Twitter, I connected back.

One day, Steven posted a request for pictures of people in dinosaur costumes with his book. My son happened to have a dinosaur costume, so I bought his book and got my son to pose holding the book. Steven didn't ask me directly. I just did it to support someone who supports me. (Of course, if he'd asked me to do it, I would have.)

Other ideas to garner attention include going to an influencer's event and finding a way to get an introduction. I highly recommend posting on social media your favorite parts of their event with pictures. Speakers *love* this and will notice. You could also apply the advice they've given, and then post on social media the results of that advice with a thank-you.

Jesse Itzler has talked about how he hired his former right hand, Amanda McCreight, into his Build Your Life Resume (BYLR) company.[39] (She's now gone on to start a company of her own, which he has enthusiastically supported). She was one of the first people to take the BYLR program

---

39 "Amanda x Jesse Itzler," Amanda McCreight, accessed March 14, 2023, https://www.amandamccreight.com/endeavors/amandaxjesseitzler.

and posted her results along the way. That got his attention, and he hired her for the amazing and surely adventurous job working alongside him as he did Ultraman races and hosted all kinds of wild adventures for his community.

It doesn't happen with one post or one comment. But being a true fan, a regular supporter, implementer, and commenter can be invaluable to many influencers. That's friction-free connecting at its best.

Of course, you can also try good, old-fashioned email or messaging on LinkedIn or another platform. But here's what you should *not* ask:

- "Can I send you my book to read and write a review?"
- "Will you please retweet this to your audience?"
- "My book is relevant to your audience. Will you share it with them?"
- "Our companies have a lot of synergies. Can we chat to discuss how we can help each other?"
- Or, the one I hate the most, "Can I pick your brain about something?"

I get more than a dozen of these a week, and while I sometimes give them a polite reply, the answer is always no. If you're trying to connect with someone else who has a big audience already, I can guarantee they won't give your message a second look.

Things that might work, however, if you ask them to contribute to your book or request advice, is to find another way to make it easy for them to say yes.

As an example, I was invited to speak at two different online summits on the same day. One made it clear my participation was contingent on my promoting the event to my list. That was an instant turnoff because it felt as if the person only wanted my participation to access my audience, not me or my content.

The other one went like this: "I see your videos each week, and I just love them. I have to ask if you would participate in this upcoming summit. We have other experts like X and Y, and we'd love to have the Book Broad participate too." I knew X and immediately said yes.

The organizers showed an appreciation for my content as their reason for reaching out. They didn't ask me for anything apart from appearing on a panel, which was easy for me to do. And they also established their credibility by naming someone I know and respect in the industry. Plus, it was an interview, so I didn't have to prepare a talk. I could just be me!

Think about what you can ask for that is an easy yes and makes the other person feel valued, not used.

Be a Sniper, Not a Torpedo

You have to be patient and focused. To achieve your goals, take the time to aim.

If you still have difficulty creating connections, send your desired influencer something of value. Robert Workman was a client of ours who successfully got his books into airport bookstores with a rather unconventional approach. His follow-up after a sales call to carry his book was sending a box of cookies.

Yep, and it worked.

My friend Scott Sylvan Bell (the Hawaiian shirt guy I mentioned in the branding section) sends amazing gift boxes full of his favorite local Hawaiian finds to people with whom he wants to connect.

If you know someone loves something, take that into account. You're taking the time to personalize your outreach, which will be far more meaningful to that person.

Who doesn't love a thoughtful gift? This is, again, where you can be a bit of a stalker. Eavesdrop to find a way you can help. Most influencers are on social media, or they do live streams or podcasts. Listen for clues as to how you can help them or connect with them.

Please don't tweet someone and say, "How can I help you?" They don't know you, nor do they really want to share where they need help. I mean, who likes asking for help? They are going to ignore you or be uncomfortable with that ask. Instead, listen and pay attention. You may find the perfect gift, whether it's a physical item or a donation to a cause they care about!

As I mentioned before, knowing someone who knows someone is a great way in. This is also where being a part of groups like Entrepreneurs' Organization, NSA, or some other community can be valuable. You can post in your group that you're looking to connect with someone, and you may just find another person who can offer an introduction.

Deliver value to others frequently. Think of others and offer support if you can. For example, you can offer to connect people with common interests, messages, or expertise as you come across them.

If you put in the work to listen and learn, and then follow up with a generous, thoughtful offer to assist people, they will remember and begin to recognize you. Often, they will ask you how they can return the favor. Voilà, you've got an easy opening.

Even if everything I've mentioned worked or you need added momentum, there is value in highlighting the work of others. Take Steven Seril, who has launched an Outstanding Creator Awards series. He gave me one, and now I'm promoting it, wearing the medal he sent to me when I shoot videos. I definitely know who he is, and now so do many more people in my audience.

Jim James does something similar by collecting experts for his podcast and then taking the best interviews and turning them into a book. I'm in his second volume of *The UnNoticed Entrepreneur Book: Fifty [More] Experts Share Their Ideas for Your Company to Stand Out.*[40]

The same approach can work if you do a series of articles, videos, podcasts, or expert interviews. Not everyone you ask will say yes, but some will. And you'll build some powerfully strong bonds with people who are influencers in their space.

All of this is work. But that's why it's effective. Most people won't do it, making it that much easier for you to stand out.

Who Is on Your List?

You need to form two teams, and the earlier you identify your players, the better.

Team one consists of people on your influencer list. When you're making this list, note what you want to ask them or why you think they'd be great for your book.

Remember, your influencer list doesn't have to be full of famous people. They just need to be names the majority of your ideal readers will know, like, and respect.

Team two consists of people on your book army list. Your book army is a network of people you know who will support the book. You aren't always going to look to these people to actually buy and review your book (because you only want ideal readers doing that ... and Amazon doesn't want friends and family writing reviews!). But they make up the basis of support that connects you to others, posts on social media, and helps build that groundswell of momentum and activity that every book launch needs!

---

40 Jim James, *The UnNoticed Entrepreneur Book: Fifty [More] Experts Share Their Ideas for Your Company to Stand Out* (Mankato, Minnesota: Capstone, forthcoming).

This list includes your friends, family, colleagues, clients, social media followers, professional or community groups, event organizers, and email subscribers. This is your LinkedIn network, your alumni list, your mom's friends, and so on. Ideally, these folks are people who will love your content and want to support you. You know most of them in person.

Even if your book has launched, having a book army you can count on is useful to rally your book for a relaunch, get more reviews, promote a 99-cent giveaway, or have an event!

Don't worry, my fellow introverts, there are plenty of ways to sell books while you hide behind your computer screen without speaking to others. But you should not rely on those methods alone if you have hopes of making it big as an author, selling a lot of books, or growing your brand or business from your book. That requires handshakes, lunches, and asking real people for help.

Chapter Summary

1. The best way to develop relationships that will support your bigger-picture goals, and possibly lead to friendships, is to make connections in person.

2. Networking and influencer outreach are marketing tactics that benefit almost every strategy and author goal. They can sell books, unlock opportunities, grow your platform, and generate leads.

3. Speaking engagements are a way to supercharge your networking, sell books, and grow your platform. Say yes to these opportunities, so that you can grow and expand as a public speaker.

4. When doing influencer outreach, look for people who are niche famous versus Hollywood-style famous. Niche influencers have fewer gatekeepers but can have just as much impact on an audience, even if that audience is smaller.

5. Focus on relationship building instead of transactional relationships when you reach out to others. Even if you don't receive any support for your book or your other professional goals, bringing people into your sphere as an author can make your life richer in many ways.

CHAPTER 7

YOUR LAUNCH STRATEGY MENU

LAUNCH DAY CAN BE DISAPPOINTING AND HUMBLING.

That's not my wish for you, but I meet far more authors surprised by a lackluster book launch than authors excited at how a launch exceeded their expectations.

There's so much hype and emphasis around a book launch that there's probably a part of you that thinks confetti, balloons, and champagne bottles are going to fall out of the sky.

Admittedly, after all the time, money, and energy you put into your book, it seems as if life should be different somehow once it's launched.

The reality of book launch day for most authors more closely resembles this:

You wake up and immediately check Amazon to see if your book is ranking. Then, after you've had your morning coffee, you beg everyone you know to write reviews of your book if they haven't already. You start your new job of "smiling and dialing" as you call in favors from connected friends to help you get attention for your book. And then you go back to refreshing your Amazon page a hundred times, wondering if you'll get an orange flag to signify that people are buying your book.

Of course, you feel a sense of accomplishment (you should!), and it is an exciting day, but the reality is that most authors come to realize the real work is about to begin. Writing a great book wasn't enough—now you have to find your readers.

A Book Launch Is Like Birth

Many people equate their book to a baby. It makes sense because it can take about nine months to get from editing and design to launch. Many authors have carried their books around inside their heads for so long, and then worked so hard to bring them into the world, that launch day has the excitement of a new birth.

The difference is that most parents anticipate a lifetime of responsibility. But most authors think the work is done once their book is released out in the world.

Launch day, or the days after launch, can lead to the harsh realization that even the greatest book is not going to sell unless you hustle to make it happen. It's the day you realize you are the parent of a book, and the minute you stop caring for this book baby, it stops growing.

When you launch your book, it's time to activate marketing mode, and let your readers know you're here to help! Even if you had a big launch, you still need to do this, by the way.

A strong launch is useful for you as an author. It was much easier for me to land a bunch of television media appearances after *More than Cashflow* was #1 overall on Amazon because that gave me and my book a lot of credibility. Launch does build momentum and makes the post-launch work a little lighter if it's a big launch, but there is still a lot of work to do to keep the momentum going no matter how your launch went.

Having a giant bestseller launch isn't always an option, though. It might be your wish, but your launch strategy is going to be more dependent on your resources than it is on your desires. Let's review what the high-level options are for launches. Then we'll match you with the one that fits your goals and resources.

These are the four strategies as we define them at Book Launchers:

- Amazon Bestseller—99 Cent E-book Launch
- Maximum Momentum Launch
- Periodical Bestseller Launch
- Phased Momentum Launch

To a point, you can combine these launch strategies. But having a higher-level picture of the primary launch strategy will help you focus your resources and tactics. Remember how we discussed matching your marketing strategy to your tactics so you get results that you want? That's what we want to do here. What exactly are these four different strategies?

I'm glad you asked!

The Amazon Bestseller Launch—99 Cent E-book Sale

Who This Is For

You have a small- to medium-size audience of engaged followers on social media or in the form of newsletter subscribers. This is usually 1,000 email subscribers or 10,000+ social media subscribers. You can get away with less if the audience is hungry and active. You'll need more if they aren't that engaged. What you want is the ability to sell 100 to 200 copies of your book at 99 cents in less than a week. By "engaged," I mean you have open rates on your emails and link clicks and your posts get comments.

Your goal here is to get that orange Amazon bestseller or new release flag. Ideally, you want to get it for the highest-level category possible, but the primary goal is to get a flag. How do you do that? Outsell the other books in your category over a period of time, ideally a week or more. To really get your audience to move, you price the book on sale (hence the 99-cents price tag) and promote the heck out of it to that engaged audience.

What This Involves

- Ensuring you've conducted good category research (more on this later) to place your book in a high-quality, as in highly relevant but not supercompetitive, category

- Setting your e-book to be for sale for 99 cents on Amazon in the week(s) before launch or during launch week

- Promoting your book through email marketing and social media to your audience

If you're going this route, I recommend you do the 99 cent e-book sale the day after launch. If you change it too soon, any sales that happened at full price pre-launch get dropped to 99 cents. If you try to change it as soon as your book launches, there can be glitches or lags, messing up any promotions you have.

For instance, say you have a six-week pre-launch. You've been promoting the book and selling e-book copies for $7.99. But then you do your pre-launch sale the final week before launch, and Amazon drops *all* the sales down to 99 cents. It's a small thing for most authors, but one to be aware of.

The goal of this promotion is to get that orange flag while your e-book is 99 cents. This means that once you've set the timing, you now have to promote the heck out of it to your audience and even run e-book sales through a variety of channels. BookBub, Bargain Booksy, or the Fussy Librarian are some we recommend for nonfiction books, but we're going to cover e-book sales more because it's an important post-launch tactic to have in your toolbox.

How to Run a 99 Cent E-book Sale on Amazon

Whether it's part of your launch strategy or something you're doing to invigorate your sales, a 99 cent e-book sale can be an effective promotional tactic. The best part is that it almost always generates sales of other formats of your book too!

If you're part of Amazon's Kindle Select Program, you're eligible to run a free e-book giveaway or a Kindle Countdown Deal. But even if you're not in those programs (my books are never exclusive to Amazon), you can still make it happen with a couple extra steps.

Use caution with giveaways (versus 99 cent sales). When you're giving away your book, you are not making any profit from it. Of greater concern, though, is the fact that readers downloading free books are not that likely to read your book, and you've devalued all your expertise by giving it away!

That's not to say you should never do free promotions. There can be times when it makes sense—for example, if you've struggled to get reviews or if the book is the first in a series and you're trying to hook someone into your ecosystem. When we do giveaways for our authors, they are typically Goodreads giveaways, which have different goals than a free-download offer solely on Amazon. (More on Goodreads coming up soon!) For now, let's focus on the 99 cent e-book promo or even a $2.99 promo on Amazon.

A Kindle Countdown Deal can work really well for a promo if you're exclusive with Amazon for your e-book. (Your print book can be widely available.) You set your sale price low and increase it slowly over a set number of days until it returns to its normal price. Your sale can last from five to seven days, and you can set your pricing in whatever increments your little heart desires.

On average, we see the best results with five-day sales that start at 99 cents and increase a dollar each day. Five-day sales also tend to have great traction. They're shorter, so you won't get that one-day sales hit that Amazon actually doesn't like, but they're long enough that readers don't miss you. For books not in Kindle Select, you can manually set the price down to 99 cents and run paid promos without increasing the price at all for the five-day period.

Not being in Kindle Select means you don't have the timer, which can create a sense of urgency for a buyer, but the sale is still effective.

Logistically, whether you're using Amazon's countdown feature or you're manually changing your price, you need to determine the timing of the promotion and then head to your favorite e-book promo sites and book your ads. If you run BookBub ads, then this is also a great time to increase your ad reach for that time period (we'll get to BookBub soon too!) and schedule out your promotions.

Plan to post the sale on your social media, email your audience, and generate some excitement for this promotion. We consistently use Bargain Booksy and the Fussy Librarian, which have reasonable rates and sizable audiences. We also use sites like Buck Books, Rifflebooks, and Goodkindles. There are always new sites popping up, and some work better for certain types of books, so search around after you've read this to find the best one for your book.

It's a good idea to plan your sale dates well in advance—especially if you're trying to hit the holiday season. At Book Launchers, we purchase space three to four weeks in advance for our authors and longer when it's the holiday season. Sites have limited space available, and some require an approval process to run an ad.

When you've picked your dates, purchased your ads, and lined up promotions, you're ready to run your sale!

Wait, just a sec, though. There's something to keep in mind before you rush over to Amazon: Once you schedule your Kindle Countdown Deal, you won't be able to edit or stop it within 24 hours of its starting time during the entire deal, ever. Amazon also requires that your book's regular price can't be changed for 30 days before and 14 days after the promotion, so make sure you've set the timing for your ads and audience before you schedule your deal.

The Maximum Momentum Launch

Who This Is For

Any author with a medium-size audience and a strong network of folks with small- to medium-size audiences that reflect your ideal reader. This is a good option if you personally have a strong newsletter list of 10,000+ subscribers, 25,000+ social media followers, and you've got some industry friends with comparable audiences. Ideally, you also have other products or services people are already buying from you, so they're familiar with your brand.

What This Involves

- You're going to create an *incentive package* for anyone who buys one or three copies of your print book. If you think bulk sales are viable, you can also have a 10-plus option.

To do this, you'll need:

- an email address,
- incentive(s),
- a network,

- social media graphics, and
- a website.

You'll also need someone to manage the incoming receipts or proof of purchases and distribute the incentives.

This is a more complex promotion than the 99-cents sale, so you'll need to prepare this at least 12 weeks before your launch. The first piece is figuring out what your incentives should be.

My personal recommendation is to offer items that are a natural fit for your book. They may supplement the lessons in your book or address problems that might arise for your reader later.

I know that sounds funny because you've likely written your book to solve a problem, but whenever a problem is solved, a new problem is created. It's why my goal is always to create new problems! I don't like old problems.

For example, if you read *Self-Publish and Succeed*, you gained the tools to write a book optimized for marketing. We offered resources to help you. (You can see a sample of what we offer for that book at https://selfpublish andsucceed.com.) And now here's this book!

Here's another example of what I mean: If your book is about getting fit and changing how you eat, your reader may need to find friends who have healthier habits. Or they may need support reworking their wardrobe now that their body has changed. Each of these problems creates the opportunity for you to offer access to a support community, course, book, video resource, checklist, or something else of value to help them with next steps.

When setting up incentives, consider creating ones that help your reader solve whatever issues they may encounter on their way to their solution. It all comes back to understanding the "outcome of the outcome" your reader desires most and continuing to support them to get there.

Remember, the key is that the incentive has to be something so valuable a reader would actually pay for it. It has to fulfill an important need for the reader in order to drive sales and expand your audience.

Besides the fact that you'll need time to create or secure incentives, there are logistics to contend with. In some cases, you need a final version of your book to circulate to your network, so they have a copy to preview or use for their promotions. You also need a mechanism to distribute the incentives. Let's break down the steps.

Here's what you'll need to do:

1. Secure and/or create your incentives.

2. Begin outreach to your network (if you weren't already doing outreach to ask for the incentives). Get on calendars early to make sure people can promote your offer the week of launch. Many folks will want you to schedule a timely interview for their podcast or live stream to promote your launch and incentives, so the sooner you get this booked, the better.

3. Create beautiful and compelling imagery for your incentives.

4. Set up a web page that showcases the incentives and their value. (A simple example of this is available at https://selfpublishandsucceed .com.)

5. Have purchase instructions and how to verify proof of sale in order to receive the incentives. If, for example, you're trying to drive people to buy from Amazon, you would make this valid only for Amazon. But if you're trying to get widespread distribution and sales, then you would accept receipts from any purchase within a certain time frame.

6. Create email and social media copy and imagery for yourself and for your network to use in sharing the promotion.

7. Set up the delivery system for your incentives. This can be a templated email with directions to access incentives, a folder in

Dropbox with links for your readers to access incentives, or a third-party system like BookFunnel.

8. If you plan on verifying receipts, you'll likely want to hire a virtual assistant or have someone on your team do this so you can focus on higher priorities during launch week. If you're using the honor system, you can set up an email address with an autoresponder that provides instructions for how to get the incentives. I've done this for single-book purchase incentives, but the higher-value book purchases (like buy three books or buy 10 books and get bigger incentives) are verified before being sent.

9. As launch week approaches, continue to secure reviews and make sure your network has what it needs to promote your book to their audiences. You can prerecord interviews, podcasts, and videos and schedule times for live broadcasts to promote the launch and incentives.

The Periodical Bestseller Launch—Lists Like the *Wall Street Journal*, *USA Today*, or the *Washington Post*

Who This Is For

This is the dream of many authors, and although it's achievable, it's not without some significant effort or cost. Deciding whether it's worth the pursuit is the first thing to think about.

I excluded the *New York Times* from this list because my focus is on independent publishing. The *Times* curates its list and almost entirely excludes books not published by a major publisher. It doesn't matter if you sell the most copies in a week. It's unlikely you'll qualify for this list without a major publisher behind you.

The other lists have criteria with their own nuances, but they don't exclude self-published books.

In the next chapter, we'll go into more detail on bestseller lists. For now, let's look at this as a launch strategy.

This is for the author who feels very confident they can sell a minimum of 5,000 print books or e-books through retail outlets in a week. It could require more than 8,000 book sales in a week, depending on your competitors.

Note that I said "retail outlets" and not Amazon. Amazon counts, but periodical lists (*WSJ* and *Washington Post* lists, among others) use Nielsen BookScan (NPD) to get their sales data.

According to its website, NPD is "the gold standard in POS [point-of-sale] tracking for the publishing market. It covers approximately 85% of trade print books sold in the U.S., through direct reporting from all major retailers, including Amazon, Barnes & Noble, Walmart, Target, independent bookstores, and many others."[41]

Amazon is just one piece of the data. NPD looks at all sales and is going to report where the sale takes place, the retailer, frequency of sales, and more. All of that data informs who makes those periodical bestseller lists. That's why you want more than just Amazon selling your book. You're looking for lots of retailers in different markets.

Of course, if you're selling direct to companies or buyers, that sale won't count toward your NPD tracking. There's also a lot of debate about multiple-book buys, especially on Amazon, and most people believe it will count as one copy sold, not multiple copies.

Bulk sales won't count, which means you need 5,000+ different buyers or need to engage a service like BookPal or Porchlight because they offer strong discounts for bulk buys. They may offer anywhere from 20% to 40% off retail, depending on wholesale discounts, and then report the

---

41 "Books," NPD, accessed March 12, 2023, https://www.npd.com/industry-expertise/books/.

number of book sales to NPD. The Porchlight website says their sales are counted accurately toward bestseller list rankings.[42]

If you have a large and engaged audience and a few groups interested in a bulk purchase, you can succeed with a little coordination in hitting these lists. If you don't have a massive following of readers anxious for your content (at least 100,000 people on social media, a newsletter list of at least 50,000, a strong network with similar-size audiences, or a strong list of corporate buyers), this strategy is probably not going to work, unless you're ready to spend a lot of money on ads to drive book sales or buy a bunch of books yourself. Or you can spend money and pay a company to get your e-book to the top of the list, but I'll talk about that in the next chapter.

This is why it really needs to be something that is important to you and, ideally, helps you achieve your bigger-picture strategic goals. What goals might align with this strategy? Well, if you're a consultant, a speaker, or a newcomer who needs to truly establish your credibility in your industry, then hitting a periodical bestseller can help. Justin Goodbread, who wrote *Your Baby's Ugly*, drove his e-book to the *Wall Street Journal* bestseller list and reported that it was a big boost to his business to have that title. Other authors claim that the title of being a *WSJ* bestseller allows them to charge more than their fellow consultants or speakers. It's a credibility boost for sure, but you must be able to capitalize on it to make it worth it.

What This Involves

The best approach is to follow the Maximum Momentum Launch steps and drive a lot of presale activity on your book. When we work with clients on this strategy, we usually look for at least 120 days in presale, so there's a ton of time to drive sales that will count during launch week. That gives the author four months to collect sales. The exception to this is if you have a killer incentive to offer and a large list of previous consumers. We had

---

42 "Bestseller Reporting," Porchlight Books, accessed March 12, 2023, https://www.porchlightbooks.com/services/bestseller-reporting.

a client who considered offering their $24 product free in exchange for a book purchase. The book didn't end up happening because of a change in their business direction, but given their large list of previous buyers and the high-value offer, I would have expected it to be very strong no matter when they made the offer.

You may see a four-month presale and think that sounds like forever. But consider this: How many *Wall Street Journal* or *Washington Post* bestsellers have you seen that don't have strong media coverage or top-tier reviews first? Editorial reviews are a keystone to getting in front of publishing industry professionals like booksellers, librarians, and top media. Editorial reviews include publishing industry outlets (like *Publishers Weekly, Foreword, Library Journal,* or *Booklist*) and print and online media. Those outlets have a minimum lead time of three to five months, meaning they have to have your review manuscript or final book in hand well before your actual publication date.

Television and radio lead times may be shorter, but top podcasts with the widest reach also have long leads. Ensuring that media cover your book is a long-game strategy, so giving yourself plenty of time in presale is vital.

Last, trying to get on a periodical bestseller list means having a book on a topic likely to make the list. A 2018 study by EPJ Data Science showed that of the 2,025 nonfiction titles that made the bestseller list between 2008 and 2016, more than half were in the biography/memoir category. They consisted of books written by or about famous individuals, from politicians to artists and business personalities. Next most popular were history and general nonfiction.[43] Now, this study only looked at the *New York Times* bestseller list, which we've already said is a curated list. It's fair to assume other periodical bestseller lists will have a wider range but will still reflect these results as well.

---

43 Burcu Yucesoy et al., "Success in Books: A Big Data Approach to Bestsellers," *EPJ Data Science* 7, no. 7 (2018), https://doi.org/10.1140/epjds/s13688-018-0135-y.

If your book is in a niche category, covers certain controversial topics, or doesn't have mass appeal, consider if the Periodical Best Seller launch strategy is the right one for you.

The Phased Momentum Launch

Who This Is For

This is the most effective launch strategy for most authors—especially if you are writing a book to build your platform—but it does require you to set aside your ego and focus on the long game of being an author. You're using your book as a tool to grow your business and establish your name in your industry. You want to sell books, but your launch may sell only a couple of hundred copies, and you have to build on that.

This is the right approach for the author starting from scratch with a small audience or none at all. Perhaps you've built a business and sold it, or you have a network that you can lean on, but your own personal platform is not that robust. This could be your perfect strategy. Possibly this book is more of a side hustle with your day job or it's something you want to write to catapult you into something new. Whatever the case, you haven't put much time and energy into building an audience, so the book is the tool you'll use to do that.

What This Involves

First and foremost, you need to manage your expectations around your book release. Of course, we all want to see momentum on launch, and if you follow the approach below and keep going with the rest of the actions in this book, you'll build momentum. But launch day isn't going to break records, and that is okay.

You need a great lead magnet and author website. Inside your book, you invite people to get this fabulous reader magnet and join your community. Then, you focus on:

- Amazon ads to consistently grow your reader base and continually have sales converting on Amazon so you're feeding its algorithm monster

- Book reviews (initially aim for 25 reviews, but keep going because more really is better when it comes to reviews)

- Media coverage, including local media, newsletters, podcasts, newspapers, radio, and any other platforms that appeal to your readers

- Partnerships, which may occur through bulk deals, your network, cold outreach, or a mix of all of the above as well as speaking engagements and conferences

- Promotions and discounts by running quarterly 99 cent e-book sales and promoting them to your audience as well as paying for features on book promo sites

This strategy starts six weeks before launch and continues for a year post-launch (and beyond) until your next book. ☺

Amazon Isn't the Only Place to Launch and Promote Books...Apple Books Is Cool Too!

The launch strategies above largely focus on Amazon, but there are some tremendous options to incorporate Apple Books and Kobo in your distribution and launch strategy plans.

In fact, both Apple and Kobo have some powerful incentives for authors to use their platform in pre-launch to drive presales.

Let's take a bite of Apple first, shall we?

Apple might actually be your ticket to making more money per book sold. Part of that comes from its readership. If you use Apple Books, it's probably because you own an Apple product, and Apple products come with a bit of a price tag.

That suggests Apple users may be more inclined to spend a bit more for books. Apple is one of the few retailers out there that does not price match —likely because their consumers are less price sensitive. You don't have to worry about that higher price getting slashed just because you're priced lower somewhere else. This can pay off for you big-time when you consider what Apple pays in royalties. You earn 70% of royalties through Apple, regardless of whether you're priced at $10.99, $99.99 or $5.99.[44]

Apple doesn't sell your book for you, but Apple Books has a secret weapon that gives it a one-up over Amazon: how preorders weigh in your rankings. One preorder sale does double the work. **It counts as a sale during the preorder period, and it counts as a sale again on launch day.** If you plan a stellar presale period and drive people to buy your book on Apple, you increase the chances that your book ranks highly.

One of the appealing parts of Apple Books is that they have a human curating their lists. When you see their hot new releases and coming soon lists on Apple, it's the result of a person's work, not a robot or an algorithm. Gaining a spot on one of their curated lists can open up opportunities and lead to even more sales.

Signing up with the iTunes affiliate program also helps you make more money with your sales. You use your affiliate code when you share your book and make extra money (7% more) from each sale. This also helps you track your analytics and conversions to adjust your marketing strategy. You can try running BookBub ads and targeting readers based on the fact that they read via Apple.

Kobo Is Kinda Cool Too

Every Canadian knows about Kobo, but in case Kobo is new to you, here's a quick rundown: Kobo is originally a Toronto-based retailer of e-books,

---

44 "Get the Inside Story on Book Sales," Apple Books for Authors, accessed March 12, 2023, https://authors.apple.com/measure.

e-readers, and audiobooks that launched in 2009 and is available in more than 200 countries. It's the second-largest e-book retailer in the world and the biggest global competitor to Amazon in the e-book market. And what's really cool is, they seem to be a genuinely great company. They're often praised for stellar customer service and have helped provide more than 20 million free books to readers stuck at home during the pandemic. Their mission isn't just reader focused. Kobo offers some awesome opportunities for authors through their free self-publishing platform, Kobo Writing Life.[45]

Kobo makes it easy to set up your book for preorder. You simply create a Kobo Writing Life (KWL) account, log in, and click e-books. From there, you create a new e-book and input your metadata, add your description, and upload your cover. Kobo's pricing tool helps you set your perfect price in more than 16 currencies. You can choose where you'd like your book to be available for sale and optimize pricing for each individual territory. And if you want to reach readers in more than 30,000 libraries, KWL gives you the power to distribute directly to them with OverDrive, a library marketplace.

On Kobo, every preorder sale has twice the effect on ranking as a post-launch sale. You don't get paid twice, but you do get double the rankings. More sales means a higher ranking for your book, and a higher ranking means more customers browsing for their next read will be shown your book's listing. Every preorder on Kobo essentially doubles your increase in visibility and discoverability. That's an invaluable extra boost for your presale strategy that Amazon doesn't offer—and it's a perk that keeps on giving once launch day rolls around.

The longer you have your book available for presale and pair it with some strong promotion, the more sales you can accumulate, and the higher your

---

45 Michael Kozlowski, "The History of Kobo and How They Changed the E-reader Market," Good EReader, August 7, 2018, https://goodereader.com/blog/electronic-readers/the-history-of-kobo-and-how-they-changed-the-e-reader-market.

book can climb within its category come launch day. This matters even more with Kobo because Kobo, like Apple, uses humans, not an algorithm, to curate some of their lists. Kobo's curators often highlight the highest preorders on their featured promotional lists, and they craft those any-where from six to 12 weeks before publication. If you want to snag a spot, plan ahead when it comes to your presale.

The perks don't stop there either. After launch day, you can keep those sales going with Kobo's promotional opportunities available through your KWL dashboard. Using the promotions tab on your dashboard, check out the current on-site sales and email promotions, such as daily deals, discounts, price drops, category features, and free e-book promotions. When you spot an opportunity, just click on the books you want featured, input your price for the sale, and submit. It's that easy to apply. Kobo's merchandising team checks out your application and lets you know if they've approved the pro-motion that you've selected.

Now, I know you're excited about being a bestseller whether you're on Amazon, Apple, Kobo, or anywhere else, which is why the next chapter is a must-read. It's all about bestseller dreams and realities.

Incentives and Freebies to Get Book Sales

When you're only making a few dollars per book sold, you don't want to spend more on incentives to get people to buy books, but incentives are sometimes exactly what people need to act!

Human nature is such that we tend to need incentives. Scarcity is a power-ful motivator, as is the fear of missing out.

Many authors rely on incentives to move books during launch week, and that can work well. I've told you how *More than Cashflow* topped the charts in its launch week partly because of the real estate investment course I was able to give to everyone who purchased three copies of the book.

This was incredibly powerful because the course sold for $299 and targeted buyers of the book. (It solved a problem almost every real estate investor faces when they start buying property—the need to access capital to do more deals.) It was free for me and didn't cost Greg (the person who had created the course) anything, except a bit of time from a person on his team who managed course registrations. If you can find an incentive that meets those criteria, you're in great shape.

Criteria for a Great Incentive / Book Giveaway:

- Does not have a per-unit cost to give away (digital giveaways work great for this)
- Provides something your ideal reader would actually pay money for
- Solves a problem that your book creates or supplements book content

So, what might work for your giveaways? Engage your creativity, but here are some ideas:

- Book you've written (audio or digital version)
- E-course
- Free access to a private group, Slack channel, or other paid membership group
- Live webinar access, where you teach something of value to support the book
- Tool or resource that people can download, like a spreadsheet, checklist, or cheat sheet
- Virtual access, live stream, or recording of an event you're hosting

These resources don't have to be yours (and sometimes, it's more valuable if they aren't). The incentive also doesn't have to be ready to go for your launch. You just need to be 100% committed to creating it in a set time frame.

For example, a live training can happen 30 days after your book launch. If you create a short e-course, the first lesson can be released 10 days after launch, and each lesson after that can be dripped out week by week. Just so long as you tell people when it's coming, and you do it, it's fine.

Managing the giveaways is another task, but there are services, like Book-Funnel, that will manage the digital side of things. You can also hire a low-cost virtual assistant through Fiverr, Upwork, Guru, or another site to check receipts and then email incentives to book buyers.

Because these incentives are only available for a fixed period of time, it might be worth it to have some short-term help. If your launch is relatively small, you can set up a link for people to register their purchase. They enter their name and email address, and an autoresponder sends them their freebie.

Of course, this means nobody checks the receipts, and someone could receive a freebie without buying the book. That said, buyers have to get the book to receive the link, so it's a low-risk and low-cost way to deliver incentives.

With all three options, you get a buyer's email address and can now connect with them via an autoresponder to build a long-lasting relationship.

Chapter Summary

LAUNCH STRATEGY	WHO IT'S FOR	KEY STEPS TO TAKE
Amazon Bestseller	Small-to-medium audience (<1,000 newsletter subscribers, similar social media) Want the Amazon bestseller flag.	Choose a five-day window after your book launches to set your price to 99 cents. Let everyone know. Purchase ad space in e-book sale sites.
Maximum Momentum	Medium audience Drive strong sales during a period of time with high-value incentives (usually in print but can be any format). Have access or ability to create high-value incentives and distribute them. Have other influencers who support the promotion.	Determine what is of value to your audience. Set up website and promotional materials for the promotion. Decide on the logistics of deliverability and qualifying. Promote the offer to your audience.
Periodical Best Seller	Medium-to-large audience Have access or ability to sell large quantities of your book in a two-to-four-month pre-launch window. Have ability (usually required) to sell 5,000–8,000 books prior to launch week. Put two to four months into pre-launch promotion to drive as many sales as possible.	Do extensive network outreach and combine the incentive package creation of Maximum Momentum.
Phased Momentum	Small audience Implement strategic plan to use the book to grow the platform and leverage it for brand and business growth.	Focus launch on getting reviews and gaining some momentum. Focus post-launch on platform building, book sales, and overall brand growth.

CHAPTER 8

THE SIREN SONG OF SALES NUMBERS (ALL ABOUT BESTSELLERS)

WHEN MY FIRST BOOK TOPPED THE PRINT-BOOK CHARTS FOR AMAZON, I tried to update my description to include "Amazon overall #1 bestseller." Amazon rejected it. It's against their policy to say "Amazon bestseller" in the description. It was also rejected from the book cover.

It seems ridiculous, doesn't it? Not only did I have screenshots proving the bestseller status, but Amazon would also be able to check it themselves and see it was true! But that is what happens when an author tries to include this claim on their Amazon listing, title, or keywords.[46]

Anyone, absolutely anyone, can have an Amazon bestseller. It's not hard, and it's not a big deal.

---

46 Penny Sansevieri, "New at KDP & Amazon: 'Bestseller' Authors Need to Prove Their Status (or Risk Getting Pulled)," AME Author Marketing Experts, February 7, 2017, https://www.amarketingexpert.com/2017/02/07/kdp-amazon-bestseller-news/.

Getting that coveted orange flag will not change your life, but for many authors, it feels like an item they must check off their to-do lists. I get that. Topping the charts was definitely one of my big wins in life. But please don't pay a company to make you an Amazon bestseller. It's definitely not worth it.

The reality is that you can get that flag pretty easily without paying anyone. There's a bigger issue, too, when you pay a company specifically for the guarantee of becoming an Amazon bestseller.

Most companies first help you choose an obscure category for your book that makes it easy to rank for. (Metadata, which includes category selection and pricing decisions, is coming up!) Then they either have their own list of people they give gift cards to buy books with or you're put in a group with other authors.

On a designated day, everyone discounts their book to 99 cents, and you buy one another's books on that day (or the assistants all make a purchase). If there's 25–50 people in the group, you can easily get to #1 in most lower-level Amazon categories. *These aren't book readers, and you better believe Amazon knows when an e-book is purchased and not read.*

Even worse than the fact that you haven't sold that many books, and the books you sold were sold to people who won't read them or post a review, **you've messed up the algorithms on Amazon.**

A friend of mind with a real estate book did this, and one year later the "also boughts" on his Amazon listing still showed books on divorce, the law of attraction, and other woo-woo type subjects that had absolutely nothing to do with real estate. It's no wonder he couldn't get his book sales moving.

Amazon also doesn't like these quick-hit blips. The algorithm rewards authors whose books have consistent conversions to ideal readers.

How Does This Amazon Algorithm Work?

Amazon is a mysterious book-selling machine, isn't it? And it has various tentacles with different lists for Amazon sales rank and Amazon bestsellers.

When you go to Amazon's product listing for a book, you see the cover, title, subtitle, and description. As you scroll down, you see books you may like and related or recommended products. Then you see editorial reviews and an "About the Author" section. Finally, you get to the product details, which has the bestseller ranking.

What is that sales rank? It's calculated by an Amazon algorithm and is not a measure of your overall sales. It's a measure of how you are selling *relative* to the other books in your category in that format (for that store —because the print store is different from the Kindle and Audible stores).

The sales rank number is not a matter of highest number wins. Lower numbers mean you're actually selling more books. This number is based only on sales, but not all sales are treated as equal. Sales that occurred in the most recent hour are given more value or weight than sales that occurred yesterday or even half a day ago. There are a lot of online sites that talk about this, but one of the best sources is David Gaughran's book *Amazon Decoded.*[47]

Sales rank is updated hourly, but it's not something that happens immediately. There's a lag. It can take hours for your sales rank to reflect a sale.[48] All Amazon bestseller rankings are based on Amazon sales rank.

Amazon made changes to how sales were ranked after too many people used gimmicks to get books flagged as bestsellers, so you're no longer rewarded for a single push of sales. Let me repeat this because I know you're still secretly coveting that orange Amazon flag. (I know it. I can read your mind.)

---

47 David Gaughran, *Amazon Decoded: A Marketing Guide to the Kindle Store* (David Gaughran, 2020).

48 "Sales Ranking," Kindle Direct Publishing, accessed March 14, 2023, https://kdp.amazon.com/en_US/help/topic/G201648140.

Amazon wants conversions on a regular basis. A one-time push plus continued sales is good. A one-time boost in sales and then no sales is not good.

You will be rewarded on Amazon for consistent momentum and conversion. Focus your efforts on generating ongoing sales, and Amazon will help you sell your books as long as you don't try to game the system.

It's also important to know that metadata matters a lot to Amazon. Choose the right categories, relevant keywords, and sell consistently so you sit beside the books your ideal reader is already browsing and set yourself up for more success.

New York Times Bestsellers

Maybe you're thinking, I don't care about Amazon. I want to be a *New York Times* bestselling author.

I get it. My ego sometimes plays tricks on me, trying to convince me that I need to have a highbrow endorsement to be in the publishing business. How can I possibly write a book on marketing a book if I have never been on the *NYT* bestseller list?

But when I tell my ego to eat a sandwich and focus on the facts, I realize that the title would make anyone feel good, and for some folks, it might translate into a higher-paying career as a consultant or a speaker. For the average person marketing a nonfiction book, however, it's not worth the lost sleep or money. It's a game, and if you're at a point in your career where you have energy and resources for the game and a strong desire to win—go for it!

For the rest of us, it's much more important to focus on the primary goal of why you're writing a book and aim for that result. So long as my books help people, support my team at Book Launchers, and ultimately grow Book Launchers by attracting our ideal authors, my books are doing their job.

As noted earlier, the *New York Times* bestseller list is curated by the editors. You still need to sell thousands of books through approved channels, and you have to be deemed worthy of their attention. The channels also need to be diverse. In other words, you have to have sales that are distributed across outlets. Amazon alone will never get you on this list. You also need to sell somewhere around 5,000–10,000 copies of your book in a single format.

If you're self-publishing, I would just pretend this list doesn't exist because you and your book have to be a unicorn to get on it.

Wall Street Journal, Washington Post, and USA Today Bestseller Lists

If you're feeling defeated, you shouldn't. Some pretty big lists are still open to you, including the *Wall Street Journal*, *Washington Post*, and *USA Today* bestseller lists.

These outlets use NPD BookScan, which collects point-of-sale data, to compile their lists.

Barnes & Noble, Hastings, Target, Walmart, Costco, Amazon, plus all the independent bookstores across the nation all report back to NPD. To qualify for the *Wall Street Journal* list, you'll likely need to shoot for at least 5,000 book sales in a week through these various channels, but some authors have reported hitting it with 3,000. Of course, the number changes week by week, depending on the hot titles you're up against in any given week. The list is also divided by format, so it can be challenging if you sell 5,000 copies split between print books, e-books, and audiobooks.

Washington Post bestsellers alternate between hardcover and paperback lists each week. They count hardcover, paperback, and e-book sales and use a combination of NPD reporting and Amazon reporting.[49]

The interesting thing about the *Washington Post* list is that it includes Kindle Unlimited books. The *Post* is also the first publisher to syndicate Amazon Charts Most Read list. This list measures the books millions of Amazon customers are really reading and listening to by looking at the average number of daily Kindle readers and Audible listeners each week.[50]

USA Today ranks all print and e-book sales from select groups of booksellers in one massive list, which can be easier to hit than a single category like hardcover or e-book.[51]

Each list has its own nuance. If making one of these lists is vitally important to you, and you don't have a strong platform, you can hire a company to get you on them. The cost is somewhere between $30,000 and $100,000 to buy your way on these lists. But that doesn't mean your ideal reader is buying your book, reading it, and wanting to hire you or put you on a stage. If you go this route and pay for placement, you had better have another way to monetize that title of "bestselling author."

Hitting these lists requires coordinated timing of sales. Most of us need to provide some sort of incentive to drive people to buy during the period of time needed to get on a list. (This is the reason why we recommend the Maximum Momentum Launch strategy in combination with the Periodical Bestseller Launch strategy from the previous chapter.) It also helps to funnel some bulk orders through companies that report individual sales

---

49 WashPostPR, "The Washington Post Launches Most Comprehensive Bestselling Books Lists," *Washington Post*, February 8, 2018, https://www.washingtonpost.com/pr/wp/2018/02/08/the-washington-post-launches-most-comprehensive-bestselling-books-lists/.

50 WashPostPR, "The Washington Post Launches," *Washington Post*.

51 "About the Best-Selling Book List," *USA Today*, last updated December 2022, https://eu.usatoday.com/story/life/books/2013/06/04/about-usa-todays-best-selling-book-list/2389075/.

back to NPD. This takes a lot of effort, and it's why most people hire a book launch coordinator if they're really serious about these lists.

Your Book Birth Plan—How Are You Measuring Success?

When I was pregnant with my son Jackson, the doctor encouraged me to create a birth plan. I could see the benefit of planning ahead, but I also had a really full plate. My second book, *The New Brand You*, launched when I was only a few months pregnant.[52] At the same time, I had licensed off all my real estate training courses and had to support the licensees, was working on a visa submission to move from Canada to the U.S., and was putting together my business plan for Book Launchers. On top of all this, I was ridiculously sick with morning (and afternoon) sickness for seven months.

Creating a birth plan just didn't fit for me. Instead, I did research and understood what was likely to happen and what decisions would need to be made when I went into labor. I didn't put any pressure on myself to have a natural birth or to do it one way or another.

My big-picture goal was simple: to give birth to my baby and not put our health at risk.

I kept an open mind, and because my definition of "success" was to have a healthy baby as safely as possible, I wasn't set on getting there in a specific way.

What happened I never would have planned for anyway. My son was born 10 days late, and I required a C-section. If I'd created a birth plan, it would have been useless, but we were both safe and healthy, so my goal was achieved.

---

52 Julie Broad, *The New Brand You: Your New Image Makes the Sale for You* (Los Angeles: Stick Horse Publishing, 2016).

Being clear on your bigger-picture goals, doing research so you understand key decisions, and leaving details a little looser might be a good approach for you as an author as well. Look at what else is on your plate in your life and business. How much pressure do you want to put on one launch day? The answer is different for everyone.

There's no right way to put a book into the world. Much of what you have been told by others feeds an outdated publishing industry or is designed by companies to sell programs and services. There are certainly optimal ways to meet your goals, but do it your way.

You're no less an author if you don't make a major list, just like you're no less a mother if you don't have a natural birth.

Remember, the launch is the beginning, not the end. If you put all your energy and effort into driving hard into launch, you may not have anything left to do the work needed to gain momentum and enjoy the benefits of your book.

From what I know about our Book Launchers authors, the ones who kept going for a year or two post-launch are the ones who really enjoy the benefits. Shell Phelps, author of *The Big Bliss Blueprint: 100 Little Thoughts to Build Positive Life Changes*, was two years post-launch when she appeared on the cover of a local magazine![53] She never stopped promoting her book and serving her audience, and it's still paying off, but it took time. Robert Belle landed his TED Global Ideas Talk more than a year post-launch, after doing every podcast interview that came his way. It's been viewed more than two million times![54]

Again, I'm not saying don't go for a list—it can be fun if you have time, energy, and drive. But for many authors, the book is a tool to achieve other

---

53 Shell Phelps, *The Big Bliss Blueprint: 100 Little Thoughts to Build Positive Life Changes* (Positive Streak Publishing, 2020).

54 Robert Belle, "The Emotions Behind Your Money Habits," TED Global video, June 21, 2021, 5:47, https://www.ted.com/talks/robert_a_belle_the_emotions_behind_your_money_habits?language=en.

goals, and your resources are best served maximizing the opportunities it can provide.

Most importantly, remember that it is never a matter of launching your book and becoming instantly successful.

It takes time for people to read your book, become familiar with your name, recognize the problem you solve, and get to know you! Even with the success of *More than Cashflow*, it took about six months before we really started to see the benefits with our businesses. I hired a PR firm four months after launch for a big second push, and it took almost a full year before things were dramatically different. I didn't launch and stop!

Part of your ongoing work involves monitoring how you're doing. Measurements are useful because they give you hard data, but it's how and why you use them that can be important. You can use your launch to measure your success in terms of book sales. Or you can look at your launch with a different lens and focus on metrics that are most likely to move the needle in the direction of your bigger-picture goal.

Measurements That Monitor Your Momentum

Sales numbers give you data that helps you understand what is working and what isn't as far as promotions and other tactics you use to sell books.

There are other things to monitor to get you where you want to go, using your book as a tool in your brand growth and business.

Instead of measuring books sold to determine whether you're successful, track what matters the most to your main overall goal by looking at:

- **Media appearances.** Track coverage, audience size, and connected opportunities for a year or two, and you might be stunned to see how much media appearances have done for your business and brand. My book-promotion efforts put me on podcasts where the audience maybe didn't buy a book, but the podcaster became a client of Book Launchers. One of Rachael Brown's goals was to be on Forks Over Knives, and her book got her the feature![55]

Tracking your media appearances with contact information is smart too, because you can go back and follow up for additional features in the future.

- **Your platform growth.** Measure the number of people entering your ecosystem (newsletter subscribers, social media followers, and people in your online or in-person groups that you manage). Use each opportunity to increase exposure to your platform. Look at what is working and what isn't, and do more of the former. Using a book to build a platform is really smart because it allows you to offer much higher value to your audience in the future.

- **New connections.** Make a list of new connections with influencers and other industry names who will help you grow your audience and credibility even more. This is something I wish I had tracked with my past books because I could say with certainty what I suspect: The books each led to new, high-value relationships with people who helped me connect with new clients, new team members and partners, and affiliates. If increasing your brand awareness is important, this would be a great metric to start tracking after your book launches. I guarantee you'll be impressed with the results after a year or two, and beyond!

- **Reviews or other mentions.** This is a powerful way to measure your impact. Track it in a spreadsheet so you can see it all in one place, and you also might uncover something that you've said that people keep mentioning in their reviews or posts. This could become the subject of your TED Talk (like Robert Belle's) or a new talk you start selling!

---

55 Megan Edwards, "For Fork's Sake: Rachael Brown's New Book Makes Whole-Food, Plant-Based Eating Easy for Families," Forks Over Knives, September 2, 2022, https://www.forksoverknives.com/wellness/for-forks-sake-rachael-brown-new-book/.

Start tracking and measuring reviews, and do things that will help you grow your reviews from free and paid sources as well as from readers! Look at what's getting reviews and do more of that. We will cover reviews soon, but this video covers what garnered reviews for *Self-Publish and Succeed*: "What's Worked to get More Book Reviews."[56]

- **Interesting opportunities or doors that opened as a result of your book.** I'll never forget Martha Tettenborn talking about how she was featured in a documentary and received a lot of other cool opportunities a year or two after her book, *Hacking Chemo*, came out.[57] AJ Coleman got a PBS show interview right after his book, *Keep Those Feet Moving*, came out.[58] Tracking your results could give you really eye-opening information a year or two (or five!) later.

It's also worth noting that all of these things are likely to lead to things that are far more lucrative than selling several thousand copies of your book. That's not to discount the value of selling books but only to highlight the fact that there are plenty of higher-value benefits. You might not give them enough attention if you haven't figured out what is most important for your goals and started tracking and recording them! You also might not spot the things that are working (and do more of them!) if you're only watching book sales.

Most people look for quick wins, but the reality is that they are successful because of time spent in pursuit of their goals—not because they did one thing right.

56 Book Launchers, "What's Worked to Get More Book Reviews," August 9, 2022, YouTube video, 7:17, https://youtu.be/H4-lsNOZcnE.
57 Martha Tettenborn, *Hacking Chemo: Using Ketogenic Diet, Therapeutic Fasting and a Kickass Attitude to Power Through Cancer* (Maple Grove Press, 2020).
58 AJ Coleman, *Keep Those Feet Moving: A Widower's 8-Step Guide to Coping with Grief and Thriving Against All Odds* (Masada Publishing, 2022).

Regardless of whether you're trying to hit a list, reach your audience, or grow your business with your book, the next piece you need to have dialed in is your metadata, so turn on over to the next chapter to get your arms wrapped around that subject. I know you might be tempted to skip it because it sounds boring. And compared to speaking, podcast interviews, promotional book sales, and bestseller lists, metadata is definitely less appealing. But it's what will sell your book even while you're sleeping, and we'll still have fun—I promise.

Chapter Summary

1. Amazon bestseller status isn't meaningful enough to pursue at all costs.

2. Amazon's algorithm rewards you for consistent conversions a lot more than a one-time hit of big sales numbers.

3. Periodical bestseller lists are a bit of a game, but if you want to play, know how to play the game and why you're playing so that you can make the most of it.

4. Being a bestseller is fun, and if it's a lifelong dream, you can pursue it for your book. But for most authors, a focus on using the book for bigger-picture goals is a better use of resources.

5. Measuring more than just book sales to determine whether your book is successful will set you up for longer-term success. You can measure reviews, media wins, new relationships, leads, and platform growth. What you measure depends on your goals.

CHAPTER 9

LET'S GET META

IMAGINE YOU'RE AT THE GROCERY STORE LOOKING FOR BANANAS. YOU look everywhere in the produce section, but you can't find them. When you ask, an employee says, "Oh! We display the bananas next to the cheese on the other side of the store."

Huh?

Now imagine there's no one to ask. You still want bananas, but while you're browsing, you see some mangoes, and you grab those. Then you think you would like some grapes. There's a display of delicious-looking apples, so you buy a bag, and then you leave. You never even knew bananas were there because they were over by the cheese.

Ridiculous? Maybe. But now imagine your book was classified as dairy when it is actually fruit. Or imagine you have to search for cheese to find bananas.

This is why metadata is so important. It tells retailers where your book belongs (fruit versus dairy) and also lets search engines know which words should make your book appear ("fruit" and "bananas" versus "dairy" and "cheese"). Metadata includes your title, subtitle, price, page count, ISBN, author name, genre keywords, and categories. It also includes the format of the book and information like who wrote the foreword, your book description, and reviews. Other details, like whether your book takes place in a certain time period or region of the world, are worth considering. For instance, if you're writing a memoir set in London during World War II, or a true-crime thriller about a serial killer set in a certain decade or a specific city, those details should be in your metadata.

Metadata impacts discoverability of your book first, but some elements of metadata will impact sales directly, including your pricing choices, book description, and reviews. Of course, your title and subtitle are essential for discoverability and selling your book to your reader too. And, as noted above, the classification of your book is vital. To do this right, you need to know about BISAC codes and Amazon categories. (Of course, Amazon doesn't use BISAC codes like everyone else—they have their own system.)

This chapter will cover the ins and outs of how to maintain fresh, relevant metadata over time to keep your book in front of new potential readers, as well as pricing strategies for both domestic and international markets. This is relevant to every bigger-picture, strategic reason you've written a book. The right metadata is vital to your book supporting just about every goal you have. That said, if your #1 goal is to make money selling books, this is probably the most important thing you can invest time, energy, and money into getting right.

This chapter is going to set you up for success, although a deeper dive into some elements, like keyword research, may be required to truly succeed.

Finally, we'll look at the pros and cons of free-book giveaways and 99 cent e-book promotions. The good news about metadata is, everything else can be changed besides your title and author name. Some things are easier and cheaper to change (like keywords or price) than others (like details on the cover or pricing if you're putting it on the book). But even after your book has launched, you have opportunities at any time to tweak your metadata and try to boost your sales.

Ready to dive in? First, let's make sure we unlock the mystery and importance of metadata with an explanation of the all-important BISAC code.

The Basics of BISAC Codes

Try saying *that* three times fast. BISAC stands for Book Industry Standards and Communications. It's a nine character code used for searching and sorting by retailers, libraries, databases, and buyers.

In other words, it's a method of categorizing your book.[59]

Make sure your readers can find you and that retailers know where to put you by choosing the best BISAC codes for your book.

Let's say you're Marc Megna, the author of *Dream Big, Never Quit*.[60] You are totally fine with being #1 in football biographies, which he was. Nice work, Marc. But you don't want to see your book sold as fiction or personal finance. The people looking for those books aren't interested in your inspirational, true-life football story.

When you upload your book to a system like IngramSpark or KDP Print, only one BISAC code is required, but it's important to know that you're better off selecting *three*. It's unlikely your book is about only one thing, and you can definitely appeal to people in more than one category. The first code you input should be the most accurate and, ideally, the most specific.

59 "BISAC Subject Codes," Book Industry Study Group, accessed March 14, 2022, https://www.bisg.org/BISAC-Subject-Codes-main.
60 Marc Megna, *Dream Big, Never Quit: The Marc Megna Story* (Marc Megna, 2019).

To begin, go through the list of codes and find the one with which your book most closely aligns. To find the list, there are paid services, but www.bisg.org maintains a list that will work for you to get this done.[61]

As an example, for a book like Rob Berger's *Retire Before Mom and Dad,* you'd start off by looking at categories under the broader topic of Business and Economics.[62]

Next, you would narrow things down by looking for the category under that topic that most closely fits your book. In this next level of categories, Rob's book would fall under Finance and Wealth Management.

Because his book is specifically about personal finance, you want to keep looking for that exact category.

Which one is next? Well, he focuses on retirement, so the most specific category would be Personal Finance: Retirement Planning. That category is going to be our first BISAC code:

BUS050040   **BUSINESS & ECONOMICS** / Personal Finance / Retirement Planning

Now, you repeat that process, starting at the top and working your way down for the next two next-best categories.

To help you with this process, here are some additional tips:

- Double-check that this is a good category for your book by searching a retailer like Barnes & Noble or your local library for the BISAC code, and see if other books with that code are similar to yours.

- Select categories that apply to your book *as a whole,* not just a single chapter.

---

61 "Complete BISAC Subject Headings List," BISG: Book Industry Study Group, accessed March 12, 2023, https://www.bisg.org/complete-bisac-subject-headings-list.

62 Rob Berger, *Retire Before Mom and Dad: The Simple Numbers Behind a Lifetime of Financial Freedom* (Glenbrook Press, 2019).

- Try not to use the general category, as it's, well, general.

- Be consistent with your BISAC codes across different formats, so the BISAC code for your print book should be the same as your e-book, audiobook, etc.

BISAC code information is valuable for all authors; however, Amazon does categories their own way.

Three Surprising Facts About Amazon Categories

Despite all of our hard work on metadata, some of our clients at Book Launchers still end up in weird categories on Amazon. That said, Amazon made some major category changes in 2023 that will hopefully dramatically reduce or eliminate this from happening.

Amazon Has Different Categories for Each Format and Each Country

First, it's important to know that the Kindle Store (which is for e-books), the Amazon Bookstore (print books), and ACX for Audible (audiobooks) all have slightly different categories.

To complicate things more, Amazon Canada has different categories than Amazon Australia and Amazon U.S.

I know that sounds like a lot to process, but even just knowing about these differences is half the battle.

You can view a specific regional store's categories by reviewing its bestseller lists. All you have to do is navigate via the sidebar. When you search bestsellers, you'll see that they compile all the formats, so then you click into each store to view categories. To find sub-subcategories, you click on the sidebar and scroll down. Then you just keep on clicking until it stops offering new subcategories. When you've done that, you've reached the deepest sublevel.

Prime Positioning Is in the Deepest Categories

That deepest sublevel? That is *prime positioning.* You want to list your book in a deep subcategory because all the books in a subcategory will show up in its parent category. For example, listing a book on leadership strategies for millennials in Business and Money would be a huge waste of time. You'd miss out on the greater visibility offered by subcategories, like Management Skills, that are more specific to your book.

Once you've found all the categories that make sense for your book, it's time to analyze them. You want to get a sense of how competitive they are and how much visibility they bring. Publisher Rocket is a fabulous, helpful tool. You also can do it manually on Amazon by looking at all of the top 5–10 books for each category you've selected. Compare them to see which categories have the majority of books ranking higher than the others.

Rocket makes it easier because the software shows you the competitive nature and sales success of each category in an easy chart. When you do this, you'll see some subcategories are really competitive. But there are some other categories where you're likely to rank even with minimal sales. One of the neat features of Publisher Rocket is this handy column that shows you the number of sales required to hit the top 10 in that category.

That said, you don't want to use only niche categories with low sales because they're not likely searched very often. The key thing here is to find a good balance. Using one of those easy-win categories is good, so long as the parent category is relevant. Then you'll want to find and use higher-volume categories as well.

Now if your book's already out, and you're trying to figure out what categories you're already in, you'd think Amazon would give you a list, but they don't. The tool you can use to determine this is BKLNK.com.

You Can Choose Three Categories

Here's where things really changed in 2023. You used to have to choose BISAC codes, and Amazon would map your categories from there. You could then email someone at Amazon to get listed in up to 10 categories. It was a really inefficient system, and it caused books to be ranked in categories they didn't belong in as authors gamed the system and algorithms made mistakes.

Now, you choose your three categories right inside the KDP dashboard.

Price Is Part of Metadata—and It Matters Too!

One thing many people in the U.S. may not know is that Canadians are jealous of how cheap books are in the U.S. I experienced this especially as a kid and young adult before Amazon came along, when I bought a lot of fiction and nonfiction books. (I devoured the Babysitters Club, Nancy Drew, and Hardy Boys series at a breakneck pace!) You see, two prices are shown on the back of every book above the ISBN: the U.S. price and the Canadian price.

The difference wasn't insignificant. For example, a book that cost $14.99 in the U.S. would be nearly at least $20 in Canadian dollars. Even at times when the currencies were close to par, the book prices diverged dramatically. This is due to import fees and hedging against major currency fluctuations by retailers and publishers.

Things have changed, but people still pay more for a book in Canada than in the U.S. As an author, you should know the international market differences, so you're not forfeiting opportunities and are able to make sales in every market where you have readers.

If your book is available on KDP, you already have access to 13 different international markets without needing to go through additional work to license your rights. Convenient, right? On Amazon, you get to choose your primary marketplace, the main market for your book. Your options include the U.S., Canada, Mexico, Brazil, Japan, China, India, Australia, Spain, Italy, France, the U.K., and Germany.

Amazon uses your book's language to determine your main market, but you're not stuck with that as your main market if you're hoping to optimize your book for increased international sales. There are many ways to do that.

You can contact Amazon and ask them to update your Browse categories in each market. You can also select keywords for international markets to increase your book's discoverability. For example, words can be spelled differently in English, depending on the location. For example, Brits and Canadians spell words like "traveller," "cheque," and "catalogue" differently than in the U.S. Consider the variations of your keywords if it's relevant to your book and to finding readers in other countries. Likewise, there may be phrases common in other countries for your topic(s), and you can use one of your seven keyword spots in Amazon to translate your top keywords for foreign marketplaces.

But you still need to think about pricing. **There are only three things that really matter when it comes to setting your book price:**

1. Perceived value of what you offer in your book

2. Pricing of comparable books

3. Your expenses

First things first: Take that category research you did, and head to Amazon for your chosen market. Review the prices of books, including print and e-book formats, in that category.

Pay attention to their:

- format and other details similar to your book,
- pricing to similar books (or even the same ones) marketed on Amazon U.S. under that category, and
- word count.

Write these down, or put them in a spreadsheet. Exclude the ones with an e-book discount or pricing that is obviously off. When Amazon clears out stock, a hardcover sells for dramatically less than a paperback. That's not a pricing strategy by an author.

Now that you've got your range or average for your Amazon U.S. market, you can figure out international pricing.

Typically, books in Canada and Australia are higher priced than U.S. books, even after taking currency exchange rates into account. In Canada, they're often about 30%–40% higher, and in Australia, they're almost always 50%–70% higher.[63]

You may not care about a dollar or two, but keep in mind, cheaper is not always better. There's a perceived-value factor that you need to keep in mind. If you are dramatically cheaper than top books, then readers may consciously or subconsciously believe you are offering less value. On the flip side, if you're selling in a country that prices books much lower, you'll be setting yourself up to collect dust instead of royalties. That means you need to do a currency conversion for your book price and also correct the price for the local market (which is an option on every book-selling platform).

Currency conversion is a great tool for determining a benchmark. Check the numbers, though. If your U.S.-dollar price converts to a funky number in a different currency, it's a good idea to round it up or down. Weird numbers can actually have an effect on buying decisions, so if your price converts to something like $15.34, you can go in and round it to a more common figure like $15.49 or $15.97 so it seems more palatable to your readers. Weird, I know, but true.

---

63 "Cost of Books in Australia Versus the UK and USA," Bob in Oz, June 18, 2014, https://www.bobinoz.com/blog/14989/cost-of-books-in-australia-versus-the-uk-and-usa/.

When you're setting international prices, you want to consider your competition and your compensation. You can use calculators on IngramSpark or KDP to determine your profit, but you have to keep in mind that if you want your book to sell, it's ultimately more about the competition and the category you're in than what you want to make per book.

What About Giving Your Book Away for Free?

Used strategically, free books can be a very effective tactic based on your bigger-picture goals. For example, to generate leads, free books (to the right people) can be incredibly effective. To get your book into the hands of influencers, free books distributed with tact and targeting can be intelligent marketing tools. It can also be an incredibly high-value gift to give new employees, contractors, or clients as part of onboarding. You'll showcase your expertise and what you do as a company in a format that has more perceived value than a brochure or a training video.

But there are downsides too. Do you remember the book bomber at the conference I told you about?

He gave away his book without any targeting whatsoever. Handing books to total strangers also didn't set his book up to have a strong perceived value.

I've given away thousands of copies of *Self-Publish and Succeed*. Maybe you met me or someone from my team at a conference and got a free copy yourself. That may be what led you to connect with us and buy this book! Then again, possibly you got this book for free.

There is an important distinction between free books we give to strangers and free books that are gifts and meant only for people who fit the criteria of an ideal reader. We aren't standing at the conference table, shoving a book in every person's hand. We have a conversation and then offer it to people who will benefit, almost always in exchange for contact information. We've also done partnerships with organizations like the Exit Planning Institute where we gave them copies of our book for each of their VIP clients. Their clients are a great fit for our service, so giving them a copy of our book adds value to their gift bags and connects us with new people who may hire us to help them write, publish, and promote a book.

You can do the same with e-books if you run ads. Someone who sees your ad is targeted, and you get their contact information in exchange for the download.

Your nonfiction book needs to have value and perceived value!

Making your book readily available too cheaply or for free doesn't allow you to easily leverage its value for partnerships and connections.

You are putting years of your expertise, education, and experience into this book. It probably took you tens of thousands of dollars (or a lot more!) and thousands of hours to gain that expertise.

If you want to be a speaker and sell your book as part of your speaking package, or you want to sell your book to corporations, you need to price your book so it has value in these negotiations.

One of the best deals I ever made was with a national real estate magazine in Canada. They needed a giveaway for their readers who subscribed to three years of their magazine. I needed exposure for my book. I got a ton of high-value exposure in exchange for giving them 250 copies of my book. If my book had retailed for $2.99 or even $9.99, it would not have had the same perceived value to them in this arrangement as the $24 book did.

Even more than that, depending on your industry, your clients probably spend a lot of money to work with you. That's true whether you're a dentist, a mortgage professional, or team member at Book Launchers who helps people write, publish, and promote books.

Your book price may reflect on your other offerings. If you give the book away for free on Amazon or price it at 99 cents, what do you think your clients are going to think—not only about the book but also potentially about your services?

Free in exchange for a promised review or free when someone opts into your newsletter are different things because you're getting something important in exchange for your book. Being strategic and leveraging your book for value, whether that value is money, ad space, or a review, is being a smart author.

Killing It with Keywords

Keywords are about discoverability. The goal here is to make sure you are found when your reader searches for a solution to the problem you solve or for a book just like yours.

We tend to focus on Amazon, but keep in mind this is also about search engines in general and anywhere books are sold. This is why we also do Google keyword research.

How should you actually go about doing your keyword research?

Step One: Think Like a Reader

I love playing poker, but I've barely been able to play since I became a mom and launched Book Launchers. (I realize this sounds funny because I live in Las Vegas.) When I get back into it, I might want to refresh my skills with a few books on the latest poker strategies. To find a good book, I'd probably go to Amazon and search using the term "Texas Hold'em."

I'm not a poker pro, but I've played way too many games to read a beginner's book explaining straddles and terms like "under the gun." If I see results including beginner's books, I might change up my search to include the word "strategy" or even "advanced." My new search might be "latest Texas Hold'em strategies" or "advanced Texas Hold'em guide."

That's what I mean when I say "think like a reader." You have to know what your reader is looking for so you can align your keywords to their thought process. When you understand that, then you'll understand which words they are most likely to use to search for the books they want.

Step Two: Use logic

Some people get really creative and try to grab every random search that might come up. Realistically, your reader is not searching for "Texas Hold'em win." Far more likely, they're looking for something simple, like "win poker tournaments" or "how to win money with poker."

Don't just string a bunch of words together in the hope that readers will find your book. Think about what they're most likely to search and the simplest combination of words.

Using logic, with your reader in mind, you're ready for step three.

Step Three: Test the Search

Go to Amazon, and see if your search works.

For example, does "Texas Hold'em" get a lot of results? Does adding specific keywords such as "beginner" make a difference? Does changing your search to another phrase like "poker strategies" help narrow your search and give you better options?

When you type your test keywords, consider whether your book belongs with the search results. If not, keep trying until you get search results that are a better fit.

Step Four: Research Keywords

Using a tool like K-lytics, you can start to get a sense of the most popular search terms. At Book Launchers, we use Publisher Rocket, KDSPY, and

Semrush to get a clear picture of what readers are searching. Then we use that data to make key decisions.

These tools are really valuable, especially when first assessing if your idea is an actual term people use. Then you want to look at the competition. Ideally, you want a term that is highly searched but not highly competitive. Publisher Rocket makes it easy to identify these terms with color coding, but you should also use your own logic because sometimes a red-coded word (meaning it has a lot of competition) is still one you absolutely want to use.

Step Five: Make a List

It's a good idea to have keywords in both your title *and* your book description (but not the same ones—use different ones). This improves the discoverability of your book in all the places readers might look for it. In addition to this, inside the KDP Print dashboard, you'll find seven keyword boxes that you can use to further clarify the relevant words for your book.

As Amazon states on their website, your keywords "should capture useful, relevant information that won't fit into your title and description."[64] This includes setting, plot highlights, themes, or key locations where the book takes place.

If your book discusses a topic in the context of a specific location, or if your target reader is a divorced person, single mom, or a veteran (or has another particular identity), those might be useful to put in your keywords.

🅘 **TIP:** Here's a pro tip for searching keywords on Amazon while you're doing your research. Do all your searches in a private browser. That

---

64 Daisy Quaker, "Amazon SEO: How to Optimize Your Product Listings (Step-by-Step Guide)," *Amazon Selling Partner Blog*, Sell.Amazon.com, April 4, 2022, https://sell.amazon.com/blog/getting-started/amazon-seo-to-optimize-product-listings.

way, your past search history doesn't impact your suggested search results and you get a "cleaner" search.

A friendly warning—avoid including words like "bestseller" in the keywords or in your book description. Making any sort of a claim about your book, like "bestseller" or "award-winning" could cause a lot of problems, with Amazon in particular. Even if it's true, if you use those words in your keywords or your description, Amazon may remove your book. You can always dispute this if you are, in fact, a *New York Times* bestseller or a Pulitzer Prize winner, and you want to put that info in your description. But if it's not a particularly prestigious label, and it can't be verified, I would just skip it because Amazon is really sticky about this. All keywords must comply with the terms and conditions of Amazon.

Other warnings straight from Amazon's KDP list of things to avoid include:

- information common to most items in the category, like "book,"
- spelling errors that you think readers may make or common misspellings,
- time-sensitive terms, like "new," "on sale," or "available now," and
- words like "Amazon," "KDP," or "free."

Here's what you can and should do:

- *Consider longer phrases.* Each of the seven spaces to enter your keywords on Amazon has 50 characters, so you can input a longer phrase, and *all* the words will be considered keywords—for example, "winning no-limit poker tournament strategies." That has less than 50 characters, and you can fit it onto one line. Every single one of those words would be considered a keyword.
- *Use those 50 characters if you can,* but don't repeat words in each box or try different combinations. They are already going to be indexed if they are in one box or in the title and subtitle.

- *Update your keywords and descriptions as often as you like*, but if your Amazon ads perform well, I'd leave them alone (more on that soon). Periodically research what's relevant and use it. As a benchmark example, we do a keyword refresh and update on our authors' books every three to six months.

- *Keep your description consistent across formats.* Don't put a different description or different keywords in your audiobook versus your e-book versus your print book.

At the end of the day, researching keywords is a huge can of worms, and we've only just scratched the surface here to give you an overview. Publisher Rocket, authors like David Gaughran, and organizations like the Independent Book Publishers Association (IBPA) and Alli all have great training options to get you current and skilled on keyword research, which is always evolving. I also highly recommend you read Dale Roberts's book *The Amazon Self-Publisher* as he talks about this and so much more.[65]

Now you know everything you need to know about where and how to sell your book, how to use keywords to find your target audience, and how to price your book for any market—including how to offer special promotional sale prices. Next up, we delve into why book reviews are crucial to your success and how to get the reviews you want.

Key elements of an effective book description

Your book description is the sales copy for your book. If your book isn't selling, it's the easiest thing you can change to try to give your book sales a boost.

Your book description is not a book summary. It's not there to highlight all the cool things you've done or all your amazing stories. Its job is to sell

---

65 Dale L. Roberts, *The Amazon Self Publisher: How to Sell More Books on Amazon* (Archangel Ink, 2021).

your book. It needs to speak directly to the reader, and you need to layer in well-researched keywords. This is copy—not content.

The description needs four important elements to hit potential readers where it matters and make them feel compelled to buy your book.

1. **Author information**, which establishes your credibility and expertise

2. **Call to action**, which asks them to buy your book

3. **Hook**, which appeals to readers' curiosity and interest

4. **Outcome**, which defines your unique approach and what they'll get from reading your book—and only your book

Here's Matthew Harmon's book, *Marijuana Hater's Guide to Making a Billion Dollars from Hemp: The Next Disruptive Industry*, as an example:[66]

An emerging industry poised for incredible growth in the United States promises big benefits and bigger profits. With the right strategy, you can cash in now. Successful entrepreneur and documentary filmmaker Matthew Harmon traveled the world researching the newly legalized super-crop, hemp—and the unlimited opportunities it holds for investors, entrepreneurs, and farmers. In *Marijuana Hater's Guide to Making a Billion Dollars from Hemp*, discover the potential of this transformative industry and your ability to grow your own lucrative hemp business. Filled with fascinating facts and insider information!

You'll learn:

Go deep into the myths, misconceptions and fascinating history of hemp and marijuana plants, which taints our perceptions today—and how that's an opportunity for you.

Innovative industries featuring hemp products, from construction materials to nutritional food, for beginner investors to consider now.

Medical hemp opportunities for the science-based entrepreneur, including skincare products and pain management.

The path to a more sustainable future using hemp as renewable energy to replace eco-unfriendly products.

Strategies to understand industrial hemp's value in America and to help change laws regulating cannabis and weed.

Now is your time for business innovation success with industrial hemp. Get this guide and plant the seed for an organic ground-floor opportunity with limitless potential!

---

66 Matthew Harmon, *Marijuana Hater's Guide to Making a Billion Dollars from Hemp: The Next Disruptive Industry* (Farmbridge, 2021).

The hook teases the massive untapped potential of the hemp industry from an investment perspective. Matthew argues there is more profit potential in hemp than other industries.

To establish his credibility and expertise, Matthew cites outlets that have featured him (building third-party credibility) and makes it clear that he's traveled the world studying hemp.

Bullet points spell out his unique approach, outlining specific investment opportunities, such as "medical hemp opportunities for the science-based entrepreneur, including skincare and pain management," that could benefit readers.

Finally, it may seem silly to tell someone on your book page that their next step is to buy the book and read it so they can enjoy its benefits. But that is exactly what you need to do. The Amazon description for Matthew's book reads, "Get this guide, and plant the seed for an organic ground floor opportunity with limitless possibilities!"

It's also important to know that the first sentence is the most important sentence of your book description. Is your description specific, or could it be used to sell any other book in your category?

Look at every sentence and ask yourself, "Does it sell the hook of your book? Will your ideal reader imagine their life differently and be curious or committed enough to buy your book after reading that description?"

How does it stack up against your competition? How is your book different and is that captured in your description? And finally, when it comes to the digital version, layer in those traffic-attracting keywords.

Chapter Summary

There are a lot of things to know about metadata, but here are the key takeaways from this chapter:

1. Categorizing your book with related books ensures your reader can

find you.

2. Pricing your book requires understanding your competition, your book's perceived value, and your publishing expenses.

3. Take advantage of international sales opportunities by checking to see if your pricing makes sense in those markets.

4. Keywords are not just highly searched words. They are words that your ideal reader uses when trying to find solutions to their problems. You need to think like a reader when choosing keywords, and then use various tools and searches to verify that they work and are most applicable to your book.

5. Giving your book away for free can have negative consequences if you don't keep your bigger-picture goal in mind. Free books should move you closer to achieving that goal.

CHAPTER 10

THE LIFEBLOOD OF EVERY BOOK—REVIEWS

NEXT TO COFFEE, BOOK REVIEWS ARE PROBABLY THE MOST IMPORTANT prerequisite for your survival as an author. Or maybe wine or chocolate? For some authors, it's probably all three! But I digress.

Why are reviews so important? It's because they are the #1 factor that feeds into not only your book sales but also your Amazon ads and helps make you eligible for new and exciting opportunities. If an event promoter or a producer you've pitched has never heard of you, they're going to go to your Amazon page to check you out. And if your book only has seven reviews? That might make them think twice about putting you on their stage or their podcast.

How many reviews do you need?

We've found that for Amazon ad performance, 25 reviews are the first tipping point. The next big tipping point for conversions with ads and even media wins is 50+ reviews. Any number over 100 is excellent.

Prepare yourself mentally for the journey that is review solicitation. Confident newbie authors often tell me that hundreds of people have promised to write reviews. Then one month post-launch, these same authors are stunned to find their books have just 20 reviews, and they don't know how to get more.

This isn't to demoralize you, but I find a good dose of reality goes a long way toward setting expectations in terms of the effort you need to get results. The good news is, there are platforms and services designed to help authors get book reviews, and I'll get to those later.

First, let's get some clarity around the different kinds of reviews you need. After that, we will review the vetted services and tools to help you on this leg of your book adventure.

To start, there are two primary types of book reviews: customer reviews and editorial reviews. For most books, both are needed. You're likely familiar with customer reviews, as they are highly visible for most products and services. Editorial reviews, on the other hand, may be something you don't know that much about, so let's cover those first.

The 411 on Editorial Reviews

An editorial book review is different from a consumer reviewer (your average reader) in that it's usually from a recognized professional (author, reviewer for a media outlet, or expert in the field).

When you post an editorial review to your Amazon page, the heat map research from Kindlepreneur shows that it's more about *who is writing* the review than what they say.[67]

Of course, you don't want to have a popular reviewer post a scathing review of your book (and if they did, you certainly wouldn't repost it to your Am-

---

67 Dave Chesson, "The Art and Science to Amazon Editorial Reviews," Kindlepreneur, last updated December 13, 2022, https://kindlepreneur.com/amazon-editorial-reviews/.

azon page), but it's important to keep in mind that your readers are really looking at the *who* of your editorial reviews versus the *what* of the content.

Editorial reviews have the power to lend your book (and you, the author) some of the reviewer's authority and credibility. An ideal reviewer is someone who has illustrious credentials and, even better, is an expert in an area relevant to the book's subject matter. The latter is great, but it isn't always necessary.

As an example, Shelley Buck, coauthor of *Leave Your Light On*, has some phenomenal editorial reviews, but the first ones you see on her online marketing pages aren't critics or authors. Instead, there's one from the CEO of Disney. Even Kristen Bell wrote a review for her. (And just in case you're wondering if it was *that* Kristen Bell, the word "actress" was added.)[68] CEO, COO, NYT bestselling author, celebrity—those are all great qualifiers for ideal folks to write you an editorial review.

I know you're asking, "Julie, I'm not connected to anybody famous, so how do I get those kinds of reviews?" You could do what a lot of people do, and that is reach out to some of the authors in your niche whom you respect. Hopefully, you've already been networking with some of them. If you're looking for cover endorsements, then the ones you don't use for your cover could be used as editorial reviews. If they're an author in your niche or genre, they would qualify as an editorial reviewer.

Keep in mind, authors get asked for blurbs and endorsements all the time.

Here are tips for getting cool endorsements:

1. Think of companies that are well known and respected by your audience. You can even ask your favorite AI system, like ChatGPT or Jasper, for some ideas.

2. Make a list that makes sense for your book.

---

68 Shelley Buck and Ryder Buck, *Leave Your Light On: The Musical Mantra Left Behind by an Illuminating Spirit* (Eagles Quest Publishing, 2020).

3. Hop on LinkedIn, Twitter, or whatever platform makes sense for you and your book, and see if you can connect with some of the company's top-level executives or even its founder(s).

4. Look for common connections, and ask for introductions if you have a friend who knows the right person. If not, reach out and ask for help (more on that in a minute).

Think how great it would look if the president of Airstream endorsed your travel book or how cool it would be to have the founder of Nobull apparel endorse your book on sport-based leadership strategies for business? I randomly selected those examples, but my guess is that those folks are not asked nearly as often for book blurb endorsements as other authors or even major CEOs. And they may find it fun getting their name on the cover of your book.

Watch for media that feature your book. If they say anything cool about your book, then you can include an excerpt as part of your editorial reviews. The same thing goes for blogs and podcasts.

We often land reviews for clients through services like NetGalley. We also submit authors to Reader Views, Midwest Book Review, and other programs. There are other paid professional review services as well—some legit, some less so. I'll get into more detail about these kinds of services soon.

Paying for the opportunity for your book to be reviewed is playing by the rules with Amazon, because these reviews are going into the editorial review section, not the customer review section. You can use the reviewer's words in your editorial review section, whether you paid for the review or not.

It's All in the Presentation

Once you've got that editorial review, the first steps are to post it on your Amazon book page and make it look impressive. My recommendation is to italicize the review text and then bold the reviewer's name and qualifier.

Formatting that bit as bolded makes a potential buyer stop and read the name and qualifier first, as in "CEO of Disney."

Use HTML for this formatting. If you have a favorite AI bot, it can format the HTML you need. ChatGPT is particularly good at this, but there are plenty of AI coding bots that can do basic HTML. Other tools like Publisher Rocket have a feature on their desktop site that will let you do that really easily. You can also ask Google how to create italics and bold HTML. It's not hard to do, and it's worth taking this extra step to make your editorial reviews look professional on your book page.

You won't use your editorial reviews on only your Amazon page, although it's one of the primary placements. You'll also want them on your author media kit, websites, and promotional materials.

As a best practice for presenting editorial reviews, we recommend creating attractive social media imagery for them. We share some of the editorial wins on our social media, so you can always connect with Book Launchers on Instagram.

At the end of the day, your #1 priority as an author marketing a book should still be to get as many consumer reviews as you can, but editorial reviews are an important piece of that book marketing puzzle too. Getting a dozen amazing editorial reviews to add to your Amazon book page and marketing materials can really boost your credibility and book sales.

Let's turn to how you actually get those reviews. For starters, one of the most important tools is ARCs.

What Is an ARC?

Have you ever heard someone say they got an ARC copy of a book? Or maybe you've been researching book promotions and heard that ARCs are an important part of getting book reviews.

ARCs are advanced reader copies of a book. They're created for the purpose of getting advance (pre-launch) editorial reviews and media coverage and enticing booksellers to carry the book. They're not usually the final version of the book, but they are very close. There may still be typos or formatting errors. Sometimes they'll even include marketing plans on the cover as background information for the media. The point of an ARC is to spread word about the upcoming release and build momentum for a solid book launch.

Traditionally, they have been labeled as ARCs on the manuscript. This labeling could appear on the cover, on every page at the top or bottom, or as a watermark lightly labeled behind the text. This kind of labeling was important in the days before self-publishing because traditional publishers often sent ARCs out well before manuscripts were finalized. This is less common now as most publishing companies have shifted to e-books for their ARCs and will put a watermark or some other electronic control on the copy. Services like BookFunnel are great tools for sending protected electronic ARC copies.

It's wise to plan on creating an ARC version of your book so you can use it to gain endorsements for your cover and other marketing materials as well as to get the review momentum going well before your launch.

What's Worked to Get Reviews—My Personal Experience

You won't always know where reviews come from. A year after *Self-Publish and Succeed* was out, I went through all my Goodreads and Amazon reviews to determine what strategies worked to get reviews and what strategies didn't seem to have an impact. After I share my findings, I'll list a few ideas that other authors recommend for reviews.

Here's what I found:

My existing audience was the biggest source.

My YouTube besties and Book Launchers clients were absolutely my #1 source. Cultivating a community of people and adding value to their lives on a regular basis means that when you ask for support, you'll get it!

NetGalley worked well.

We went through IBPA to get a reduced rate on a NetGalley review, and it resulted in at least a handful of reviews. More on NetGalley in a second.

Booksprout was hit and miss.

Booksprout is another paid service, and I tracked four reviews back to them. (I'll explain how they work shortly.) That said, we use this service for our authors and get mixed results. It's worth trying, but it may or may not result in reviews for your book.

Goodreads giveaways generated activity on the site.

While I can't be certain that this resulted in much in terms of Amazon reviews because this was before Amazon automatically posted Goodreads reviews, it did generate activity.

Asking, begging, and celebrating every review was fun!

For many months, I posted thank-yous on social media. We also held a reviewer party, where we made sure everyone won something. If you submit a review of this book, shoot us an email at team@booklaunchers.com with a screenshot of the review, and we'll be sure to thank you and invite you to our online or real-life parties too!

Our reviewer party was super fun, and I was able to provide content, have fun, and reward attendees with swag. Every review was helpful—especially in the beginning.

What Didn't Attract Reviews for *Self-Publish and Succeed*

The biggest strategy that didn't work was *hoping* reviews would appear for different formats. The audiobook has sold decently well, and yet I didn't get very many audiobook-specific reviews. I know a few YouTube besties tried to post audiobook reviews and had them removed, and I didn't take a proactive approach to get those kinds of reviews. (You can post a review of *Self-Publish and Succeed* on Audible now, if you'd like.)

Audible doesn't include Amazon reviews, so when someone goes to their Audible app, it may look far less impressive than their reviews on Amazon.

The other thing that didn't work was asking for reviews in my newsletter. It's impossible to tell, but the links where I ask for people to "click here and post a review" didn't see much action. They may have served as a reminder for some people, but they didn't move the needle anywhere near as much as places like Goodreads, Booksprout, or NetGalley or as much as leveraging my wonderful community and just asking people one-on-one!

How to Ask for a Review

Because of the importance of reviews, this is a subject we continually discuss in our biweekly launch letter and over at BookLaunchers.tv, so I highly recommend you connect with us there for all the latest tips and ideas.

When the opportunity arises, ask for a review. But how you do it is important. The last thing you want to do is annoy someone when you ask them for a favor.

Openings to ask for a review may look like this:

- Someone says they read your book and loved it.
- An interviewer asks how they can support you.

- You've received an email question from someone that your book can answer.

You'll know the opportunity when it comes. Seize it.

How you ask someone for a review depends on your personality, of course. It also depends on the person and context. Here are some of the ways I ask:

- Can you help me by posting a review on Amazon so I can find other readers like you who will benefit from the book?

- The greatest gift you can give an author is a review of their book on your favorite book-buying website.

- Please help me have more impact with my book by posting a review.

- Please, please, please post a review, and you'll be my friend for life.

- If you post a review of the book, please email it to me, and I'll get you on the list for our next reviewer party.

If you're emailing people, do it one-on-one, and keep track of who promised to post a review. Don't be a total pain, but be brave enough to follow up once or twice to get them to follow through on their promise. You need the reviews.

Next up, let's talk about some of the best services and additional tools you can use to drum up those all-important reviews.

Review Services and Tools to Make It Easier

Paying services to help you get reviews isn't the same as paying someone to review your book. You need book reviews as an author, and while you can't ethically pay someone to give you a positive review, there are some great legitimate review services out there that will help you find a reviewer.

At Book Launchers, we use Goodreads, NetGalley, BookSirens, and Booksprout for our authors. New services are always popping up too, so ask around your favorite forum or check out our latest videos on BookLaunchers.tv to find new ones.

You can also pay services like *Kirkus, Publishers Weekly*, Reedsy, and BookLife, among others. Some are expensive, but sites like *Kirkus Reviews* and *Publishers Weekly* carry a lot of weight with libraries and bookstores. If getting wide distribution is part of your plan, it might be worth the investment.

The best book review sites for you depend on your book category, your overall strategy, and your goals for your book, as well as whom you're targeting with your book. The ultimate goal is the same on every site, though: to increase your exposure, find new readers, and bump up that review count. Fiction authors have even more services to help them (as well as e-book and audiobook sale services too, but that's a different topic!).

Goodreads

Not all sites make sense for every author. At Book Launchers, while we submit some books for *Kirkus* or *Publishers Weekly*, we most often use Goodreads.

This is the single most popular review site in the publishing industry and the top online community for both book lovers and authors alike. As of the writing of this book, they claim to have more than 140 million members worldwide.[69] Yeah, that's a lot of readers!

Even better is that Goodreads reviews now appear on Amazon. (Amazon owns Goodreads, so integration makes sense.) When someone posts a review on Goodreads, it does double duty.

---

69 Cybil, "Goodreads Members' Top 72 Hit Books of the Year (So Far)," *Goodreads* (blog), June 6, 2022, https://www.goodreads.com/blog/show/2302-goodreads-members-top-72-hit-books-of-the-year-so-far.

While every author and their books should be on Goodreads, you need to decide for yourself how much time and energy is worth investing in this platform.

That is largely going to depend on the genre of your book and its desired audience. Memoirs do better on this platform than hardcore financial investment books, for instance. Past reports have shown the audience is primarily females in the U.S. under 35 with a graduate school education.[70] If your reader is likely to be in that audience, this could be a great place for you to invest some time.

One pro tip and a word of caution

When you create your Goodreads account and connect it to your Amazon account, *do not connect via Facebook or Twitter*. Also, if it's possible—and it might not be possible because you have to tie it back to your Amazon account to select the books that are yours—set it up with a different email address than you use for those social media accounts.

Let's face it, Amazon already has way more information about us than most of our closest relatives have, maybe even our significant others. Even so, any little step you can take to keep things separate can help you retain as many reviews as possible. Amazon has been known to remove a lot of reviews in sweeps, and many authors believe that these kinds of connections can make it easier for Amazon to remove reviews from people who have a connection to you (whether they are friends or family, or not!).

The strategy here is to get people to add your book to their virtual bookshelves and write reviews. You also want other users to see your book in their friends' feeds. Hopefully when they see it, they add your title to their reading list too. It's like a 90-million reader game of telephone.

---

70 "Who Is the Average Goodreads User? You'll Be Surprised!," Goodreads, January 13, 2017, https://www.goodreads.com/author_blog_posts/14538341-who-is-the-average-goodreads-user-you-ll-be-surprised.

Bottom line, get in there, create your Goodreads account, claim your books, put up a nice 400-by-400-pixel headshot of yourself, and voilà! Now you're ready to use your Goodreads account for the greater good of your book promotion. This is the absolute minimum any author should do.

Here are three more ideas:

Run a Goodreads giveaway. This is something we do on a regular basis for our clients. If you want to drive more attention to your book for a fee, this option can add value in getting you more reviews and a whole lot of potential readers to put you on their want-to-read list. All active giveaways are listed on the giveaway section of the website, and your fans can link to it and encourage their friends to enter the giveaway too.

Once upon a time, Goodreads giveaways were free, but you had to mail physical copies. These days, it costs a fee of $119 to run a Goodreads give-away (or $599 for the premium giveaway option), but you can also run them using e-books, so at least you don't have to handle addresses, ship-ping, and printing costs for your winners. Instead, winners are emailed their copy from Amazon. That makes things easier.

Are Goodreads giveaways worth doing? If you have a limited budget, and you're a nonfiction author, I'd probably spend my money on a NetGalley promotion (read more about them later) to get high-quality reviews from the right readers versus spending my marketing budget at Goodreads. But again, this varies. It's worth doing 20 minutes' worth of research to click around the site and see what kind of books are being given away (especially books in your genre or on similar topics to yours), and the responses these offers get. Typically, memoirs are a great fit, as are self-help, fitness and health, and mindset books.

Promote your book with paid ads. The reality for many nonfiction au-thors, especially business and finance authors, is that your ideal reader probably isn't spending a ton of time on Goodreads. Do your research before you decide to invest in their pay-per-click ads. It's a simple ad platform, and it could be a great way for you to boost your book sales, but check first to see if your ideal reader is on the platform.

Engage with the platform. There's a spot on every author page for a Q&A, just waiting to be filled! You can also create a list of books and share it on Listopia or add your book to other lists. Your book will get up and down votes on these lists, so it needs to be relevant to the topic.

Bottom line, the tens of millions of readers who use Goodreads are always looking for their next read, so you belong there. Whether you spend a lot of time on Goodreads depends on whether your ideal reader is likely to be hanging out there or not.

NetGalley

NetGalley is an online service that connects book publishers with reviewers. As an author (or publisher), you can pay to list your book with NetGalley, and they release it to their database of professional readers. These are reviewers, members of the media, bloggers, librarians, booksellers, podcast hosts, and others who just really love books. These readers can then request a digital ARC of your book for review.

This can be an effective marketing tool for your entire author brand, not just your book, because your book is made available to people who want to read it in their professional capacity. A NetGalley promotion offers your ARC for six months (or you can do shorter three-month promotions if you purchase through a service like IBPA or Xpresso Book Tours). It also highlights your book in the "Recently Added" and "Read Now" sections of their database, as well as in the section specific to your title's categories. That way, all users see it on the website.

The best time to start using NetGalley to get reviews for your book is six to eight weeks before it launches.

Reviewers are most interested in reading and reviewing a book *before* it's launched.

That said, if your book is already out in the wild, NetGalley will still accept your title. It's a fee-based service, so it's really up to you to decide whether it makes sense for you post-launch or not.

What Does NetGalley Cost, and What Do I Actually Get?

The cool part about how NetGalley[71] works is that a reviewer typically posts reviews to their NetGalley profile and also to Amazon, Goodreads, and sometimes blogs or other media. Each review from NetGalley gives you more exposure than a typical Amazon review. The reviewer's doing this for free, and they're getting your book for free, but they are motivated book reviewers. In most situations, reviewing books is related to their occupation. We see a lot of librarians, bookstore employees, and journalists who write about books posting reviews. However, they are specially vetted to post reviews on NetGalley.

NetGalley also gives you a certain amount of control over who is going to review your work through their database. When someone requests your ARC directly through NetGalley, you get access to the book reviewer's profile and can approve their access to your book or not. You can see reviews they've written and reject the request if you think they are unfair or not a good fit for your book. If you go through another service like IBPA or Xpresso to get the discounted listing, you will not have the ability to reject the request. It's a trade-off for lower-cost access.

A Word on NetGalley Reviewers

Brace yourself for a 4/5 review (or worse). Even if the reviewer shares a glowing review, they often tag it with a four-star rating. What we've found is that these are reviewers who aren't your average readers. Because they are often people from the book world, they are saving their five stars for what they consider the absolute best books.

---

71 https://netgalley.com

If you've invested in creating a top-quality book, this shouldn't deter you. We still like the service because it's trusted in the industry, you are likely to get a handful of reviews, and sometimes these reviewers are in a position of power and influence where they can get your book into other places.

For example, one of our clients got a NetGalley five-star review (hooray!) from a librarian who said that she was going to recommend the book be listed in *all* of the libraries in her library's system. That's the power of Net-Galley reviews. If you get a great review, don't forget to actually use it to promote your book. Post it on your author page, website, and social media.

How to Get the Most Out of NetGalley

NetGalley has a widget and some other share links. Use these to get the word out so people in the database find out about your book's availability. You can't automatically assume that people will see your listing if you're not promoting it.

You should encourage people to give your cover a thumbs-up on NetGalley because that helps it get featured.

BookSirens and Booksprout

BookSirens and Booksprout are like NetGalley in that they are review sites set up to deliver your ARC copy to readers and reviewers. But these two sites are more for the average reader versus the person in the book industry. Just like NetGalley, though, they focus on getting your ARC securely to book reviewers and bloggers and your book army. BookSirens boasts more than 30,000 readers across a variety of genres with an average review rate of 75%.[72]

You first send your book to the BookSirens team for evaluation so they can confirm that it is a quality book they want to offer to their users. Once it's

---

72 "What Is the Expected Review Rate?," BookSirens, last updated March 6, 2023, https://support.booksirens.com/article/52-what-is-the-expected-review-rate.

approved, your book will be added to its category where users can discover it, download the ARC, and start reading.

BookSirens also supplies you with a direct link to send to your book army. That means those folks can hop on over and securely download their ARC for free. You also have the option of choosing whether your reviews are posted on Goodreads, Amazon, or both.

Booksprout is another option to consider if your main priority is a pre-launch review push.

Similar to BookSirens, Booksprout is a review site that automates the delivery of your ARC to more than 40,000 users. And even your own book army can't beat their average review rate, which exceeds 79%.[73] We've been testing this service at Book Launchers with really mixed results. My book, well after launch, got four reviews from a single Booksprout listing, but the other books we tested didn't see any results.

It's worth noting that we've experienced the same thing with BookSirens. Some of our clients, however, have had good results getting reviews.

In other words, be ready to test different services, because some things will work, and others won't.

Whether you go with BookSirens, Booksprout, or both, they're easy-to-use, effective sites if you need a little help getting reviews. If this is your first book or if your book army looks a little sparse on the pre-launch battlefield, one or both of these review sites could be your answer.

Change Your Mind—Change Your Results

Are there other ways to get reviews?

---

73 "Booksprout," Booksprout, accessed March 14, 2023, https://booksprout.com

Well, sure. You just have to ask for them, as we discussed. You can do that in person, via email, on your social media, at the back of your book, and on your knees or from seated or standing positions.

I know. It feels needy or demanding.

Plus, you're too busy.

But after all your hard work, you've earned the right to go to people and ask, "Will you help me by writing an Amazon review?"

If you've followed the Book Launchers #NoBoringBooks process, and you've invested in creating a great book, you should be proud of your book! Plus, here's the thing: **You wrote your book to have an impact, didn't you?** That's not going to happen if nobody buys your book, and they are unlikely to buy a book that doesn't have reviews.

Writing a book to help others walking along a similar path is generous and noble, and you can look at reviews as something you need to do to help your reader, not just you. In turn, grateful readers will thank you by writing more reviews and growing your readership and fan base. Everyone has to get started somewhere.

Stick with it. You've got this.

Chapter Summary

WHERE TO FIND YOUR REVIEWERS

TYPE OF REVIEW	WHAT IT IS	SERVICES TO USE	TIPS OR POINTERS
Customer reviews	Reviews posted on the book-buying site or a site like Goodreads from readers. These can be people you have in your sphere of influence, but Amazon prohibits reviews from friends or family.	Booksprout, BookFunnel, Goodreads giveaways, NetGalley	Ask your readers, clients, colleagues, and anyone who is not your friend or family member to help you find your ideal reader so your book can have the impact you intend. Keep asking—you've earned the right to ask, *and* your reader needs you.
Editorial reviews —paid	These are reviews from industry professionals that go in an editorial review section on the Amazon page. They can lend massive credibility to sell your book to bookstores or libraries.	*Publishers Weekly*, *Kirkus Reviews*, NetGalley, Readers' Favorites	There are a lot of services (many, like *Kirkus*, are very pricey) that will read your book and write an editorial review.
Editorial reviews —influencers	These reviews are to borrow credibility and make your book stand out to your reader. The identity of the reviewer is more important than the content of the review.	Ask ChatGPT or your favorite AI to find influencers for you. Use LinkedIn to find the right connections. Ask your network who might be connected to people your reader will find credible.	There isn't one way to approach this, but I find either a polite but direct ask or a longer-term relationship-building exercise are most effective.

CHAPTER 11

THE LOW-DOWN ON LIBRARIES

THERE'S MONEY TO BE MADE WITH LIBRARIES, BUT WE'RE NOT TALKING big bucks. If you care only about making money, this chapter isn't for you.

If, however, you've become an author to make an impact, enhance your authority, or give back to the community you live in, then you're going to love learning all about library listings.

Selling books is important to access readers. But for many authors—especially those who want to help others trying to get through hard times —getting your book on the shelves at libraries is a must.

A library listing doesn't mean a big payday for an author because the book could be read a thousand times, and you're paid only once when the library buys the book. That's not quite true of e-books and audiobooks, depending on the system and how the library lists your book. But it is true of a physical copy of the book. Even so, libraries still represent a valuable book-marketing opportunity.

Getting your book listed at libraries allows you to build an audience at the grassroots level in your local community and provide support and resources to patrons, including those who may otherwise lack access. It's also a way to continue to gain exposure, grow your platform, and discover new, unexpected audiences.

Even better, a successful program at one library can generate more avenues for you to explore. And people who sit on library boards are often very successful local businesspeople or educators. I always look at book marketing as one door leading to another, which leads to another. And if you have the right topic for the library audience, and you're an author who doesn't have a big audience yet, your local library could be the place for you to test your material, your training, or your workshop while selling some books and building your brand.

A library might not be your place if you've written a book for high-level executives and CEOs and your goal is to land six-figure consulting gigs. But for authors who've written books on personal finance, immigration, education-related subjects, subjects for teens or young adults, grief, or hobby-related subjects, a local library could be the perfect partner.

Now one quick note before you start approaching libraries: P-CIP blocks make it easier. Your library may still buy your book without the P-CIP data, but the cataloger who enters the book into the system could reject it.

The P-CIP block is a Cataloging in Publication record (CIP data), a bibliographic record. It helps libraries know where to file books. If you haven't filed for a Library of Congress listing, or you didn't successfully secure it, you can pay to have this created for your book. This data block allows librarians to properly catalog your book. (Remember the Dewey decimal system from school—yes, that is part of this.) Without it, some catalogers won't do it (so your book won't be listed), while others may try but may not get your book exactly where it should be.

Again, it's not required, but if you plan to make a big push for library listings, investing in this could be well worth your time. You can hire someone to create this block of data for you on Reedsy.

Library Live Events 101

Most community libraries love supporting their local authors. There's a good chance that your nearby library is ready and waiting to become your #1 fan. That said, in meeting many librarians at American Library Association conferences (where I've had the pleasure of speaking on the topic of self-publishing), I must warn you that they get a lot of authors approaching them asking for help. They see a lot of badly put together self-published books. You must stand out by showcasing why their patrons will benefit from your book and your event, not asking them to give you support. Please don't go into a library asking for them to help you. Be prepared to show them how you are going to be of service to them and their community.

Libraries are interested in doing all kinds of things to get people in the door, and they want to make use of the space they have. I've held many different kinds of events at libraries. Some have beautiful spaces where you can host a class, offer a book reading, or even do book signings. Check out your local library—you might be surprised and impressed at what they have available.

My local library in Las Vegas (the Summerlin Library) even has a theater, where they host plays and other productions! On top of that, they have several event rooms for hosting readings, clubs, and other activities. Check out your library's space, and chat with the person in charge of programming to explore your options. Then, let your creative juices flow.

Organizing a book event can seem daunting at first, but the process is easier than you might think. How easy, you ask? I've broken it down into seven steps:

Step One: Make a List

Make a list of five or more libraries in your area. An AI search engine can help, along with using one of the many mapping services to find libraries near you. You're shooting for public branches you can drive to or reach by public transportation with relative ease.

Step Two: Research!

Hit up their websites to research individual library programming. Most library branches have online event and activity calendars, and this is the best place to start your research.

You might be surprised at their diversity and robustness. Many libraries host weekly or monthly book clubs. From month to month, these often revolve around topical subjects or current events, and there may be an upcoming topic that's a perfect fit for your book. Libraries also hold events to coincide with holidays, awareness months, or other celebrations. Some even host things like creative writing workshops in November for NaNoWriMo. Get a sense of what kind of programming the library likes and what events are coming up to figure out where your book might fit in.

Does your book have a tie-in to something already in the works? Great. If not, you'll have to pitch a new event to promote your book to the library. In either case, you're ready to move to step three.

Step Three: At Dawn, We Plan!

What kind of event will you host?

Authors often default to hosting typical readings and book signings, but this is the least desirable thing for a library to host. In fact, at the American Library Association LibLearnX event where I spoke at a workshop session on self-publishing, an entire discussion erupted about boring author readings. One woman said, "We'd rather hear what you didn't put in the book or what your process was for writing the book! Most people want to read the book, not sit there and hear a tiny part of it read to them!"

Chat with other authors or even your local librarians to see what is of interest or what has worked in the past (and how you can improve upon that). There are so many options. I've offered short workshops at libraries to teach a small part of my book to the audience. It was free, but it was a great way to build my list, sell books to the library, and connect with my local community. Just keep in mind your goals and resources, as well as the capacity and interest of the local library.

Here are a few ideas to get you started:

- Author reading
- Audience Q&A
- Book club
- Local author panel (has the added benefit of your intersecting with another author's audience)
- Party to celebrate a book award, your book launch, or an awareness month
- Virtual events that include interactive quizzes or games (like Kahoot!)
- Workshop or some other sort of interactive activity (especially if you have a workbook)

Research your audience and understand their demographics and interests. We've spoken to librarians who said popular topics include resume building, career advice, home buying, immigration support, ESL, local stories, basic personal finance, and books that will engage a teen audience.

Step Four: Pitch Your Event!

Once you have your event plan in place, the next step is to get in front of the person in charge of programming for the library. For nonfiction books, your best bet is probably the adult services or programming librarian. There's often a youth services librarian who specifically handles children's and young adult books. When in doubt, just reach out to the library branch and ask whom you should talk to. You can always reach out to the reference librarian.

Making an appointment to speak with the right person face-to-face is a good idea so you can pitch something they want. Then you can send an email reintroducing yourself, sharing a bit about your book, and then putting one or two sentences together on what you're planning. If possible, suggest how your event might tie into what they've already got going on or align with the particular interests of their membership base.

If the library likes your idea, it's time to put together a one-page plan. You don't have to map out every little detail, but it helps to have a general outline. This should include a summary of the event, including schedule, costs, supplies, date, time, the number of people you expect to attend, and of course, your marketing ideas. You'll also want to ask if you can sell books at the event and if you need to pay any kind of fee.

Sometimes, a library will even have a tiny budget to pay you for your appearance. More often, you'll be doing it for free but are welcome to sell books, and the library will help you promote the event.

These are details to discuss before you finalize event plans. *Be sure to emphasize how you're going to promote the event as well.* Libraries are always interested in new ways to attract community members, so your assistance is important. Additionally, most libraries don't have the marketing expertise to draw a crowd, so the success of the event is on your being a great promotion partner.

Step Five: Prepare and Promote

You got the green light? Okay! That means it's time to get ready, get prepped, and promote. Spreading the word is vital to this event's success. Most libraries put up posters and advertise the event on their websites and newsletters if they have one.

Meanwhile, you need to hop on your social media and start rattling some cages! If you have a newsletter, send out an invite.

Post regular reminders, starting at least a month in advance. If you have an email newsletter list, use it. Reach out and let everyone know about the upcoming festivities. You can even potentially get posters printed and put them up at your local coffee shop, gym, or other popular community spot. That kind of visibility can be great. After all, this is a local event celebrating a local author.

Find out if the library allows food or drinks, and if so, bring some tasty treats for your guests to enjoy during your reading, talk, or workshop. Send out reminders the day before, and make sure you've posted again everywhere on your social media.

Finally, remember to bring copies of your book to sign and sell. And if you're ordering them, make sure you've ordered them at least a month in advance to make sure they arrive in time.

Step Six: Execute

The day has come! Get there early, and set up as needed. Your attendees may need certain materials, including pens or paper, so make sure they're available and that there's plenty for everyone. Bring a sharpie or two for signing books!

Since your event probably won't be gigantic, greet everyone as they arrive. And don't forget to introduce yourself before the event kicks into gear. Some attendees might know you, but others will not. Remember, you're not just there to promote your book. This is a perfect opportunity to create connections with the potential to do more than sell books.

Ideally, have a friend at the book table, helping to sell books and hand out your materials. After the event wraps up, let your audience know that you're signing books, and give them a chance to approach you directly with questions or comments.

Step Seven: Thank the Library

This is a best practice tip that benefits both you and your relationship with a library over the long haul. There's a good chance that the library probably won't charge you for their event space. And they almost always buy a copy of your book to add to their bookshelves if you're selling it at an event. Your library deserves love, so make sure they get it. Thank the librarian in person right after your event, and let them know that you'd be interested in participating in other events in the future. Bring a receipt book because many libraries have actually paid me cash for the book and needed a receipt! And of course, post pictures and a happy note on their social media pages filled with your gratitude for their hospitality.

How to Approach Libraries for Listings

All right, now that you've got your local events rolling, it's time to get people requesting your book in your area and beyond! Usually, when you host an event at the library, they will buy a copy of your book. But here are two other ways besides events to get library listings:

First, let everyone know that your book is out and that they can request your book from their local library, either in person or online. The key is this person has to be a member of that local library. Unlike the Amazon marketplace, where there's not much a friend or family member can do to help you promote your book, *libraries don't care if it's a relative or friend of the author requesting the book.* They only care about serving their membership. That means these requests can absolutely come from family or friends.

If you're focused on a specific library, you can make it even easier on friends and family by letting them know whom to contact to request a book. If they're more inclined to go to a library in person, provide some directions, like telling them to ask for the circulation desk or the main help desk. The library staff should be able to direct them to the right person to make requests, but any help you can provide along the way to your friends and family will be a bonus!

If they will be requesting your book on the library website, check to see if the library has an online "Request an Item" or "Ask the Librarian" feature. In that case, the person requesting your book will need the title, your full author name, and maybe even data like the ISBN. (Most libraries will be able to search by title or author name.)

Second, credibility in the library world comes from those paid reviews we covered in the previous chapter, so you need them to sell your book for library listings. I've met many librarians who complain about the authors who don't make a case why their book should be carried by the library. Having a sell sheet could be a great way to do this, but high-quality editorial reviews are an incredible help. A review in *Kirkus*, *Publishers Weekly*, or *Foreword* will be highly regarded by librarians.

When I was at the 2022 American Library Association conference in Washington, D.C., I heard from many librarians who consider these types of reviews important. And when I spoke with the folks at OverDrive about lists they make for libraries, they said they use sales data. But they also look at published editorial reviews from those sources to decide which books should be featured in their system and their library e-book listings.

Librarians have told me that without the gatekeeper of a publisher to ensure quality with self-published books, they rely heavily on reviews or authors. It's up to you to show that you are heavily invested in the quality of your book and that you have credibility.

One additional thing to note is that librarians are book lovers, and they're intensely focused on patrons. If you have a high-quality book that is in demand and will help readers, librarians will be interested in it.

Oh, and a fun fact for you—libraries often buy books from Amazon.

All right, now that you know the basics of how to make your book attractive to librarians, let's introduce you to some of the other tools you can use to get your book onto library shelves.

What Is WorldCat?

Imagine you could visit a library anywhere in the world and browse its bookshelves. Or even better, imagine that your book was available to readers not only in that library but also in thousands of other libraries worldwide!

How is that possible? It's all thanks to a site called WorldCat.org. WorldCat includes catalogs for 15,637 libraries in 207 different countries. Plus, it contains over 512 million bibliographic records in an astounding 483 languages. That represents more than three billion physical and digital library assets. And the number of people accessing all of this? More than 100 million.[74]

With WorldCat, you can search for books, videos, music, and any other physical items you can check out of your library. Think of it like a Google search specifically crafted for bookworms. The database can also help you discover new digital contact, like downloadable audiobooks. It doesn't just search your nearest library either. It searches the itemized collection of many, many libraries all at once to help you locate what you're looking for nearby.

---

74 "Inside WorldCat," OCLC, accessed March 14, 2023, https://www.oclc.org/en/worldcat/inside-worldcat.html.

WorldCat can help you find research articles or digital items that can be directly viewed or downloaded, right from their database. It even has historical documents and photos, such as local newspaper articles and digital versions of rare items that are usually unavailable to the public.

Once you find what you need, you can add items cataloged in WorldCat to personalized lists, and there's no limit to how many lists you can include in your profile. You can group items in all kinds of ways, like titles owned by your library or other WorldCat libraries. You can also share your lists with friends, colleagues, and other users.

A record of your book here has the potential to connect to tens of thousands of libraries and millions of people throughout the world. It's like the greatest PR firm ever.

To add your book to WorldCat, you need an Online Computer Library Center (OCLC) member institution that carries a copy of your book in their catalog.[75] OCLC is a global library organization that provides shared technology services, original research, and community programs for its membership and the library community at large.[76] Once your book is available in one of those libraries, check WorldCat, and confirm the accuracy of your listing.

Library of Congress Listings—Why They Matter

If you love the smell of books, you should definitely visit the Library of Congress in Washington, D.C. Besides being a beautiful building, it's a place many authors dream of having a book listing.

---

75 "Together We Make Breakthroughs Possible," OCLC, accessed March 14, 2023, https://www.oclc.org/en/about.html.
76 "Frequently Asked Questions," OCLC, accessed March 14, 2023, https://www.oclc.org/en/worldcat/library100/faq.html/.

Not being listed in the Library of Congress does not mean you won't get library shelf space. That said, it definitely helps you get more library listings if you are listed.

To be accepted, your book must meet their requirements, which can be viewed on the Library of Congress website.[77] Essentially, they want titles that will be widely acquired, and the title page or the copyright page shows that it has been published by a U.S.-based publisher.

It doesn't mean a self-published book will be rejected, but you shouldn't be surprised if it is.

As much as I love libraries, it's not going to be a tactic that makes sense for every book because not every audience will borrow books from the library. Let's talk about something that does make sense for most authors—how to use ads and paid promos to boost your signal.

Chapter Summary

1. Libraries are great author partners if your ideal reader is likely to be a patron.

2. Being active with libraries is a great way to build grassroots support for a book and have a meaningful impact on communities.

3. Be creative when considering your event options for libraries, and remember you have to sell yourself and your book. While librarians like to support local authors, they won't do it out of the goodness of their hearts. It needs to be something that benefits their community. Do your research, and be prepared when you pitch your book or your event to your librarian.

4. Library listings are not typically the way you'll make a lot of money or even sell a lot of books, but for the right authors, they can open doors to bigger and bigger impact (and income) opportunities.

---

77 https://loc.gov

5. The best way to get into your local library is either by making a request (you or someone else) or by hosting an event. Of course, writing a high-quality, popular book itself will get you into libraries. Paid reviews from respected sources are also a way to attract librarians' attention.

CHAPTER 12

DOES MONEY SOLVE ALL BOOK-SELLING PROBLEMS?

LET'S TAKE A STACK OF YOUR HARD-EARNED DOLLAR BILLS AND LIGHT them on fire, shall we?

That's how running paid ads can feel. I get it. I've spent a lot of money on ads that didn't produce results. And the reality is that when it comes to book marketing and book selling, money alone won't be the only thing you need to succeed.

If money *were* the only thing you needed to sell books, it would actually be easier. Of course, financial resources absolutely help, but unless you're fine with taking a match to your money, there are fundamentals you should know first.

And one of the most important fundamentals is that the answer to almost everything in marketing is…

You won't know if your selling tactics are any good until you test them. Another author's "proven formula" is not necessarily the ticket to your audience or your book.

Consider the first few hundred dollars you spend on ads as an investment in your education, not money that's going to bring an immediate return.

And know that ads amplify only what is already happening. In other words, if your book is not selling at all, you need to fix fundamentals first. More ads won't solve the problem.

As far as those book fundamentals are concerned, we'll touch on them here, but that is really what *Self-Publish and Succeed* was all about. If you haven't read it, then it would be a great resource. If you have read it, this will be a quick refresher.

One Size Does *Not* Fit All

If there were a guaranteed way to sell books, publishers would be a lot more profitable, books wouldn't bomb, and we'd charge a lot more for our services at Book Launchers.

Many of our authors started without much of an existing audience and have gone on to have incredible results—a documentary feature, a TED Global Ideas Talk, thousands of books sold in bulk purchases, dream publishing deals, and so much more. We get results for most of our authors, but it's never one thing that works for every author, and it's never *only* what we have done. It's also rare that anything major happens after one month of marketing support. In many cases, the real results came six months post-launch or longer!

Book marketing is a team effort that requires the author to be involved as much as anyone else over the long haul. Don't believe anyone who claims to have *the* proven system or promises you overnight success.

Fundamentals First—Paid Marketing Second

Make sure your fundamentals are strong before you start paying for ads. This is important, no matter what bigger-picture goal or strategy you pursue.

Speaking of your bigger-picture goal, paid ads are a good tactic for almost every goal. It's just important to understand your desired outcome —growing your audience, selling books, and driving leads into a funnel for a business or product. But before you spend any money, let's make sure your book is ready for the paid ads spotlight.

A sales page needs to convert viewers into book buyers when you send people there. If you're driving traffic to a page, and your book isn't selling, you have to fix that page and stop spending money until it's fixed. This could mean changing your cover, your book description, getting more reviews (remember we see 25 reviews as the first real tipping point for a book's performance), or even revising the first 20 pages of your book so they pop for a reader.

Conversion is the most critical variable when you pay for ads. When people land on the page, do they take the desired action you want them to take? Do they buy a book? Or give you their email address? That's what conversion is, and that's why you should care about a reader's experience on your book's sales page.

If your book's already selling even a bit, then paid ads can add fuel to the fire. If you're using paid ads to try to ignite a fire that's never been lit, the wood might be wet, and you could be wasting your time and money.

Test One Thing at a Time

It might be tempting to try to run ads everywhere right away, especially if you are impatient for results.

But in the world of books, tracking is imperfect. If you run Goodreads, Amazon, BookBub, Facebook, and banner ads all at the same time, you likely won't have strong tracking on all the platforms. As a result, you will likely not confidently understand your results or be able to pinpoint where tweaks would help.

When you test or add (or remove) one platform at a time, you're able to notice when something starts working because sales will increase. This is because people almost always need multiple touch points. Maybe they saw your ad, then heard you on a podcast, and that was enough for them to make the purchase. Or it could be someone was told about your book over dinner, and then your ad pops up the next day.

In other words, rarely does any one thing trigger a book sale, and it's impossible to really know what works and why. Through a process of elimination, you can discover whether a sales increase is due to an ad or not. Adopting a marketing approach that layers tactics, one at a time, can help you identify what creates tipping points and what doesn't do anything at all.

We'll cover a few of the tactical aspects of ads in this book. But please know that entire books are written on each of these subjects. To truly do it well, you should read books by Dale L. Roberts or David Gaughran that go into more depth and provide detailed instructions.

Amazon Author Central

Amazon Author Central is a free tool that Amazon has given authors to increase their visibility, create their author brand, and sell more books. It also ties back to ads.

Once you've created your account (just head to Google and ask for instructions on how to set up your Amazon Author Central account), you will see your books for sale on Amazon and links to view your profile on a variety of Amazon pages in different countries. From your account, you can access NPD BookScan data, including sales sorted geographically. You can also use your account to follow the Amazon sales rank and customer reviews of your books.

Whether you've already set up your Amazon Author Central page or not, I'm going to run through some best practices, along with some dos and don'ts.

Best Practice One: Upload a professional author photo. Do not post a selfie! Get a professional photo.

Best Practice Two: Include your well-crafted bio—ideally, a version with keywords. If you have multiple books available for sale, I recommend using a more general bio that covers your credentials, awards, degrees, fun facts, and what's relevant to your most recent book. You should also include social media and website links here. Amazon encourages you to upload your biography in other languages, so you may also want to look at using translations (and double-check them for accuracy, just to be sure).

Best Practice Three: Link your books to your account.

Ideally, your author page should list all editions of your book. Used copies of out-of-print books may still be available if someone lists them for sale. Many customers appreciate being able to find them, so Amazon makes that kind of sale possible and doesn't remove them from your author page.

If a book is incorrectly attributed to you, you can contact Amazon support to have it removed. Just look for the contact links in the "Help" section of your author account.

There are other things you can do like linking your blog feed, uploading images, and adding video, though it appears video is disappearing from platforms in some countries.

Best Practice Four: Add your editorial reviews.

To do this, select the Books tab, and choose the book to which you want to add reviews. Select Add under editorial reviews and follow the instructions. When you're done, don't forget to preview the review to make sure everything looks right. Then make sure you hit Save.

Once your profile is created, check back every three to six months to give it an update. Check all your links, and make sure they're still working. Then add any new content you think should be there.

Sales Data

When you've got promotional activities on the go, you want to be able to view the sales data easily. This is where you can do it for Amazon. To view your sales data, go to Reports plus Marketing. Once you're there, two specific reports are worth checking out.

First, you'll want to view your Amazon sales rank report, where you can see your books in all formats, along with how they rank. The second thing to look at, which I think is even cooler, is the BookScan report. I like this one because you get geographic breakdowns. For instance, let's say I had a big buyer for one of my books in Cincinnati. If I ran ads or planned live appearances, I might use this information to focus on areas where I have an existing fan base. I can leverage the momentum that is already there with some kind of event or promotion.

An amalgamated spot allows you to see your customer reviews first by format and then by Amazon site. In other words, you can see activity on different Amazon marketplace sites in one place. This is a cool feature.

In addition to all of these great Amazon Author Central tools I've shared, Amazon also has a way to make your page look a little more appealing using what it calls "A+ content."

A+ Content

A+ content is a visual section on your book's sales page that can include charts, photos, quotes, and other graphics or visual images. It's displayed in a section called "From the Publisher," which appears *below* the book cover, description, and Buy button but *above* the section for reviews and product details. It's really intended to support a buyer's decision to buy the product (your book!) by making your page more attractive and engaging.

A+ content lends a visual punch to product listings on Amazon, and that can't hurt your sales.

If your book is published or on preorder through KDP, it's eligible for A+ content.

Because Amazon is ever-evolving, I recommend checking their latest "how to upload" information. For our purposes, let's think about what will appeal to your ideal reader.

This is intended to sell your book, so the copy must pop, and the images must be appealing. If you're not going to invest in making that happen, skip the A+ content. And remember, this should supplement your book description and book cover. Don't include a picture of your cover—they have that already. You could include enticing quotes from inside your book or images that aren't on the cover but fit with the content and will entice a reader. You could also add powerful reviews or blurbs.

Avoid promotional or time-sensitive language. Words and phrases like "free," "bonus," or "on sale today" are not going to get approved. Leave out your book's price too, and don't include any links or copy that directs users to any site other than Amazon.

Look at other authors in your category for inspiration if you need ideas. This is an evolving space, so it's best to check around for the latest trends and ideas.

Amazon Ads

If your big goal is to sell books, you absolutely must be running Amazon Ads. For most authors, Amazon Ads is a smart supplement to every bigger-picture goal.

Amazon Ads work. It's putting your book quickly and easily (and often more affordably than many other advertising options) into the hands of willing readers.

We run Amazon Ads for our clients at Book Launchers. Based on what we've learned through educating ourselves and our own experience about what works and what doesn't, here are three tips for giving Amazon Ads a go:

- **TIP ONE: Set your budget at $5 or $10 a day.** This is an easy thing to fear, especially if you've done Facebook ads! Facebook seems to magically spend your budget every day, and it doesn't matter if you get results or not. Amazon won't spend your budget like that.

  We actually find it challenging in the early days of running ads on a book to get enough clicks to hit that modest budget. That's because Amazon's ads are charged on a pay-per-click basis. You only pay when people click, and you're not setting your click rate anywhere near what you might pay on Google for a click. It can take a lot to hit a $5-per-day budget because you're setting your click rate at something like 15 cents to 50 cents per click. Now, if you set this too low, you won't get enough data to make decisions that will help you optimize your ads.

- **TIP TWO: Consider your initial costs an educational expense, not a financial investment.** You need data to educate yourself and make decisions, and it's rare you're going to get a positive return on investment (ROI) on your first month of running Amazon ads. However, if you're not getting a positive ROI after 60 to 90 days, that needs a close review.

- **TIP THREE: Understand advertising cost of sales (ACOS).** ACOS is the percent of attributed sales spent on advertising within 14 days of clicks on your ads. This is calculated by dividing total spent by attributed sales. If you've got that at 100% or less, it is a good thing, but it doesn't mean you're making a profit because it's not considering your royalty rate—only the sales price!

When you get an ACOS of 50% or less, your ads are likely profitable, and it's time to spend more money, because you're making enough money to reinvest it in more ads to generate more sales.

A high ACOS doesn't mean ads aren't working, though. If your overall book sales do well, keep ads going because they will likely be impacting your overall sales and turning them off will cause sales to dip. Tweak them and try new things to try to get better results, but a full shutdown could hurt your overall sales. We've seen authors turn ads off because the results don't seem great, and then their entire accounts see sales dips. Again, this is because there isn't one thing that sells a book, and ads aren't always the thing that leads to the sale, but they can contribute to it.

Amazon ads are simple in principle—definitely much simpler than Google or Facebook—but even so, you have to know how to get that ROI. The biggest thing you really do need is to manage your ads and spend time tracking them on a weekly basis, at a minimum. In terms of must-have tools for running Amazon Ads, besides Publisher Rocket, I also highly recommend you grab Brian Meeks's book, *Mastering Amazon Ads.*[78] There are also Facebook groups and Amazon courses to guide you along the way.

Paid Ads for Social Media Platforms

Of course, you can run paid promotions on Facebook or other social media platforms for your book too. For a nonfiction author, **the best play for social media ads is almost always to drive traffic to an opt-in page rather than a book sale.**

If your goal is only book sales, you will likely want to skip social media ads completely as a nonfiction author. If you're hoping to grow a platform or business with courses, consulting, or high-end offerings, then your book

---

78 Brian Meeks, *Mastering Amazon Ads: An Author's Guide* (Martello, IA: Brian Meeks, 2017).

could be a tremendous entry point for your entire funnel. In that case, whether you sell your book on social media or even give it away for free, social media could work really well for you.

One tactic many marketers use is called a "free-plus-shipping funnel" (or something similar). The ad is designed to first collect contact information, using a small fee to cover some of the costs, and then upsell the buyer into much higher-paid and higher-margin offers. You'll typically see these offers at $7.99 to ship the book to a reader. This doesn't break even for the author, but the goal is the connection to the reader and the upsell on the back end.

That's why knowing your #1 goal is so important. A social media ad strategy isn't going to turn your book into a bestseller, but it might help with obtaining contact information and back-end sales. It can also contribute to book sales in the long run because you'll gain a platform, and you can leverage that platform to grow book sales.

Most authors benefit from running ads that lead to email addresses if they have good offers on the other side of that connection.

At the same time, ad costs are so expensive that you would be very hard pressed to get a strong return on your investment with running ads direct to a book sale. Fiction authors who want to hook readers into a series do it with some success, but their ad costs might be lower than nonfiction authors (who compete with businesses buying ads for the same keywords and similar audiences).

We run Google and YouTube ads to a video sales letter and have a video ad that sells *Self-Publish and Succeed*. It gets people to visit https://selfpublish andsucceed.com, where there's an offer to buy a book and get some bonuses. We don't make money on this sale at all because our ad costs plus the printing and shipping costs are higher than the $18 we charge, but it gets us contact information for the same cost as a normal opt-in, so we continue to run these ads. It's a business strategy more than a book-sale strategy, which is my point.

Apply only the tactics that help you achieve your goals with your book.

Now, there's another book platform that you should know about as an author whether you seek featured-deal promotions or ads, and that is BookBub.

BookBub

You likely have heard of BookBub featured deals. These almost-mythical features have been known to sell more than 1,000 copies of a book in a single promotion. While not always true and definitely not always a strong ROI, BookBub featured deals remain a coveted prize.

It's understandable, given that they email millions of readers daily and that the lists they send out are curated for those readers. They move books, but for nonfiction authors the return isn't always there because the fee for a BookBub deal can be greater than $500 while your books sell for 99 cents. This really requires that your book is set up to lead into other money-making opportunities or serve as the entry point into your ecosystem of books and other materials.

My book *More than Cashflow* landed an international featured deal many years ago. It barely broke even, but it sold almost 500 e-books. We've had a couple of clients land BookBub features, but their costs were not recovered by book sales or royalties.

BookBub, at its core, is a book-discoverability site, similar to Goodreads. Its purpose is to help readers find new books and authors. BookBub also has features that help an author market their book through deals, ads, new release announcements, and more.

They have a subscriber list of close to three million. Of course, not all three million subscribers get notified of every deal. BookBub curates their lists, so readers get only what they want. At the time of this writing, 1.4 million subscribers were interested in general nonfiction. Two million were interested in biographies and memoirs, and so on.[79]

Typically, a BookBub deal is 99 cents, but sometimes a $1.99 or $2.99 e-book will be featured. The book must be priced at least 50% off its normal retail rate for this promo, but you probably need to get closer to 90% off to be accepted. It also has to be the best price that has been available for the last 90 days, so be mindful of the impact other 99-cents sales you may run can have on your book's acceptance here!

If you've never submitted for a featured deal, here are a few things to know about the process:

First, be flexible with your dates when you apply for a feature. If you have a preferred time frame, submit at least a month in advance.

Every application is reviewed by a human who is familiar with what the BookBub audience clicks on and purchases. That person looks at the same things a buyer looks at, including your book's cover, book description, editorial and consumer reviews, and any awards you've won.

If your book is widely distributed (which is their preference versus being exclusively on Amazon), you need reviews in different places so that they feel good readers will want your book.

Second, you likely will want to accept their featured deal, but BookBub won't put a mark on your book if you choose to refuse a proposal. Sometimes, you may be asked to go into a different category or offered an international deal, and it's okay to say no if you don't think it's a fit.

Third, there is a comment field in the submission. Use that space to highlight things that might not be obvious. If you've won some major awards, or you have an endorsement from someone really big, this is the perfect place to put that. A really killer editorial review could be highlighted here

---

79 https://bookbub.com

too. Don't repeat anything that is obvious on your book page, like your book description, but leaving this blank is a missed opportunity. Remember you are appealing to a fellow human being.

Finally, mark your calendar to resubmit after 30 days if you are rejected (and you likely will be rejected many times). Many authors submit for years before they finally get accepted. You're competing against some heavy hitters to get those few coveted featured-deal spots, including traditional publishers and big-name authors. It's not unusual to be rejected. Make improvements to your product pages and your platform, and keep trying.

In the meantime, you don't need to abandon BookBub. It's a big player in the book-ad space, but it's important to go in understanding that BookBub is very different from Amazon or any other platform. Shake off the idea that it's going to function the way you expect, and be ready to start fresh. The best resources I've found on BookBub ads are from BookBub itself and author David Gaughran. I'm listing his book on the resources page at https://selfpromoteandsucceed.com.

Here are a few other things to note about BookBub, especially if you're used to running ads on platforms like Amazon. Their ad traffic is driven by a featured-ads newsletter, which means the traffic comes in waves. You see a spike and then nothing, and another spike and then nothing. Their audience is also more drawn to fiction than nonfiction, so it's not super lucrative for nonfiction authors.

It's also highly visual, and your ad performance will be really dependent on the quality and appeal of its appearance. Be ready with a bunch of images, and test them out! The good news is that it's easy to start with all formats and platforms and turn off the ones that aren't working for the images but keep the ones that are.

My excitement with BookBub ads was largely related to the fact that I could promote audiobooks directly with them. There aren't a lot of platforms to do this. Of course, my first time doing these ads, I found that after spending $325 on audiobook ads, despite strong clicks, I had sold about five books. The click-through rate was doing really well on this one ad, so I left it. After a month, I dug into the data and realized that even if 100% of the audiobooks sold on Apple were as a result of the ad, the ROI was abysmal.

It definitely takes some persistence to get the ads working and some spreadsheet work because the tracking is even more imperfect with BookBub than it is with other platforms. This is improving slowly, but it still requires spreadsheets and affiliate links for the various platforms so you can track which ads perform and which ones don't.

One last thing to note for BookBub is that the targeting is based on authors, not your ideal reader. With social media ads, you might target demographics or interests. With Amazon, you may target keywords. But with BookBub, it's based on authors. This means you have to figure out other authors who appeal to the reader you want to reach.

What I discovered, however, is that it's actually less about the authors themselves and more about the number of their BookBub followers. This is not as directly correlated to the popularity of the author as you might think.

Take Joanna Penn or David Gaughran as examples. We target their books for Amazon Ads for *Self-Publish and Succeed*. Their readers will like that book, and it goes well. This is BookBub, not Amazon, though, and their follower numbers are too low to do much, so I have to widen the list to more high-profile writers like Brené Brown and Tim Ferriss. These authors are not a direct fit for my audience, but they have a lot of followers and are better performers than the more niche authors.

At the end of the day, only ad space at market giant Amazon works well for authors of all stripes. BookBub may or may not be for you.

Paying for book sales is a great strategy when your book is already selling well. If you have a budget for testing different ad platforms and running ads, you will likely find a place that works. Just remember, when you test ads, focus on conversions, and try one new tactic at a time to succeed in the long run! Let's move on to public relations and other types of exposure to help you build that brand and get your book out to more and more readers.

Chapter Summary

Here's a quick summary of the paid promotional options we discussed in this chapter and how they relate to different bigger-picture goals.

AD PLATFORM	BEST TACTIC FOR WHAT STRATEGY	MOST IMPORTANT TIP
Amazon	Selling books	Start your budget at $5/day and increase it as much as you can while still maintaining an ACOS of under 100%.
		Be mindful of overall book sales on Amazon, not just ad conversions, because ads can generate sales indirectly.
BookBub	Selling books Getting featured deals	BookBub is great for e-book sales when you are running a deal. Their featured deals are emailed out to large lists of people looking for their next genre-specified deal.
		Ads on BookBub require visual content to be on point. It takes Canva or a graphics designer and a lot of testing to master the ads.
Goodreads	Getting reviews Building relationships with readers	Goodreads giveaways give your book more exposure and gain more reviews. You can also run ads on Goodreads, but make sure your ideal reader is a person likely to be spending time on the platform. Not all nonfiction books will perform that well on Goodreads because this is an audience that generally tends to be fiction readers or consumers of memoirs or self-help type books. Business and finance books don't tend to do as well here. Goodreads reviews are viewed on Amazon, so getting people to review your book on Goodreads can lead to a lot more Amazon reviews, which is great.

AD PLATFORM	BEST TACTIC FOR WHAT STRATEGY	MOST IMPORTANT TIP
Social media and Google ads	Building your platform Using your book to feed into a funnel	Your ads are not likely to generate a positive ROI on the sale of your book due to the ever-increasing cost of ads on these popular platforms and increasing print costs. Using your book as the lead to a "free-plus-shipping offer" or to promote an opt-in offer where you upsell the reader can be the best approach with these platforms. An example is https://self-publishandsucceed.com where we sell the book and (mostly) break even after ad costs to begin building a relationship with the reader. Fiction authors more often find success with social media ads because they use the first book in a series as a loss leader to pull readers into an entire series. Nonfiction authors with many books might consider a similar strategy.
E-book sales	Selling books	We've talked about 99 cent e-book sales in previous chapters. You can find some great sites for promoting a 99 cent e-book for varying fees.

CHAPTER 13

DIY PR THAT'S A-OK

ON THE SET OF CTV VANCOUVER, I COULDN'T BELIEVE THE NUMBER OF cameras in front of me. I had been told to ignore them and focus on chatting to the host of the morning show.

For the first minute of our conversation, it was going fine, but then she stopped looking at me. She asked me a question and turned away, while at the same time motioning for me to keep talking. With her other free hand, she frantically signaled to someone on the side that she needed something. I realized she didn't have a copy of my book and was trying to get it for the rest of the segment. Meanwhile, as a cameraman pushed his camera closer to me, I did my best not to look at him and concentrate on what I was saying.

Ahhhh, live TV. There really is nothing like it. Zoom interviews just don't have the fun or energy or anxiety of being in a studio.

It's really fun to do media interviews, and you might be excited at the idea of being on local or national television, but getting that three-minute segment isn't as easy as sending a press release. Nor will it likely have the impact on your book sales that you hope. That doesn't mean it's not worth doing—especially if your goal is to be known as a thought leader or to gain more speaking engagements. Television interviews can be really useful for those goals. Let's get into how you can land some great media.

How to Pitch Yourself to Media

A press release is good for corporate announcements or mergers, management changes, and new launches. It doesn't get you media coverage—especially if you send it through a newswire service. What actually works is crafting targeted pitches for specific outlets. It's what our team of marketing and PR professionals do for our authors every day at Book Launchers. Now you can do it for yourself if you want.

Media Outlet Pitching 101

First, put on your research cap.

You need to find potential media outlets that may be interested in what you can contribute to their audience. To begin, you'll need a list of relevant, active, and niche-driven media contacts that publish content within your area of expertise. Please don't waste your time or money on a media list someone else put together. You can, however, ask your AI bot of choice (like Jasper or ChatGPT) to begin the research for you. It will need your vetting, but it's better than starting from scratch.

For example, you could ask it for a list of your local news stations, then ask for a list of the producers of the business segment or the reporters who cover your area of expertise, like health or education. Of course, you can do your own research online for this too!

Researchers are also easy to hire on Upwork or Guru, and they often have databases with media contacts, which can be a great shortcut.

After you have an initial list, see if the outlets publish content relevant to your book. If so, grab the producer's contact information, which is usually found in their website bio or social media. Compile a spreadsheet for easy organization and access. This way, you can also record each time you reach out with your pitch and follow up.

Online resources also contain contact information for members of the media. Sites like Muck Rack or Cision can give you information, but they are pricey and aimed at big publicity firms and agencies. Kimanzi Constable has started a new service called PR Pitches, which might be more valuable to authors. It's more affordably priced on a monthly basis with a strong database of speaking, PR, and corporate consulting. Another good starter resource could be Anewstip.com. It requires you to sign up, but it has a free option for research. I also like HARO - Help a Reporter Out for uncovering media opportunities. Good old-fashioned social media outreach can work to introduce yourself as well.

Second, craft your pitch.

This is not one pitch fits all. Customize your pitch based on whom you're pitching and whom they serve. Are they a magazine journalist, a podcast host, a TV host, or a book reviewer? What topics do they usually cover? Your pitch needs to highlight how you and your book can help them with their specific audience—specifically, how it fits in but stands out from what they normally discuss.

Yep, your research hat is still on. But now, instead of looking at whom you're targeting, you're researching what you're pitching. No two outlets are the same, even if they're within the same genre or cover the same type of topics. That's similar to books, right? *Game of Thrones* and *Lord of the Rings* might sound like the same thing if you describe them in a general way. But every fantasy fan knows that the two are worlds apart.

The same could be said for nonfiction books, of course. Of the countless real estate, financial, or memoir books out there, what makes each unique to their readers?

If you answered, "Their hook," imagine me giving you a high five right now, because I am!

A well-crafted hook makes your book stand out and also makes your pitch stand out. Individualized pitches tell media outlets why they should care about you and how you can bring value to them. That's the hook you need when pitching to the media outlets you've got your eye on. When I was in the real estate space, I built a really strong relationship with the editors at *Canadian Real Estate Wealth* magazine. I read months and months of their back issues. I knew the kind of tactical, numerical articles they liked, and I knew some of the topics they hadn't covered that were within the range of topics they liked to cover.

I sent a pitch for two articles I could write, and why they were perfect for the magazine. Sure enough, I was invited to write one of them. After the first article was submitted, I followed up with a new pitch, and I ended up being a regular contributor. I even graced two covers! This partnership led to me being a keynote speaker at their events across Canada many years in a row—and my business was heavily promoted in every magazine and many of the ads they ran outside of the magazine too.

You can imagine what that does for a goal of being a known name in the industry. It was an enormous boost to my brand and reputation across the country to get that regular exposure from the only major magazine in the industry for investors.

It didn't happen in an instant, but it all started with a good pitch. The time I put into researching and thinking about how I could offer something different but similar to what they had already covered paid off for years and years.

Just like how you crafted a hook for your book, a successful media pitch highlights an audience problem and the solution that you and your messaging provide. You could even reference another expert in your space, perhaps someone else they covered, and say something like "I saw that you had Eric Brotman featured in issue 32. He did a great job sharing why retirement can be a new phase of your life versus the end of work. My strategies for choosing a low-cost country to live in during this new phase of your life could be the perfect angle for your audience to follow that story. Complete with my detailed research on the three best places in the world to retire to, I can offer tips to make it work with health insurance, finance, and family." Then include a sentence or two with your bio.

Devote time to diving into the outlet's website and social media. Scroll through their past content, and figure out how your expertise can help their audience by solving a problem or adding value to their lives.

When the media contact at that outlet reads your pitch, it should be specific and targeted enough that they can see you did the work and took the time to research who they are, who their audience is, and what you're looking to give them. If you present a strong enough hook, they should be able to see just how they can present it to their audience right off the bat.

💡 **TIP:** Do not start the pitch off by saying you're a big fan if you're not legitimately a big fan. I spoke with a podcaster who says he gets about 40 pitches a week, and almost all of them start off that way. If you're legitimately a big fan, show it by saying, "Your interview with Sally made me cry. It should come with a tear warning."

Keep it short, clear, and direct. A snappy subject line under 10 words and a pitch no more than two paragraphs is what you should aim for. And if two paragraphs seem too short to say what you want to, then go back to that part where we talked about hook and messaging.

A hook is called a "hook" for a reason. You're using it to bait the person reading it so they want to learn more. Even in pitching, your hook should be one or two sentences max.

The third step is to send your well-crafted, well-researched email.

💡 **TIP:** You should always attach a professional media kit. It should include your bio, sample speaking topics, headshot, book description, and any social media links. (We'll get into details on media kits in just a moment.) Be sure to also offer to send them a copy of your book, either physical or digital. Even if they pass on your pitch, you never know what could happen if they decide to pick up your book anyway. It never hurts to send a copy if they say they're interested.

And now for the fourth step: Wait. Then wait some more.

After you send out your pitch, patience is most definitely a virtue. Media pitching is not an overnight thing. It can take weeks or even months to hear back from outlets, unless (sometimes) your book or expertise can be tied to breaking news or a time-sensitive event. It's important to remember to keep your chin up, and don't be discouraged if you don't hear back right away. Our team does a round of outreach, then follow-ups, more follow-ups, and even more follow-ups. The number of times we have a win come in three to six months after the initial pitch would surprise you, but it doesn't surprise me anymore.

Give it two weeks, and then follow up with another personalized email. Any sooner and you risk bothering and annoying them or getting sent directly to that dreaded spam folder. The best wins, though, can come from follow-ups. Check back in after a couple of weeks.

Carefully considering and crafting each pitch you're sending can be a slow process, but it's worth the time and effort. All that research and writing may mean that you get to do only 20 pitches this month, but that's okay. Better to have directed pitches with two to four yeses than throwing away your time and money on pitches that will get you absolutely nowhere.

Timing is even more important to keep in mind when it comes to media. Podcast hosts often have a backlog of interviews and can be months ahead on scheduling. If you want media appearances to coincide with your book launch or some other event, you have to start pitching weeks or even months in advance. It's also worth noting that a pitch sent in mid-December could get lost in the holiday shuffle. You're probably better off either saving it for the second week of January or getting the pitch in by the end of November if you can, unless your pitch is very specific and tied to current news or events.

Fifth step: Be ready for last-minute opportunities and short-notice invites.

You are busy, so it might be tempting to skip answering emails or calls from numbers you don't recognize, but you could miss your big media moment. We landed a client on a PBS show because there was a last-minute guest cancellation. Our initial pitch hadn't received a response, but a month later, we got a call asking for our author to appear the next morning!

Especially when it comes to TV, you can get bumped for a big news story or brought in due to a lack of news. Programs are often booked the day before, and the first potential guest to answer the phone gets the spot.

Media does not wait. If you are not ready, they will move on to the next source. When a good media opportunity comes up, be as flexible as possible with your time so you can take advantage of it.

But What About Press Releases? Do You Really Not Need One at All?

A well-crafted press release can be part of a media kit and can accompany those well-crafted pitches we just discussed. Book bloggers or print media like local magazines can take the press release, tweak it a little bit, and publish it or use it for background after an interview, saving them time.

In other words, the press release does the work of producing content for some media outlets that choose to use it verbatim or as background to supplement an article. That's where there is still value in a press release. For most authors, though, it's really not worth paying a lot of money to get a press release written or distributed. You're better off to take that money and research specific media that may be interested in your pitch and your angle and create that all-important short, very personalized pitch.

For example, if you're Amani Roberts, author of *DJs Mean Business*, you'd be better off pitching all the DJ podcasts, DJ news, and other specialized media first, using concise, targeted pitches instead of writing a press release and distributing it to mass media. While his book could potentially be picked up as something cool for the general media to talk about (because you get to learn interesting business lessons during a night in the life of a DJ), the reality is that mainstream media is unlikely to be as interested as an outlet that covers the industry.

Whether you write a press release or pitch your book by email without one, the most important thing you need to know is that your publishing a book is not news. **It's not a big deal to anyone other than you and your family and close friends.** So, don't just write something like "There's a new must-read book out right now!" That's not a hook. What you need to figure out is what is relevant and timely or new in your book or your personal story.

You may or may not need a press release in your media toolbox, but one thing you'll definitely need is an author media kit. Next up, I'll go into what you need to know to create one or to improve your existing kit if you're already ahead of the game.

Author Media Kit Creation Tips

Author media kits are an important tool in your book-marketing toolbox. Sometimes they're called a "press kit," and it's typically an electronic document to be emailed or downloaded from your website. We make them so they are easily downloaded but also look great when printed.

Every media kit we do at Book Launchers is a little different, as we tailor it to the author's strengths, goals, and project. Some things will be different. But every single media kit has the following sections:

- Front and center, **a picture of your book with your title and subtitle and your name.** The front page of the media kit should immediately grab attention with its great design and your cover.

- Your **book description and metadata.** This should include information like the ISBN, available formats, pricing, word count, and publication date.

- Your **contact information**, including where to connect with you online. Specifically, make sure you include your email address, phone number, up-to-date social media account links, and anywhere else that showcases your expertise and credibility. If you're working with a publicist or a marketing team, their contact info can go in this section as well.

- An **author bio with your professional author photo.** This bio should contain key details that are relevant to your book and the area of expertise you're highlighting. My current bio doesn't mention my MBA in real estate and finance or any details of my time as an investor. Instead, my bio details include my author awards, Amazon bestseller status, and Book Launchers because those details are most relevant.

- **Interview topics or questions.** If you're looking for media attention, you need to give them some ideas of what is a good fit and what you should be asked. Ideally, include questions or topics that will be of interest to larger audiences. The idea here is you want to make it as easy as possible for an interviewer or journalist to interview you. By providing five or so topics or questions, you let the outlet know where your expertise lies and the type of topics you cover with ease. Don't be afraid to get specific. For example, let's look at a generic topic:

- Tips for new parents

The audience (parents) is obvious, but the angle isn't. A media member won't automatically know what you offer in terms of tips, how you can help, or even what's interesting about your pitch. Instead, let's try a more specific topic:

- Three unusual tips to get more sleep as a new parent
- Why ice baths make you a more patient parent
- How to nurture other relationships in your life when your new baby seems to take all your love and time

By adding a few more details, you generate interest. (Pro tip—hosts, journalists, and media outlets *love* numbered lists or tips. It translates well for the audiences they're hoping to capture. Look at the headlines on *Huffington Post* or another news site, and you'll get a sense of the kind of titles that get attention and clicks—those are similar to what will be attractive in a pitch topic.) We'll cover sound bites in a second, but thinking about how you can deliver high-quality content in 20- to 30-second chunks is a savvy media move.

Spend some time narrowing down your questions, and imagine what would be most interesting to you if you heard it for the first time. What would pique curiosity and invite discussion?

- **Testimonials or endorsements** if you have them. These are best if they come from other established experts in fields related to your book's topic or anyone else with name recognition, like a celebrity.
- **"As featured on" or previous media coverage details.** A media kit is meant to establish your expertise and be easily used by a media member to get all the info they need for a story or interview with you. If you've done media interviews and appearances, had speaking engagements, or have recognizable clients, use logos to

showcase that. (Pro tip—images or logos are easier to view than blocks or lists of text, so use them when you can.)

- **A book excerpt, article, or advertisement about the book.**

- Finally include **a link that can be used to easily download pictures of your book cover and your author photos.** If you know you're going to be printing these kits on a regular basis, then you should get an actual URL.

What I would recommend is to find a template that you like and visit Upwork, Guru, or even Fiverr to hire someone with great graphic design experience to make your media kit. Make sure to have your brand or book colors available for them. Finally, you don't want this file to be too enormous to email. Ask your designer to compress it to one megabyte or less.

Author Media Kit Use Best Practices

1. Remember, *the media kit is an all-purpose tool.* You still need customized pitches to get results. The media kit doesn't do that work for you.

2. When it's done, *don't mass mail your author media kit.* It should have a place to live on your website, and it will be used either after you have a pitch that gets a nibble of interest (or sent out as an attachment with a well-researched, targeted short pitch). If you get that nibble of interest, that's when you send your reply and the media kit.

3. *Get your press kit documents proofread* before you start using them. These are professional documents meant to put your best foot forward.

4. If you hire a designer on Fiverr, there's an option to get the source file for an extra fee. I highly recommend you do that. Similarly, when you hire someone on other sites like Upwork and Guru, *ask for that source file* because chances are you're probably going to

want to change or update these documents at some point in the future.

5.   Review the kit carefully before using it. *Does what you drafted showcase who you are and make you and your book look compelling and stand out from others in your field?* It should.

6.   *Do your research on how editors, journalists, or hosts prefer to receive media kits.* Some like attachments, so you can send your media kit as a PDF. Others prefer links, so you can include a link to download. Pay attention, so they don't immediately put your media kit and pitch in the spam folder. At Book Launchers, we include ours as an attachment, but we have established relationships ahead of time. If you're not sure, ask!

Your author media kit is important. It makes it easier for media to feel comfortable calling you an expert because a lot of the work they have to do in researching you is done for them in this package. It also shows you're a professional, because you've invested the time and money in yourself to assemble a professional package. And while we focused on its purpose for media, it really is an informational brochure that helps anyone interested in you or your book learn more.

How to Leverage a Media Appearance for Success

Your work paid off, and you're booked for an interview. All that's left is hair and wardrobe, right?

Well, not exactly. You need to be ready for that appearance with sound bites and be prepared to leverage all the benefits of the media appearance.

Media appearances are awesome! Being interviewed on live TV is absolutely one of my favorite things. Yes, it's high stress, with so much happening all at once. But it's also a huge adrenaline rush, and it's fun and exciting.

You feel like a real expert when you get to drop knowledge bombs for two to four minutes on a news segment.

As exciting as this all is, the sad reality is that TV appearances rarely sell books.

If you do it right, though, the actual media appearance is only a quarter of what you do to get the full value from it. Let me say that again. *It's not just the media appearance that has value. It's what you do with it afterward.*

We're going to cover what to do to leverage it in a second, but first let's make sure you're media ready!

Sound Bites

Do you know what's better than giving an awesome interview? Getting quoted from that interview over and over, and over again, and having that one interview lead to others. The next thing you know, everyone is talking about you and your book. Often, all you need for that to happen are some well-crafted sound bites.

Learning to talk in sound bites for interviews will not only save you time when prepping for media appearances, but it also makes it easier for outlets to quote you directly and for listeners to remember what you've said.

A good sound bite is snappy, easy to remember, and hits on a key point in 20 seconds or less. There are various types of sound bites, but to make it really easy for our clients, we teach them to prep three different kinds for their book-promotion interviews.

Type 1: Quotes

What is something you say, or even a popular line from your book that others quote? Here's a couple from *Self-Publish and Succeed* that I use all the time:

- "Your book might be about you, but it's not for you. It's for your reader."

- "Focusing on becoming a bestseller makes you the product, not your book."

- "One of the biggest mistakes authors make is putting their book on Amazon and then figuring out how to sell it. The work should have been done before they even started writing!"

If you're familiar with me or Book Launchers (or our YouTube channel), you've probably heard me say these lines before. You might have even memorized them yourself.

Once your book has been out for a bit, you can pull out your Kindle app and see what people highlight to help you find a sound bite. If you're not sure how to find this, just go to the little lines you see on the top left, and click Popular Highlights. You'll see that people highlighted quotes that they found impactful.

Type 2: Comparisons

How can you draw comparisons between two unusual things to illustrate a point in a memorable way? This can be a brilliant way to create a lasting visual picture in the mind of a viewer or listener!

Take Ted Lasso (if you haven't seen *Ted Lasso* the TV show, do yourself a favor and watch this show; it's so good), who said: "Taking on a challenge is like riding a horse. If you're comfortable while you're doing it, you're probably doing it wrong."[80]

Just make sure if you're going to use metaphors in your sound bites that there is a clear parallel, otherwise your listeners will walk away confused.

---

80 Darkseid, "Ted Lasso Coaching Taking on a Challenge Is Like Riding a Horse," February 7, 2023, YouTube video, 0:09, https://youtube.com/shorts/cx0U3h7Xdiw?feature=share.

Type 3: Triples

Next, try to hit triples. Here's an example: "At Book Launchers, we help professionals and subject matter experts **write**, **publish**, and **promote** a nonfiction book to build their business and grow their brand." Write, publish, and promote … one, two, three.

If you have three simple steps or a point that has three descriptors or three bullet points that you can share, memorize it. The human mind likes things that come in threes. If you can deliver three key points, three simple steps, or three ideas in a single sentence, your point will come through powerfully in an interview. And because the art of threes makes our brain happy, that point is more likely to stick with your listeners. Bonus points if you can make a triple that is an alliteration like media, market, and money or publish, promote, and profit.

Learning to talk in sound bites might take some trial and error. Brainstorm some sound bites, and share them with your friends or family. Do they think it's something they would remember? Does it effectively illustrate your main takeaway or point? Does it make them curious to hear more about you or your book? Over time, you should continue to develop your sound bites, and keep them on note cards near your computer or wherever you do your interviews.

When you prepare for your interviews, it's a huge relief to have them. With strong sound bites and note card reminders, you can rock the house, get invited back, and build your profile and platform with every media appearance.

Make the Most of Every Media Moment

Closing the Zoom meeting or walking out of the studio after an interview doesn't mean you're done. Now it's time to make that one media appearance count in a big way.

You need to:

Post it on social media. This is the thing that gives you credibility. You were a featured expert for a third party. Woo-hoo!

Use the best image from the appearance for your ads. This is especially true if you're on TV. The image can be really powerful for your ads and promotions. A picture of you on TV or a feature on a major media doesn't look like an ad, which means you can potentially get a lot of clicks if you add an interesting call to action or a promise in the text attached to it. It also quickly establishes you as an expert.

Put the media logo on your website and media kit. Yes, that means you will be doing the whole "as seen on" thing. People ascribe importance to appearances, and showing that a third party deemed you an expert worthy of interviewing helps establish your credibility.

Now, many people do those three things already, but here are two things that aren't as obvious:

Repost on social media. This time, use a lesson learned from being on TV or mention what you talked about. In other words, talk about one of the questions you were asked and the answer you gave, or an answer you would give today. You had a great media appearance! Spread the word! William Hung, author of *Champion by Choice* and a former *American Idol* contestant, does this brilliantly. He repurposes his moments on *American Idol*, on stage with Ricky Martin, and many other major public appearances. He never just reposts, though. He always shares new lessons, along with behind-the-scenes memories.

Follow William's approach, and use the best moments over and over and over again because not everyone sees your content the first time. In fact, the way social media algorithms work these days, you're lucky if 20% of your audience sees any one of your posts, so use them again. Just change up the messaging a little each time to share a lesson that others might find useful.

Follow up with a thank-you. Show your gratitude to the media outlet, and open the door to another appearance. If you have the budget, send a gift basket with a thank-you note and a few relevant topics you could speak on in the future. Make sure you include your card and maybe even another copy of your book, if you can. And if something newsworthy happens in the future that hits your expertise, reach out and suggest an angle you can address. If you were a good interview the first time, they will be highly likely to invite you back.

Media builds credibility. It also gets you seen, which is really valuable when you want to become the known expert in a space. It may not sell a lot of books, but you can leverage it to do much more for you and your business. Hopefully, these five tips help you make the most of any media coverage you land for your book.

Now that you know how to take the media world by storm to promote your book and grow your reach, let's talk a little more about podcasts in the next chapter and why they're important for authors.

Chapter Summary

1. Media appearances aren't always going to directly sell books, but they are perfect for growing a brand and becoming a recognized name (and using your book to get there).

2. Mass press releases rarely result in media coverage. Instead, you need to use a targeted and well-researched pitch to get high-value appearances.

3. Research your media opportunities with an attention to detail. Understand the most interesting angles of your topic, and prepare a short, pointed, and personalized pitch. Attach or link to your media kit or press release.

4. Prepare sound bites in advance so you have quotes, comparisons, and triples to give an audience some gold nuggets to remember you by—especially if you do a short segment.

5. Leverage every media appearance by showing up prepared, posting it afterward on social media, and sending a thank-you. Repost the best images with lessons or other insights you can share.

CHAPTER 14

THE POWER OF PODCAST PROMOTIONS

PODCASTS USED TO BE SOMETHING YOU COULD DO IN YOUR COMFY PAJA-mas in any room of your house. Nobody could see you, so you didn't have to be camera ready. Those days are gone since the majority of podcast interviews now also include video.

Podcasts have also become incredibly mainstream. Many celebrities have their own podcast, and a podcast exists for literally every niche these days. That means there's going to be a podcast (or a hundred) that covers the topic of your book, as well as another hundred that are interested in you because of your own personal story. You have an eager audience out there waiting for you, but you need to get the attention of the hosts.

I know you're asking, "Do podcasts sell books?"

Well, some do. I've definitely bought books after hearing about them on podcasts, so I know it's possible. But personally, having done more than 100 podcast interviews, including many to promote one of my books, I can tell you that I haven't ever seen a podcast episode drop and have a massive, immediate impact on sales.

Nonetheless, I still think podcasts interviews are well worth doing if you have any goal other than to sell books. Here's why:

1. It's marketing for your book, your brand, and your business— and the majority of podcasts record remotely, so you can do it at home. There's been at least five podcasts I can think of that sent clients to Book Launchers, even if I can't be sure they sold books. A new client is far more valuable to me than a book sale.

2. It gives you a lot of feedback and practice in mastering how you tell your story, share your message, and gauge response to your tips. You can see patterns in what hosts ask, when they get excited, or what makes them laugh. Doing this effectively is what led Robert Belle to uncover the winning topic for his TED Global Ideas Talk!

3. The long shelf life of a podcast with links back to your book and website pays off over time. Often people discover a podcast, decide they love it, and then listen to the entire backlist.

4. Niche podcasts can be a gold mine because they tend to have really engaged listeners. They'll buy anything the host recommends, and the host may even promote whatever else you're doing outside of the book if it's a fit for the audience. That can lead to a lot of incredible opportunities beyond a book sale. Unfortunately, identifying these podcasts in advance isn't super easy, but when you hit one, you know it! Ally Fallon's podcast, *Find Your Voice with Allison Fallon*, has been one of those for me with Book Launchers and *Self-Publish and Succeed*. She and I really connected, and she's sent a lot of her clients to work with us. In addition, we've had several people join our Book Launchers service after hearing that interview. I don't know if it sold books, but it created a personal connection to someone who shares a lot of the same values and was a very profitable interview for the business.

5. Connecting with a podcaster helps you build relationships. Take advantage of the minutes before and after your interview

to connect with the podcast host. Ask them about their projects and goals. Podcasts are a door to finding speaking opportunities, consulting gigs, new clients, new friends, and more leads. If you can be a great guest, create cool and memorable talking points, and put out a clear call to action for listeners to connect with you, then you will have the opportunity to sell books and potentially build a valuable and profitable relationship over time. Remember, podcast hosts talk to a lot of people, so they could become a great referral source for you as a speaker, businessperson, or author!

How to Decide Which Podcasts to Pitch

Be forewarned and forearmed: There are some terrible interviewers out there. The majority are decent, but there are a handful who are stiff and limit the interview to prepared questions. You can mostly avoid those by listening to one of their podcast episodes first!

Even with screening, a bad interview can still happen. Podcasts are produced by people, and people have bad days. Do your best. Remember it's a privilege to have any audience!

Most interviewers love what they do, though. They make you feel at ease and do a great job of promoting you, and you can feel their connection to the audience.

How do you target the most popular podcasts? Some data exists on downloads, but the podcast distribution systems are so fragmented it can be hard to identify the real listener base. Try looking at comments, social media engagement, and rankings on specific platforms to give you a sense.

Next, let's talk about how you find and book a podcast.

One way is through services like PodMatch, which is set up like a dating service for podcasts and potential podcast guests. You pay a fee to sign up, and then you set up a profile page with your bio, photo, and topics. From there, you can search for possible matches, or hosts can find you based on what they search. Both guests and hosts are vetted by PodMatch. You can even schedule on PodMatch's platform. It's a great option to find new podcast opportunities and develop strong relationships with hosts.

Full-service agencies like Interview Connections and Interview Valet also connect hosts with experts. Or, when working with a full-service company like Book Launchers, you can get pitched to multiple podcasts. Once you actually have a podcast appearance booked, what should you do to make your participation a success?

How to Prepare for a Podcast Interview

Once upon a time, I used to prepare for every podcast interview. I'd listen to an episode or two before the interview. This was awesome for rapport because I could comment on past episodes, I knew the format, and I was prepared for oddball questions. It always set the interview off on the right foot when I was able to say what I liked about the show.

Eventually, my schedule made that impossible. I've also done hundreds of interviews, so I am very confident and comfortable that I can deliver.

That doesn't mean you should do what I do, though, especially if you are new to interviews. Even with experience, it can go wrong. There are a few times when a host was very unhappy I hadn't listened to their show beforehand. A couple of times I was not warned about a curveball question that the host asked on every episode. If I'd listened, I would have become familiar with signature questions some hosts ask all their guests. It can be something out of left field, like "Tell your 10-year-old self about the biggest mistake you've made, and why they should still make that mistake." "If you were to start a business today with only $100, what would you do?" Or the worst one: "What's something about you that nobody knows?"

You need answers for these curveballs so you don't get totally thrown off. That's why preparation makes a difference.

As part of your preparation, put the host's name, the podcast name, the topic of the call, what they call their audience ("Team Flynn," "Bosses," "Fire Nation," etc.) on a note card and put it in front of you. There may come a time when you forget those details in the middle of the interview, and having them handy will save you from making an embarrassing mistake.

You can also write your new sound bites on a card so you have them for easy reference!

If an interviewer sends you a list of questions in advance, don't script out your answers. Review them and think about key points you'll make, but your real goal is to create a connection with your host, and you're only going to do that if you're engaging in an organic conversation and enjoying a natural back-and-forth flow.

Also, just a heads up that you should stay familiar with your book. It seems funny to say that because you wrote it and probably reread it half a dozen or more times. But believe me, you can start to forget some of the things you wrote. I've been caught off guard by a few really well-prepared hosts who say, "On page 83, you reference a story that really changed your approach. Can you tell me more about that?" And I'm frantically pulling up my book and trying to recall what I was talking about!

Preparation makes a difference whether you're experienced or not, and it's essential for your first interviews. If you ever find yourself feeling as if podcasts aren't getting results, come back to this because it could be that you're not bringing enough intention and effort into every interview. Which leads us beautifully into how to make the most of every interview whether it's your first or your 50th.

How to Make the Most of Your Podcast Interview

Often when an author has done a dozen podcasts but feels nothing has happened as a result, it is because they are missing the mark somewhere.

Let's make sure you aren't. It's important to make the most of every opportunity that comes to you, so here are my five best tips for making the most of a podcast interview.

1. **Stay value focused, not sales focused.** Seed your book in the conversation only when it makes sense to bring it up. Good interviewers will be sure to do that for you so that you don't need to do it at all yourself. Ideally, you can just focus on having a valuable conversation.

   If you give your best, people will ask to do business with you. Some will buy your book while others invite you to speak or connect with you.

2. **Set your intention at the start that this will be the best interview yet.** You can ask the podcast host if they're promoting anything or if they'd like to bring something that's important to them into the conversation because you can help them do that. These things can go a long way in creating synergy in your interview that lets both of you shine. Podcast hosts talk to a lot of people. If you reach out to them as partners, they will be much more likely to remember you, refer you, or even do business with you. Making it the best interview yet may not sell books (though it might!), but it will make you memorable!

3. **Create a clear call to action.** Your host is likely to ask, "Where can people connect with you and buy your book?" *Give them a single link to a website* that's your download. For example, you can go to https://booklaunchers.com/7steps to download the seven steps to write and publish a book that will sell. Let them know they will get your contact info and links to buy your book that way too! This way, you're driving them to your site to get your freebie and join your email list. You can build a relationship with them and invite them to buy your book afterward.

   You can even go the extra mile and create a special freebie that you are *only* giving away on podcast interviews. You can close the interview with "I have an amazing checklist that will give you the steps and resources to do everything we discussed today, and your [insert audience name] can go to the link and get this extra special thing I'm just doing for you guys."

4. **Turn one into many.** At the end of a podcast that you've crushed, the podcaster is likely to say, "Hey, how can I help you?" This is your opportunity to say, "Amazing. Yes. Thank you. If you know another podcaster whose audience I'd be a good fit for, I'd love it if you would connect us." One podcast can lead to many, many more when you consistently do this and stay top of mind by sending a thank-you or a follow-up email after the interview. If someone is a really great connection or did something special for you, send something by mail! If you establish a good working relationship, it's also possible that you may get invited back again and again until you become a regular. This happened with me on *Talking Wealth*. I've been on that show at least six times, and they've interviewed more than a dozen of our authors. They have now turned all the podcast interviews into an online TV show too! It's quite exciting to develop those kinds of relationships. So, my message to you is keep in touch and say thank you.

5. **Share your episode far and wide once it becomes available.** Post the link on your website, your social media, and more. Some hosts make this easier to do than others, but either way, this is an opportunity to reciprocate and build credibility. Other hosts considering you for their show will see this too, and it's always appreciated. Some hosts, like Jeffrey Feldberg of *The Deep Wealth Podcast*, will even offer you the raw interview to repurpose. Jeffrey told me that our episode was cocreated, and we're both owners of the interview, so I can use it for whatever I want to. For instance, I can turn it into social media content or excerpts for YouTube. If you still struggle with what to put

in your email newsletter, struggle no more! You have a lot of content that you can share when you're doing podcast interviews.

As I mentioned before, my interview on the podcast *UnNoticed Entrepreneur* became a chapter in a book that was eventually picked up by Capstone, an imprint of John Wiley & Sons. How fun is that? All I did was show up for an interview and sign a waiver, and now I'm in another book.

Many podcasts can have a big impact on your business, brand, and overall book momentum. It's important to understand how podcasts can help, so now that you know, don't overlook these opportunities! Remember Martha Tettenborn landed a documentary from a podcast interview, and podcast interviews led Robert Belle to a TED Global Ideas Talk.

Podcasts are a wonderfully easy way to connect with new readers, get your name out there, increase the links going back to your website (which is always useful), and practice both your interview skills and talking about your book. Another great place to talk about your book is live and in person at bookstores. In the next chapter, I'll tell you what every self-published author needs to know about selling your book on bookstore shelves and putting on live events at stores.

Chapter Summary

1. Podcast interviews are a great way to hone your message, build your brand, and meet interesting people.

2. Research podcasts before you pitch them. It's wise to listen to a couple of episodes to make sure your message will be a fit.

3. Prepare for your podcast interview by listening to at least one episode and making note of the host's name, podcast's name, and their community's name before you get on the podcast. Also, if you have a specific topic you're going to cover, writing down some bullet points is a good idea too.

4. Be camera ready because most podcasts are now recorded on video.

5. Leverage your podcast interview into new opportunities by teaming up with the host to make it the best podcast interview ever. Ask for more interviews and podcast contacts at the end of your interview. Send a thank-you note later!

CHAPTER 15

BANGING ON THE BOOKSTORE DOOR

"CAN YOU DIRECT ME TO THE COOKBOOKS?"

"Do you work here? Can you help me find …?"

"Where are the bathrooms?"

These are some of the questions I get asked at every single bookstore event I do.

Bookstore signings weren't all I dreamed they would be, but it is a bit surreal to see your book on the shelf. There's just something so cool and validating about finally seeing your book for sale.

Widespread bookstore distribution may not be what you really need to achieve your goals. For most authors, it's going to be more of a personal goal than an achievement that really moves you toward the impact and income you desire. Plus, the math is kind of scary. (We'll get to that later.)

Local bookstores, however, can help you and your book gain exposure and sell more copies.

To get a bookstore to carry your book, here's what you do: First, plan your sales approach. Large traditional publishers have sales teams who pitch the books they want to promote to bookstores. If you self-publish or have a small publisher, you typically have to be your own team and head into the store with a sales sheet on your book.

A sales sheet is similar to a media kit, in that it's meant to give retailers quick and easy info about you and your book. But unlike a media kit, a sales sheet's goal is to get the retailer to order the book for their store. It can be a PDF or printed (if you're approaching a retailer in person) and should be only one page.

On your sales sheet, you need to include several items:

- Cover image and, if possible, your author image
- Details of your promotional plans for the book, including local media or events
- Metadata on the book
- Noteworthy editorial reviews or blurbs
- Prior media exposure and awards or recognition
- Short book description
- Where the book can be ordered wholesale (for example, IngramSpark)

If you've already prepared an author media kit, you're way ahead of the game!

Remember, stores want books that sell. They have limited shelf space and small margins. This means your job isn't to convince the bookstore manager that you tell an incredible story that will mesmerize readers. Your job is to show them that you're going to send eager buyers to their store to spend money on your book and (hopefully) other books too.

Another thing you can do is to pitch an event at the store. Ask if they're hosting authors for book readings or Q&A sessions. If so, you can offer your contacts, clients, emails, and social media accounts to help them promote an event you host.

Tying into an awareness month (if applicable to you or your book topic) can work wonders, too, especially if it's one the bookstore already wants to promote. Most bookstores stock books for upcoming events and have you sign copies that they sell later.

This is the strategy I used to get widespread bookstore listings for *More than Cashflow*. I had about 10 different bookstore events across Canada, and I pushed sales hard. It worked, and other stores saw the sales numbers and ordered books. A decade later, some bookstores still carry my book.

The second step is to discuss listing and wholesale discounts with the store. Once they're interested, now they've got to buy copies. If you're set up through Ingram, then your bookstore can order from them.

Most bookstores require a 40% discount, which means setting your Ingram wholesale discount at 55%. That said, you may be able to strike a deal somewhere in between since you're going to do a lot of work to drive traffic to the store. Alternatively, many bookstores may offer to do a consignment deal, where you get paid after your book sells.

Finally, fulfill your promise once your book is listed. Just holding a book signing isn't enough. You have to have a marketing plan to sell books during the event, and even after.

My bookstore appearances did much better with a radio interview the day of the signing or the day before. I also emailed people in the local market and suggested they come by and say hello. Posters around the area can help. But remember, if you're not famous, you have to sell the hook of the book and the benefit you offer. **It's not about the reader getting to meet you, because they don't know (or care yet) who you are.** Keep that in mind, because the number of people who are going to come out and see *you* is far fewer than the number who are coming for the expertise you offer or the tips you can share.

Following through after the event to help sell books can help, especially if you're working with an indie store. One store in Ottawa brought in 26 books for an event, but a snowstorm swept in, and we didn't have a good turnout. They had 10 books left after my event. This was a big deal. I could have bought them from the store, but I decided to send an email to my list and promised a free one-hour consultation for anyone who went in and bought all 10 books. Within days, the books were gone, and the store loved me and kept a copy in stock on an ongoing basis for many years.

If your local sales do well, you may find yourself faced with the opportunity to sell books with a retail bookstore chain. That raises a lot of factors to consider, so we'll get into that in a bit.

Case Study: Airport Bookstores

Do you dream of seeing your book for sale in the airport? We've had several clients at Book Launchers make that dream a reality, but none did it quite as well as Robert Workman, the author of *Hired Gun II*.[81] Walking through airports on sales trips, he'd pop in and get the manager's name and phone number. He'd call them and find out where they bought books and what made them carry a book. He was determined and would follow up conversations with a box of cookies and a thank-you. When he got a listing, he would tell all his traveling colleagues and friends to buy his book at that store. Sales at one store make it easier to get a listing at another. Bit by bit, he unlocked the keys to 15 different airport bookstores.

You can find book-selling opportunities everywhere. The trick is to be patient and persistent, have fun with it, and uncover the opportunities as Robert did. He did it for fun, not necessarily because airports were going to make him rich.

---

81 Robert Workman, *Hired Gun II: Blasting Business Politics* (Direct Media Marketing, 2019).

Now, if your book is targeted at people like you, think about where you go on a regular basis. Walking around with your eyes open, as Robert did, is a simple yet brilliant exercise in creative marketing.

But reaching out and following up also requires preparation. When Robert called airport bookstore managers, he had the tools he needed to convince them that his book would sell. These included a professional book cover design and a well-designed author media kit, including endorsements.

Sometimes, it took Robert a week of phone calls to get the person actually buying the books on the phone.

Not surprisingly, given his background in sales, his process boiled down to prospecting, calling, and sending the information by email with a media kit attached, and then following up. If the bookstore is part of a big chain, the only way that any individual manager can buy a book is if the big chain headquarters ships it to them. They cannot always make independent buying decisions. What did Robert do?

He'd head over to Federal Express, wrap his book in really nice tissue paper, and put it in a box with a half dozen cookies in a Mrs. Fields tin. He attached his business card and included a cover letter with the media kit printed on really high-gloss, heavy stock. Then he would call a week later. His strategy resulted in book orders from airports in Anchorage, Dallas, Los Angeles, Miami, Omaha, and San Francisco!

Now that you know how to sell your book to a store, you have to be ready for them to buy the book. For that to happen, we need to talk about IngramSpark.

The Bookstore Catalog of Choice: Ingram

KDP has a global-distribution option, but bookstores won't buy from Amazon. The money doesn't make sense for them, and many don't like

Amazon, so they just plain won't buy from them. If you want wider distribution, you need IngramSpark to gain access to the Ingram catalog.

When you upload your book to IngramSpark, they ask for your wholesale discount. A wholesale discount is how much a wholesaler actually pays for your book. Wholesalers include online retailers like Amazon as well as brick-and-mortar retailers like Barnes & Noble and Costco. These retailers sell your book at its list price. And if they can't make a profit from selling your book, they won't buy it, plain and simple.

In other words, the retailers are doing a Jerry Maguire: "Show me the money!"[82]

If you pursue bookstore distribution, you don't just compete with self-published books. In fact, your biggest competitors are books published by traditional publishers. They already have a little spot carved out on the shelf. The major publishers literally pay for display space.[83] (Haven't you ever found the top 10 bestseller stands suspicious? I mean how can there be three John Grisham books in the top 10 at once?! They paid for that spot —that's how!) To interest retailers, you need to offer a 53%–55% discount.

You also must make sure you've checked the "return and destroy" box when you upload your book and choose your settings. Bookstores won't buy books if they can't return them, which leads into why bookstore listings can be riskier than they're worth. And, if you're cringing at the thought of your book being destroyed, read on.

---

82 Kychristmas1, "*Jerry Maguire* (Tom Cruise)—Show Me the Money Shortened," February 27, 2012, YouTube video, 0:057, https://www.youtube.com/watch?v=TuQC5hhhqkY.

83 Alan Rinzler, "Shelf Wars: What Authors Need to Know about Bookstore Visibility," Alan Rinzler Consulting Editor, April 13, 2010, https://alanrinzler.com/2010/04/shelf-wars-what-authors-need-to-know-about-bookstore-visibility/.

Bookstores Might Not Be Worth It

When I self-published my first book, *More than Cashflow*, I wanted everything traditional published authors get and more. I busted my butt to get my book into bookstores all across Canada. And it worked! I got widespread distribution. But I also got an unexpected and unwelcome surprise: Many of my books were returned six months later. And guess who had to foot the bill for all those returned books?

It's not the store, and it's not Ingram. It's the publisher, and when you self-publish, that means *you*.

Six months after a huge book tour across Canada, I got hit with a $1,200 bill for returned books. Thankfully, by then I'd already pocketed more than 30 times that amount in book royalties, but it still really stung.

Bookstores haven't presold your book when they buy it. They buy it and hope it sells, unlike print on demand, when your book gets printed only when someone buys it. A lack of sales is what leads to returns. If your book sits on the stores' valuable shelf space for too long collecting dust, they need to get rid of it. And it's not their loss to absorb. It's yours.

In other words, as I mentioned earlier, you have to reimburse them for the returned copies that didn't sell.

After wholesale discounts, depending on the book (size, type, and price) you probably made about $5 per copy.

The bookstore probably paid about $9 or $10 for your book. You're not paying the bookstore back for what *you made* for the book, you're paying them back for what *they paid*. In other words, you made $5, and you're paying them $10. Yup, you lost $5 per returned copy on a book that didn't sell.

Here's what that looks like in a formula:

What the bookstore paid – what you got paid = the extra charge you have to pay for a return

$10 – $5 = $5

The situation got even worse for me because I didn't check the "return and destroy" box. Instead, I checked "return to author," and that meant I paid for *delivery* for every individual copy sent back to me. Instead of it costing me two times what I made, it cost me two and a half times because I then had to pay $3.00 per book for the return. So here's that formula:

(What the bookstore paid + the delivery charge for each book) – what you got paid = the extra charge you have to pay for each return.

($10 + $3) – $5 = $8

At the time, I thought I could resell the books. I also cringed at the thought of my book babies being destroyed.

Big mistake.

If a bill for $1,200 shocks you, imagine if you had an entire chain of bookstores purchase your books but then go out of business or have to close their locations for three months for a pandemic. All your books could be returned. That's really ugly.

Here's some more disturbing math: I probably sold a maximum of 600 books total to the stores that first year.

Unfortunately, through Ingram you don't get to see who's buying books, so you don't get to know what percent of those are bookstores. But I was in the trenches, so I think my estimates are solid. Here's the math I warned you about. Brace yourself because this gets a little ugly.

Let's say I sold 500 books in stores and netted $5.80 per book for a total payday of $2,900. Then I had to pay $1,200 for returns. From book sales, I netted $1,700 before tax. Then I had to pay my book tour expenses: hotels, marketing, airfares, and the PR person I hired.

Thankfully my speaking engagements and other business initiatives in each city were profitable, or that would not have been a good financial move.

When you think of that? I mean … whoa! I can tell you I won't be doing a bookstore push for any other books I self-publish.

If you don't want to give up on bookstores completely, keep these things in mind: Online is still good. The 55% wholesale discount and issues with taking big risks with returns are not the same with digital sales through Barnes & Noble, Chapters Indigo, or other chains like Walmart. Those chains sell your book online, and you can set your wholesale discount to 40%. You make more money, even if there is a return.

I must say, it feels incredibly validating to see your book on the shelves of a bookstore. But just being on the shelf does not mean it will sell. This is true, especially since your title will likely be spine out, not cover out, on a shelf where someone has to really search for it. The only way to sell books is for you to generate that demand.

If you decide to sell online only, you can market the book, keep more dollars sold per book, and not worry about the bookstores returning your books and costing you more money. If you still want a few select book-stores to carry your book, become a great bookstore partner because selling local can be really smart and worthwhile, especially if you want to contrib-ute to your community's economy.

If a bookseller knows you and likes your book, they'll talk you up and sell it to walk-in customers or include you in their newsletter. It's worth being in a few bookstores if:

- a bookstore is excited about your book,

- you can sell your book on consignment, or

- your book is ordered at a discounted rate that's compatible with your overall strategy.

In the next chapter, we'll turn our focus to one of the most powerful content-marketing strategies for anyone looking to be known as an expert in their industry, build a platform, or have an impact—video marketing, featuring YouTube.

Chapter Summary

1. Bookstores won't buy from Amazon, so you need to be listed in the Ingram catalog via IngramSpark to sell your book to a local bookstore or others outside your community.

2. Bookstores need to make money, so you have to set your wholesale discount at 55% on Ingram so that the store gets 40% and Ingram gets 15%. If a bookstore returns your book, it's a net loss to you as an author. This means every book returned is a net loss to you as an author.

3. Author book-signing events can be a great tool to get more bookstore listings, but take the time to understand your goal and purpose in doing them. Also make sure you've marketed the event well because getting people to attend bookstore signings isn't as easy as you might think.

4. Wide bookstore distribution might not be a good fit for your overall goals, given the risks. Be sure to understand your reasons for pursuing it and whether it's worth the work and potential lost revenue.

5. And last but not least, when you show up at your bookstore event, check for the location of the cookbooks and the bathrooms because you'll be asked.

CHAPTER 16

SPEAK AND SELL

IT WAS A MULTISPEAKER EVENT, AND ONE OF MY PR FRIEND'S CLIENTS was the only speaker with a line to her table afterward.

Why? She had a book for sale and offered to autograph copies.

Thanks to the conference, and her book, she received invitations for two more speaking engagements. That kind of synergy can happen to you too.

Many authors write a book to become a speaker, and whether you are a speaker or that's your goal, it makes sense to be an author. Speaking and books go so well together they are like peanut butter and jelly or fries and ketchup. Yum.

Getting speaking engagements is one of the best ways to sell your books, make money, and expand your reach. Your hosts will often buy a copy of your book for every person in the audience, or you can sell books at the back of the room. Books can be icing on a speaking contract because they amount to higher fees.

For someone just starting out as a speaker, you may not be able to command a contract rate, but you should be able to ask for participant emails or sell books (maybe even both). I did many talks where my payment was a kind of barter—either books sold to the event organizer or at the back of the room. It's well worth it to do this if you have a larger impact or income goal and the audience is a great fit!

How do you make that happen if you're not yet a speaker?

Once you have a book, if you've done a great job of creating a hook and a compelling read, it's quite likely speaking opportunities will find you. My second book had a chapter called "You Are Who Google Says You Are," and that chapter alone generated multiple speaking engagements without my pursuing them at all!

Still, it's never a good idea to leave anything to chance.

First, **come up with some super cool and compelling topics**. If you want to be a keynote speaker, you need to develop a signature talk.

Steve Multer, a professional speaker and event emcee, wrote *Nothing Gets Sold Until a Story Gets Told* to complement his already successful business.[84] The book is all about how to tell a great story as a presenter—a skill that every business leader needs to know. Sometimes, the audience is small, but often the stakes are high because you need to have an impact and influence your host's organization.

Steve's book has a great tie-in to his profession, and his speaking engagements offer clear and compelling topics for organization managers

If you're new to speaking, I'd suggest getting a copy of his book because it might help you think of stories you can tie into your message.

---

84 Steve Multer, *Nothing Gets Sold Until the Story Gets Told: Corporate Storytelling for Career Success and Value-Driven Marketing* (Message Master Media, 2023).

Make a list of three to five talks that you can give, and create interesting titles that will generate curiosity and focus on the benefits of your chosen topics. Here are some talk topics we've helped Book Launchers clients create:

Shaun Hayes, author of *The Gray Choice: Lessons on My Journey from Big-Time Banking to the Big House (and Back)*

- "Business Ethics: How to Keep Your Decisions from Straying Off Track and Derailing Your Business and Life"

- "Entrepreneurship: Smart Risk-Taking or Dangerous Decisions? How to Tell the Vital Difference in Business"

- "Motivation & Inspiration: From Perfect to Prison—Lessons from a Multimillionaire Turned Convict on Staying the Course Through Life's Ethical Gray Areas"

Dr. Virgie Bright Ellington, author of *What Your Doctor Wants You to Know to Crush Medical Debt: A Health System Insider's 3 Steps to Protect Yourself from America's #1 Cause of Bankruptcy*

- "An Insider's Look at Medical Bills: Three Steps to Manage Medical Bills and Stay Out of Debt"

- "What Your Doctor Wants You to Know: How to Dig Out of and Avoid Medical Debt"

- "Secure Your Financial Future: How People in Their 20s and 30s Can Arm Themselves Against a Lifetime of Medical Debt"

Mark & Kristen Krikke, authors of *You, Me, and Airbnb: The Savvy Couple's Guide to Turning Midterm Rentals into Big-Time Profits*

- "A 5-Star Stay: How to Use Airbnb to Make Home Ownership Affordable for You and Your Family"

- "Master the Art of Midterm Rentals: Build Cash Flow and Get More Quality Time with Your Family"

- "Mom CEO: Create Your Stay-at-Home Business with Short- and Midterm Rentals"

Once you have some compelling ideas for talks, assemble the necessary materials.

You need a great *profile picture* and a *bio* that is short but packs a punch. It needs to clearly highlight why you are *the* person to speak on this topic and what makes you that person. If you did a good job of creating an author bio, you can probably pull from that, but be sure to highlight your tangible successes and experience. This is also the time to name-drop the big companies with whom you've worked or done presentations and speeches. This is not the time to be shy, okay? You're trying to get other people to put you in front of their audience. Also important are references or testimonials from past speaking engagements.

You can even create a *speaker one sheet*, which summarizes your speaking business and is a simple sell sheet for your talks. We have examples on the bonus resources page at https://selfpromoteandsucceed.com.

Finally, you should create a speaker reel. While this is the most important task, it's also the most challenging when you're starting out. This can feature excerpts from one talk or several, if you've been speaking for a while. The reel shows clips of you speaking to an audience and audience reaction and engagement. It also highlights brands or events at which you've spoken and usually has a soundtrack. When you book paid gigs, you need a reel unless you've been referred or the event booker has seen you speak. You can start without this, but know that paid gigs may be initially harder to get.

Start planning your pitches. Start small and focus on individuals or organizations that are going to have some interest or gain value from what you have to share. Are you a member of your local chamber of commerce, a women's business association, or business owners' group? What about any other kind of association or a Meetup group that's relevant? A lot of my early speaking gigs—and actually, many others later on—took place with

Meetup groups because they had a huge following, and sometimes, it was the perfect audience. These groups were excellent for book sales too! Even though there might be only 50 people in attendance, I would often sell a book to every single person!

Just like with your media pitch prep—do your research. If you don't have a personal connection to a group, then make sure your pitch is researched, focused, and all about how you'll benefit their audience.

When you start submitting to larger events, you'll complete speaker submission forms. As you find events near you (or with your ideal reader in the audience), you can look on the website for these forms.

Your goal with your first few talks is to get an audience for you and for your material. Do what stand-up comedians do—talk in front of people in a place where you can afford to fail and test your material. In other words, start small. Find an open mic night or another place where you can do an unpaid talk for a small group of people to see what works, and what doesn't. If it goes well, you can collect reference letters from those organizers.

When you reach out to people about speaking engagements—even in small venues—make sure the pitch is about them and what you can do for them and deliver to their audience. That's super important. You can get started by finding groups through Meetup.com, LinkedIn, Facebook, and good old Google. Just search away. Let's say you're looking for entrepreneurs. Look for local entrepreneurial Meetup groups, local business groups, etc.

What you're really looking for is a group that meets regularly and typically has a speaker. Even at my local mom's group, a potty training expert came to speak to us for $20 apiece. That's not a lot of money when you only have 20 people in the room, but she also offered potty training consultations and sold a handful of $500 consults along with copies of her book. She probably made $4,000 for a few hours of her time—not bad for a pretty casual gig.

As you do these smaller events, if you're good, and your content resonates with your audiences, you're going to find bigger ones come up. You're also gaining practice, confidence, and a track record that's going to help you when you start submitting speaking applications to larger events.

Getting a speaking engagement is a start, but what should you do once you actually land one?

How to Prep for a Speaking Engagement

A lot of authors think that they can write a book and get paid for speaking without any preparation. The truth is that this rarely happens. In fact, your progress will feel slow, until suddenly you're like Shell Phelps, author of *The Big Bliss Blueprint*,[85] standing on an international stage. That's not where she started, but she just kept going. (Can you tell I'm enthusiastically cheering her on? I am so excited for her!)

If you've never given a talk before, you really need to be ready for it. And there's a lot more involved than putting some PowerPoint slides together and delivering your expertise. (If you want some amazing tips, I highly recommend you check out Dan Fraser's book, *Kickass Presentations*.)[86]

Workshops are very different from keynotes or breakout room talks. You'll almost always find me speaking in a breakout room or a workshop format because I am teaching. If you're going to be sharing something that will change the audience's perspective on something, you'll be on the main stage giving a keynote. You'll want to iron that sort of thing out first, and realize that most speakers start in breakout rooms.

Have the core of your presentation rehearsed and ready. If you haven't done work on a signature talk, it can be really useful to at least have a core talk structure outlined and ready to go. Sometimes, these opportunities

---

85 Phelps, *The Big Bliss Blueprint*.
86 Fraser, *Kickass Presentations*.

appear on short notice. On one occasion, I was exhibiting at FinCon for Book Launchers, and a speaker didn't show for their talk on turning your book into money-making content. I was able to step up because I'm always prepared to give a talk and share content, and that one little speech generated more activity at my booth than anything else I did the entire event, and in the next year after the event, we had two clients join with us from that impromptu talk.

If you need help preparing a talk, there are lots of great speaking coaches or programs to help you.

For instance, Michael Port and Andrew M. Davis wrote a great book called *The Referable Speaker*. (As I read it, I was delighted to see a feature on the Book Launchers author of *Mean People Suck*!) Michael compared how actors prepare for the show *Hamilton* on Broadway with an improv show. Tickets to *Hamilton* cost hundreds of dollars, while an improv show ticket may be priced $40.[87]

While all of the performers are skilled in their craft, what you're getting when you go to an improv show is (mostly) a spontaneous performance. Meanwhile, *Hamilton* is precise, practiced, and highly professional.

As a speaker, do you want to be a performer in an improv show, or do you want to be an actor in *Hamilton*? Are you rehearsed and ready? You should be. You can't afford to wing it if you want to effectively communicate your message and succeed.

And as it turns out, you already have an amazing tool to help you prep your talks for speaking engagements: your book!

---

87 Michael Port and Andrew M. Davis, *The Referable Speaker: Your Guide to Building a Sustained Speaking Career—No Fame Required* (Page Two Press, 2021).

Creating a Talk from Your Book

Your signature talk can come right out of your book. In fact, your signature talk and your book should support and reinforce one another so that you're presenting a cohesive brand.

But you don't have to stop there. You can mine your book for all sorts of topics. What I find often happens after you develop a signature talk is that you now have a core story to plug into different lessons or training elements for *all* of your talks. This allows you to have material that works every time along with flexibility to customize the talk for each audience so it resonates.

Another important thing to consider when you start to structure your talks —and really, *any* story you tell onstage—is a three-act story structure.

This type of story structure is a foundational framework in Western storytelling. And guess what? You actually *are* already familiar with this structure through movies, TV shows, novels, and more—you just may not know it yet. Learning the moving pieces of this structure is very helpful because when you become a speaker, you also become a storyteller.

How does a three-act structure work? Here's a crash course:

Act 1 is the *setup*. This is the inciting incident. It's the thing that sets you off on your adventure. For *Alice in Wonderland*, it's Alice's curiosity about the rabbit that sends her off on her adventure. Another classic is Alec Baldwin's speech in *Glengarry Glen Ross*. You know the one. The gist is "Sell or be fired. Always be closing." Basically, it's the call to action that leads up to the next act.

Act 2 is the *confrontation*, or *conflict*. This is where things get intense. It's often the midpoint, and it's when a lot of things pile on top of each other and really create a challenge that seems insurmountable—as in, you're never going to overcome it.

And then comes act 3, the *resolution*. This occurs after the climax, the peak of the action. Ideally (in my world, at least), this is where everything gets wrapped up with a bow.

If you want to get really into this stuff, you can also read about the hero's journey, a story framework that takes this three-act structure and explores it in more depth, adding character archetypes and steps along the way. Book Launchers client Scott MacMillan released a book titled *Be the Hero of Your Life*.[88] If you're looking to dive more into the hero's journey in your life, this is an excellent read.

Have you ever wondered why we like to watch movies and TV shows and read books? It's because they take us on a journey. They spark our imagination with a situation where something goes wrong or some kind of tension builds up and then resolves at the end.

That's exactly what your signature talk should do for your audience. If you can tap into the way human brains are programmed and primed to want to hear stories and go on that journey, your talk is going to be all the more memorable.

How to Apply the Three-Act Structure to Your Talk

It's time to apply this amazingly helpful structure to constructing your talk.

Act 1 is where you set up the situation. In this case, what is the audience's goal? What do they want for themselves, their lives, their career, their businesses, their health, their relationships—and how is this linked to your area of expertise? What is the obstacle that the audience sees as being in the way of them achieving their goal? And more important, what is the underlying

---

88 J. Scott MacMillan, *Be the Hero of Your Life: Ditch the Excuses, Take Your Hero's Journey, and Find Your Life's Purpose* (Mobes Publishing, 2019).

real problem that they may not recognize, but you, as the expert on this topic, understand and can identify for them?

This is where you create the tension for your audience that you're going to resolve by the end of the talk. Act 1 is also where you bake in your credibility as to why you are uniquely qualified to help them.

Act 2 is the framework you use to get the audience where you need them to go. Because you've written a book, you already have a lot of content. If you have a step-by-step process in your book, take a few components and use it here. Integrate some audience interaction, such as questions or activities. Make sure you also pepper in real-life client examples to bring your message home in a concrete way.

Finally, act 3 is the resolution. This is where you give your audience their next steps. What are the things that they can do on their own, and what are the things that they can do with you? You've got it. This is where you plant your call to action for them to purchase your book. The call to action could also be for them to hire you or your company. The real trick, though, is to make sure that at the end of act 3 you've left your audience with the inspiration and motivation to work toward the better vision for their future that *you* see is possible for them.

Now that you have the tools you need to get started creating and booking your talks, how can you make sure to make the most of any speaking engagements you land?

How to Leverage Speaking Engagements

For years, I did a lot of speaking engagements that didn't pay me speaking fees. Hello, real estate industry. These days, many events charge speakers to step on stage, so it's even worse than not getting paid!

The reason they can charge (and people will pay) is because a smart speaker can leverage that talk into tremendous value for their business, so knowing how to do this is vital to your success.

Whether someone else books you for speaking engagements or you do it yourself, you need to plan ahead so you can make the most of every gig. Here's what I recommend:

- *Promote your participation in newsletters, social media, and on your website.* You're doing this for two reasons: First, it boosts your credibility (and lets people know you are a speaker, which can unearth future opportunities). And second, event organizers appreciate your helping them get the word out. This can often lead to their referring you to other events or giving you opportunities around their platform, like video interviews, blog posts, shout-outs, and reposts.

- *Research, plan, and leverage media coverage of the event.* Smart event planners, especially of larger 100-plus-person events, typically arrange some sort of coverage around their event. The things to look for when you're pitching the event to media are opportunities for a human interest or news story related to the event, because the media isn't interested in promotions. Make yourself available for interviews, and introduce yourself or ask to be introduced to on-site bloggers and others so you get exposure through follow-up posts or articles after the event is over. If you aren't prepared with an angle or don't know whom you're looking for, you'll miss out, so do your research in advance.

- If the event is a decent-size one, it can be worth it to *hire a professional photographer and/or videographer to shoot a demo reel and photos, including headshots.* This is great for your portfolio and can also be used for social media, your website, and media outlets that ask for professional images.

- *Collect email addresses with a feedback form.* I've got to give a huge shout-out to speaking coach Carol Cox. She caught me speaking at Podfest in 2018 and gave me this brilliant suggestion: Ask the audience to turn in a feedback form at the end of the talk and include a simple offer to join your newsletter list. You'll find that 30% to 60% of the room signs up. Platform growth, baby. You also might learn a few things that the audience really liked (or wished you'd covered).

- If the organizers of the event didn't buy books for the audience, and you're unpaid, *ask if you can set up a table at the back to sell books.* Many events now have designated author areas where authors can sell books. This is good, but being able to sell right after your talk is best because people will be primed and ready to learn more from you.

- Assuming the talk goes well, let the audience and the organizer know you're looking for more speaking engagements and *ask for referrals.* For the audience, this is a little trickier, but as people come up to you afterward and say how great it was, let them know you'd love to do more, and if they know of any events you'd be a good fit for, you'd appreciate a connection. Do the same thing with the organizers.

- If you can, *ask for testimonials from the organizer.* Letters of reference are ideal, but a great testimonial can really help too. Just because a speaking engagement doesn't put cash in your pocket directly doesn't mean it's not worth doing. In many cases, event organizers will buy books in exchange for your speaking. In other cases, they will be more than willing to help you get something out of it. Think about what you need and ask for it.

- This is optional, but if the event was a great one for you, or the event organizer made your experience special, I highly recommend that you *send a thank-you card with a small gift* to the event organizer. This will help you stay top of mind for future events as well as increase the likelihood of getting that endorsement letter or testimonial.

In general, the larger the audience and the more experience you gain, the more value you can expect in exchange for your talk. Before you know it, you'll be getting paid to speak to most audiences. And eventually, you'll have gained enough exposure and clout to generate a lot of income and book sales from every opportunity, including unpaid ones.

Of all the possible marketing tactics, speaking done well is one of the few that is almost guaranteed to sell books, make an impact, get your name known, boost your credibility, and catapult your platform. Granted, public speaking may not be something you want to do, but I really recommend you try it! For those of you who prefer to stay out of the spotlight as much as possible, let's move on to the wild and wonderful world of audiobooks and how to market an audiobook if you decide to record one.

Chapter Summary

1. Speaking and book sales go together like peanut butter and jelly, so if you're not speaking now, it's something to seriously consider.

2. Creating a list of high-value topics that generate interest and curiosity is a great first step to show an event organizer what you'll bring their audience. Remember it's about what value you can provide the audience.

3. Consider creating a speaker one sheet and demo reel if you plan to do a lot of speaking. These are investments in your speaking career that will pay off quickly.

4. Leverage speaking engagements to support your bigger author and business goals by asking for referrals to other engagements, collecting emails for your newsletter, selling books at the back of the room, hiring a videographer or photographer, posting

engagements on your social media, and asking for testimonials from event organizers.

5. It's okay to start small—in fact, it's the best way to begin if you don't have much public speaking experience.

CHAPTER 17

ALL THINGS AUDIOBOOKS

WHAT DO YOU THINK? ARE AUDIOBOOK CONSUMERS WHO LISTEN TO books considered readers?

I'm not sure. But whether you think they are or not, it's worth spending a moment on audiobook marketing. Audiobooks are widely considered one of the fastest-growing segments of the publishing industry. Many books, even traditionally published books, don't have an audiobook format for their book because of the (to date) high cost of production, though this is rapidly changing given advances in AI narration quality and acceptance.

There are some distribution decisions that impact your marketing choices, and that's a bit of a rabbit hole. For our purposes here, I'm not going to go too deeply into that, but they generally involve money, reach, and marketing.

Audible also continues to squeeze authors and their profits. It's a bit gross, the power play they have made, but that isn't a topic for this book. Ultimately, if you want your audiobook to be available to library listeners, as many of our Book Launchers authors do, then you must make it available widely (and not exclusively through Audible) so it can be requested through platforms like OverDrive at the library. We do this through Findaway Voices, but there is also Author's Republic.

There are also some good options for selling your audiobook direct to buyers (stay tuned for the next chapter)—it's a pretty fabulous way to make more money per book sold and get contact information. BookFunnel is probably the best option right now for selling direct to an audience, but there are more options emerging constantly in the audiobook space.

Before I give you my marketing strategies, I have to emphasize that an audiobook with a bad title or a bad cover has the same problem as a print book or an e-book with a bad title and bad cover. Design is just as vital when it comes to your audiobook.

Bad narration on Audible can also cause you problems because books are rated on performance. And, just as reviews are vital for the success of your book in print and e-book, it's also important you get Audible-specific reviews because they are the only reviews shown on the Audible app.

Assuming your audiobook, metadata, and design elements are good to go, here's my audiobook marketing advice (regardless of your bigger-picture marketing goals):

- **Ideally, launch your audiobook at the same time as your print and e-book.** We've done audiobook launches after a book has been out for a while, but driving traffic to sell an audiobook isn't that easy. And generating media interest based solely on the release of an audiobook is almost impossible if it's simply an audio version of your book. If there's some new fresh content only in the audiobook that is relevant to something happening in the world or a trending topic, it makes it easier, but driving traffic just to an audiobook is not that effective.

It's best to market your book and have all formats available at once so buyers can choose! If you don't have the audiobook ready when you launch, you lose sales that would have come from folks who consume books only in audio form. The reality is that someone won't check back later to see if you've produced an audiobook—you've lost that sale.

- **Make it a habit to tell people your book is also available in audio.** You'll see people's faces light up when they prefer audiobooks and you tell them you have one! Plus, they may know other people who wanted the audio version, or perhaps they haven't finished reading your book, and they would prefer an option to listen to it to make that easier.

If your book is sold on Audible, there is a great feature called Whispersync. Whispersync lets readers switch back and forth between reading the e-book on their Kindle and listening to the audiobook on Audible, without ever losing their place. Maybe they get home from work, after they've been listening to your audiobook in the car, and they sit down to read the e-book. And voilà! They're in the same place. I did this while reading *Never Split the Difference* by Chris Voss.[89] I also found it beneficial to be able to review and highlight what I heard while driving.

Some readers will buy both versions for these reasons. Granted, one is at a discount, so less royalties for you, but it's a bonus sale, selling to the same person twice. And now the readers are happy because they can listen and read interchangeably. Telling your audience your book is also available in audio just opens the doors to a lot more sales.

- When you do live appearances and you're selling physical books, **have a QR code available for people who might prefer the au-**

---

89 Chris Voss, *Never Split the Difference: Negotiating as if Your Life Depended On It* (New York: Harper Business, 2016).

diobook version. You can even have them buy the audiobook on the spot and give them a free print book, pen, or other incentive. If they walk away, they might forget or lose motivation. Get them to buy it while they're there.

- **Post samples of your audiobook on SoundCloud, and then embed those on your website.** Also share them in your newsletter and pretty much anywhere you're talking about your audiobook. Once you've uploaded a file to SoundCloud, they have an easy embed function. You can also use that embed code in newsletters or as an email signature, if your email provider allows it. You can even upload a free audio chapter and give it away to people who listen to your podcast interviews. That's a great way to build connections with potential readers, customers, clients, or even partners.

- **Use the free code to get audiobook-specific reviews or for reader giveaways to generate interest.** When you upload your book, you receive codes to give away free audiobooks. If you have ACX codes, the listener can get an Audible version of the book. If you use Findaway Voices, they give you 30 one-time codes for a free audiobook that you can give away to anyone you'd like. Listeners can go to a designated site to redeem your code to listen to your audiobook on any of Findaway's free author-direct mobile apps. If you pursue professional reviewers, bloggers, or podcasters, you can give them one of your codes. You can also do reader giveaways. If you're on a podcast or doing a live event, you might want to give away an audiobook using these codes to a few audience members. I also use them for thank-you gifts for someone who's been a great supporter or for someone who did something extra for me.

- **Chirp and BookBub are now available as paid audiobook-promotion spaces.** Watch the market for more, as I expect this will continue to grow along with the interest in audiobooks. Supporting Cast is a service I'll use with this book promotion to offer copies of the audiobook for free to buyers of the print book. I'll also set up a sales page, like https://selfpublishandsucceed.com. This sales page, however, will be a direct audiobook sale using Supporting Cast as the distributor. Then I can run Google or social media ads with links to the audiobook and track conversions. To date, I've found limited value in paying for a lot of audio-specific promotions, but I recommend testing the waters if you have a bit of a budget for paid promotion.

- **Pursue audiobook-specific reviews.** If you're listening to this book, please head to Audible.com afterward to rate and review it! I would be so grateful. There are a few review sites specific to audio. One that I've seen work really well, consistently, is Audiobook Boom (now freeaudiobookcodes.com). Again, it's worth testing because different books get different results. Some of the many sites you can check out include the Audiobook Blog, the AudioBook Reviewer, Audiobooks Today, Audiobookworm, and Karen Commins.

- **Enter audiobook-specific awards to gain more credibility for your book and help sell it.** The biggest is probably the Audie Awards from *AudioFile Magazine*. There's also the Independent Audiobook Award for us self-published authors. The IBPA Benjamin Franklin Award also has an audiobook category, which is a well-known and highly respected award in the publishing industry. There are more and more of these types of awards out there, and my feelings about them remain the same: An award win is really what you make of it. In and of itself, it doesn't do much to sell any books. You have to be the one to leverage recognition into credibility, promotion, and sales.

Promotions have been a staple of e-book marketing since the beginnings of BookBub. But there are not as many promotional services for audiobooks, largely because Audible controls the price. You can't set a promotional price for your book if you're using Audible. I think this is part of why more promotional services haven't cropped up yet. But as more authors go wide with their audiobooks (especially after Spotify bought Findaway Voices), you're going to see more opportunities to promote your audiobook at a discounted rate.

We're always talking about the best places to promote books, and we'll keep you up to date on emerging audiobook platforms. Make sure you visit https://selfpromoteandsucceed.com and join our biweekly launch letter, so you get all the news on book-promotion opportunities.

And now, as promised, here's what you need to know as an author about Chirp.

Chirp for Audiobook

Chirp is a sales platform developed by BookBub, and it brings the best audiobook deals right to readers' inboxes. It's simple. You sign up, and then they email you with audiobook deals of the day or the week, along with featured deals curated by BookBub. If you're on the hunt for something in particular, you can specify your favorite genres, authors, or titles, and Chirp will match recommended deals to your interests. The deals are time sensitive, but you can also shop the rest of their audiobook library and buy directly from the site. They also have an app, so you can listen to your audiobook or download it to your device.

While Chirp focuses on helping readers score hot deals, you can find most traditionally published and a ton of self-published audiobooks available for the regular retail price. So, what does that mean for you, dear author?

Chirp's unique distribution model relies on deals, not a credit or subscription model with a bunch of fees. Unlike audiobook services like Audible, a buyer doesn't have to sign up for a service they may or may not use or commit to a pricey monthly plan just to get their hands on one book they want. If your book catches a reader's eye, they can simply purchase the book in the app and start listening. The whole process is really easy.

By joining Chirp's library, you can potentially reach a whole new audience ready to take advantage of a great deal without any hassle, and you're giving your book's discoverability a big boost. Even better, you're not giving up control of your price. With Audible, you don't get to choose the price of your audiobook, but on Chirp, you do. Since you're the one setting the price, you don't have to rely solely on their featured-deal option to offer readers a discount. You can lower your price in the library whenever you want and run your own promotions outside of Chirp as well.

One disadvantage is that you must be partnered with Findaway Voices to sell your audiobook on Chirp and take advantage of Chirp deals as an author. Unfortunately, Findaway Voices does get a small cut of the sale, but that's for their service. For some people, that might be a deal-breaker, and there's no way to sell direct on Chirp to keep all your royalties. You have to go through Findaway Voices.

If that's not a deal-breaker, and you don't mind the limited availability, the process to submit your audiobook to Chirp is easy. And submitting and listing your book as a featured deal is free. Yep, I said "free." We don't get very many breaks like that as authors, so you've got to take advantage of it where you can.

As long as you're not exclusive with ACX, you don't really have anything to lose by submitting to Chirp and broadening your audiobook's audience horizons.

Now that you're armed with what you need to know about marketing audiobooks, we'll look next at some creative book-sales strategies, including how to sell from your website and dig up new sales opportunities.

Chapter Summary

1. Audiobook consumers are an opportunity to reach more people with your book and compete in a market that has far fewer titles.

2. Remember to let people know your book is available in audio format. It's a simple step that adds punch to your outreach and marketing efforts.

3. Audiobook marketing is still new, but there are platforms like Chirp that allow you to do some specific promotions. This requires you to be set up through Findaway Voices, so you can control your audiobook price.

4. Audible doesn't allow you to set your audiobook price, so it's difficult to use for promotions.

CHAPTER 18

CUT OUT THE MIDDLEMAN—SELLING DIRECT TO YOUR READER

RICH DAD POOR DAD STARTED OUT BEING SOLD IN CAR WASHES, AND after the right person found it, momentum grew rapidly.[90] You really won't know where your book will find its audience if you don't try different things.

Using retailers to distribute your book (online or on bookstore shelves) is important, but it's not the only way to grow your reach and make a bigger impact. Sometimes, a little creativity can be the key to getting your book into the hands of more readers through less traditional tactics.

One way to do this is by selling your book directly on your own website, and we'll get to that in just a bit. Another way to do it is to think outside the box about where you can and should sell books—from a table at the

---

90 Chandler Bolt, "SPS 056: How I Sold 46M Copies of My Self Published Book with Robert Kiyosaki (Turning Your Book into a Brand & a Board Game)," Self-Publishing School, March 24, 2023, https://self-publishingschool.com/podcast-056-robert-kiyosaki/.

back of the room at your live events to anywhere your target reader frequents in the real world. I've sold books at my dentist office, my CrossFit gym, and at the library. I know authors who have sold books in garden stores, chiropractic offices, gift shops, and travel agencies. You are never limited to bookstores or Amazon.

Every single step you take in book marketing can lead you to newer, cooler, and bigger opportunities. Let's start with selling direct and get to the more creative ideas next.

Selling Books Direct

Selling books to readers cuts out the middleman, which means you can make more money and potentially build relationships. But there are lots of pros and cons to consider.

When you sell direct, first of all, you can charge any price that you like. Of course, that doesn't mean anyone will pay it, but you are in control of the price. You can also offer incentives for readers to buy books.

For example, if you wanted a print copy of *Self-Publish and Succeed*, I could bundle in the audiobook version of the book. When you sell direct to buyers, you also get data, like their contact information and the links that brought them to your website.

Now, how to do this? For a long time, we used Lulu Press to sell *Self-Publish and Succeed* at https://selfpublishandsucceed.com. It was a great setup because Shopify was the cart, Lulu printed and shipped the books, and we collected the data and money from the sale.

This wasn't terribly lucrative, however. After we paid for ad costs, we paid Shopify, PayPal, and Lulu their respective printing, shipping, and merchant fees. That said, once it was all set up, which was a bit of a pain, it was very hands off, and the data was delivered directly to our customer relationship management system.

It was also a simple way to handle direct sales because I ran ads. It allowed me to track conversions from those ads, so we could turn off unprofitable ads and add more money to the ones that were converting. But even more important, it allowed us to get the contact information of book buyers, so we could send them emails and build long-term relationships.

Amazon never tells you who buys your book, so it's much better to end a conversion with a contact. Building the long-term relationships was especially important because we barely ever broke even on the books after ad costs, and that's okay because the ultimate goal is that somebody reads the book and then wants to hire Book Launchers or take one of our courses.

We stopped using Lulu halfway through 2022 because they raised their print prices several times and then announced a further increase and also increased their shipping rates in the U.S. This brought the cost of printing and shipping a single print book to more than $16 per copy, plus we had to pay Shopify and PayPal fees. Even if I sold a book for $20, I was not going to break even, so there was no margin left for ad costs or any profit at all if somebody just came direct to the website and bought the book.

To make it even worse, we got a lot of complaints because Lulu was taking two weeks to deliver a book to a buyer. We even had somebody submit a chargeback complaint to PayPal against us because they hadn't received their book after 12 days.

In this day and age where almost anything ships and arrives within two days (when there aren't pandemic-driven supply chain problems), that is completely unacceptable. We had several angry emails from people saying they would never trust our service if we can't send a book out in a few days. Keep that in mind, too, if you decide to do this on your own—it's a commitment to quick turnarounds.

The good news is, the alternative is cheaper, but it's more labor intensive.

We're currently buying cases of books from Ingram at a net cost of $5.44 per book, plus our shipping cost. When we buy a carton of 30 and ship it to an address in the U.S., our shipping is roughly $50, so our cost per book works out to about $7 per book doing it this way.

If we print through KDP Print, we cut a dollar off the top for each copy. Now the trick is that we then have to mail the book to the buyer, which is done via media mail, and our operations manager has to drop them off at the post office. To make shipping from home a little easier, we use Stamps.com, which allows us to print labels at home, so it's nice and easy.

It costs us $3.49 to print a media mail label and then have it ready for the post. Doing it this way costs us just under $11 to send a book, plus the time it takes to print the label and ship them off.

If you're selling lots of books, like hundreds and hundreds every month direct, it might be worth doing a large print order to get a discount, especially if you're doing a free-plus-shipping funnel and you're charging something like $7.99 for the shipping.

Once you sell a lot of books, you can consider warehouse options, but this is for high-volume direct sales (more than 1,000 per month). The only other way that I really know of that will work is to access your KDP account and ship author copies direct to buyers. I don't love this option for domestic buyers because the book comes from Amazon when somebody thought they were buying it from you. But I like doing this for international buyers because it's much more cost effective than shipping a book from the U.S. to another country.

Personally, if somebody's buying a book direct from me, I would like to have it look as if it's coming direct from me. You may also want to include a card, promotional materials, or stickers, and you can't do that if you're using Amazon.

Direct to your reader also means selling at trade show events and other places, where you're actually taking credit card information or cash from the buyer. If you do this, I strongly encourage you to send receipts via email so you build a connection and can follow up on their purchase, ask for a review, or make some sort of an upsell offer.

If you aren't doing that, you at least should invite the reader to join your email list at the time of purchase.

Stripe and Square are great mobile payment apps to handle purchases at events, and you can automate email receipts for buyers, which allows you to follow up on the purchase.

If you sell direct in person, you should have cash on hand for change and take that into account when you price your books. It's probably easier to sell your book for a round number to avoid needing to handle change.

Selling E-books and Audiobooks Direct

Now, that's just print books. For selling e-books direct to buyers, Book-Funnel is the choice most authors make. They have a robust system that allows you to do this and still keep a lot of control.

They also recently announced an integration with ThriveCart, which solves issues for more sophisticated authors selling direct who may want to offer upsells as part of every book purchase. ThriveCart also has a system that automatically calculates sales tax, along with other features.

ThriveCart comes with a heftier integration fee, but this might make sense, depending on the model for your author business. Other platforms that many indie authors use to sell e-books direct include Payhip, Gumroad, and E-junkie, to name a few.

Payhip could be a great option if you want to build an entire funnel of offerings, like courses or membership sites. I've not used them personally, but I know some authors who do, and they're pretty happy with how the system works.

Selling audiobooks direct has not been very easy to date, but services coming on board now may make it easier. The most exciting for authors is BookFunnel. Other services, like Gumroad, which podcasters use for membership sales, could be rigged to work for it. Supporting Cast, which is a podcasting platform, is getting into the audiobook-sales space. Connecting it with Stripe allows you to sell your audiobook direct to listeners, and their platform creates a secure copy of your audiobook for that buyer so they can listen to the book as they would a podcast.

It's easy to get excited about selling direct, but it's extra work, and of course, it's totally on you to send the audience to buy your work. Make sure it's worth it by assessing the advantages and how they align with your bigger-picture goals. For example, if you're using paid ads for platform building or using your book as the first step in your bigger business funnel, this is a great tactic.

The upside of using Amazon and Barnes & Noble is that they bring buyers to their platforms, and if your book gets in front of the right buyer, it could sell itself. Their platform also has buyer trust. When you sell direct, you have to make sure you can drive the buyers to your pages or your platform and that you can establish enough trust that someone will pull out their credit card without knowing who you are.

As part of brokering your own sales, you need to build a lot of elements, including a sales page. This page needs:

- images,
- a payment method connected to a bank, credit card, or service such as PayPal,
- a privacy policy,
- a return policy, and
- sales copy.

You also need to figure out if you need to charge sales tax. In most cases, you probably don't unless you're selling more than $400 of books in any one state in a year. Some of the platforms like BookFunnel make setup more straightforward, but it still takes work, and I recommend you work with an accountant.

Selling in Person—How to Prepare for Author Signings and Selling Books at the Back of the Room

When you sell books directly, you need to look like the professional author that you are. Here's a quick checklist, so you can make sure you've got what you need to succeed:

- **Sharpies for signing those books.** One of the best parts of selling physical books direct to readers is that people ask for the book to be signed. People love having signed copies! Bring fine-point Sharpies or whatever you prefer. You can use a pen, but a Sharpie looks official.

- **Sign-up sheet for your newsletter.** Do this old school. Put up a sign offering your reader magnet, and provide a sheet of paper with a spot for their name and an email address. I've tried QR codes, but unless it's at a conference that gives you attendees' names and email addresses automatically, it's not going to work well. I've tried texting systems and so many other ways for people to connect with me and get on my newsletter list, but nothing works as well as just getting them to pull out the pen and write it down. One other thing you can do is have an iPad there for them to enter in their name and email address right on the spot. Either way, don't expect them to do anything after they walk away because few will.

- **Pens for people to use to sign up for your newsletter or make notes.** Bring lots because they grow legs.

- (Optional) **A display shelf** or way to stand the books up, so the covers face out. This can be a cheap magazine stand or some other fancier book stand. We often have a box that we put down on a table and cover with a white tablecloth. We lean books against the box, and also use book stands we bought online for a low cost.

- Depending on the event, you should have **at least 20 books on hand and/or a QR code** that takes purchasers to a universal link to buy the e-book. Also provide a QR code for buying the audio version that you hopefully have for your book as well.

- **Table cover to hide the ugly event tables.** I would go with black because I can't tell you how many coffee stains are on our white one. Your tablecloth doesn't have to be branded, but when you do events at libraries and bookstores, it should look nicer than the ones the event is likely to provide. You can buy a cover at Michaels, a local craft store, or an event store for a pretty low price. You can also order a branded one from Vistaprint or services that make banners. (I'll list some in a second.) If you order a branded one, make sure it has your website on it.

- (Optional) **Stand-up vertical banner with a call to action** that will attract your ideal reader. You could put your cover on it, but you may want to make it stand out in some other way because people will already see your book cover on your table. Instead, have a great blurb or an endorsement and the formats and logos of where people can buy your book.

- **Way to collect payment.** I would recommend a cash box with change (and a receipt book) as well as a way to take credit cards. You can use Square or Stripe to collect credit cards with your mobile phone. So many people don't carry cash anymore, so this is really important.

I use BoothPop! for all my banner needs. I just have really enjoyed working with them, and they have a graphic designer who works with you, so you don't necessarily have to hire or outsource that job. They're a little pricier than Vistaprint, which holds a 50% off sale twice a year.

You can have other branded items like postcards, pens, bookmarks, or even fancier merchandise like journals, water bottles, or T-shirts to give away or sell. It's not necessary, but if you have a business behind your book, it can be good exposure.

Promotional Partners Are Everywhere—Are You Looking?

I met a woman who ran a gift basket company and liked to find a really great book or two to include in her arrangements. She said she was often able to strike great deals with self-published authors for buying 100 books at a time. She said she always sourced the books on her own based on the basket theme (new-mom gift basket, graduation gift basket, wedding gift basket), and she had to have a decent margin between what she paid and the perceived value of the book.

That's one idea. Here are some other out-of-the-box ideas that you can use to sell books or open the door to new opportunities:

- Consider companies you discuss in your book in a positive light. Write that list down, and make sure they know about your book. Speak with them about how they can leverage your book to their advantage, which will also likely help you with your book sales and promotion.

- Try placing your book "for sale" in stores. This means you leave a copy behind. You're out the cost of a book, but you might sell it. One of our authors is currently approaching all the running-focused retail stores in his state. When that is done, it will certainly be something I cover on BookLaunchers.tv because it's going to be a great lesson-learned piece! We've had authors sell books at chiropractic offices, travel agencies, gyms, and other places of business that were a fit for their books.

- Pair up with some other local authors, and set up a book table at your local farmers' market or craft fair. The expense of a table isn't as high as you might think, and if you share it with other authors, it could be a fun and affordable way to sell books. The best part is that it doesn't matter if you are all in different genres … people will come to the table because they see books!

- When your child's school or sports team or your nonprofit group asks for donations for silent auctions, you can give them your book along with something else relevant to the subject of your book. My idea might be a "budding-author kit" complete with our journal, mug, pen, this book or *Self-Publish and Succeed*, and maybe even a one-hour call with me or a writing coach.

- One author I spoke with said he was planning to take books to all of his kids' football games because the parents of high school students were his target market.

- What establishments do you frequent? In *Self-Publish and Succeed*, I tell the story of an author who wrote her book at a tire shop, and the tire shop promoted her book when it came out. If you have a regular coffee shop, restaurant, gym, massage therapist, bowling alley, or other popular venue, be brave and let them know that you have a book coming out and that you're looking for places to display, sell, and promote it. This is how my dentist and my CrossFit gym displayed and sold my book!

- If there is a product your book promotes, or it provides a good cross-promotion opportunity, why not reach out to the company that owns the product? This can be especially good if it's owned by a smaller company seeking to grow. They might also be looking for great promotional opportunities. You may find a cool partnership.

- What about selling your book new on a place like AbeBooks, eBay, or Etsy where you'd normally see used books?

Always remember it's never one thing you do that leads to the results, it's *all the things* you do that combine to create momentum and uncover the opportunity you didn't even know you wanted!

Getting creative with your book sales and how your book can help you reach your professional goals is one thing, but what do you do if your book isn't selling, or your sales trickle off? In the next chapter, I'll walk you through Book Launchers' signature process for how to boost flagging book sales.

Chapter Summary

1. If your goal is to build a business on the back end of book sales (especially if you're running paid ads), selling direct is a savvy way to collect contact information and offer upsells after someone buys your book.

2. Selling books in person requires a little extra prep so you can look like a professional. Having items like permanent markers, a tablecloth, a way to collect and process payments, copies of your book, and an enthusiastic attitude can go a long way.

3. Selling direct takes more effort to set up, and there are more logistics involved (like how to deliver your book to readers), but it can be worth it to make more money and learn about your buyers.

4. Get creative about how you reach readers with your book. You don't need to sell your book in bookstores—in fact, having a book in unusual places almost always gets it noticed. Whether it's a running store, garden store, gym, or a specialty gift shop, you can find a cool place to get your book in your readers' hands.

CHAPTER 19

WHAT SHOULD I DO IF MY BOOK ISN'T SELLING?

THIS CHAPTER IS DEVOTED TO SOMETHING THAT HAPPENS TO NEARLY ALL authors at some point: Your book stops selling. It's hit Cricketsville.

Time to scrap it and move on to the next thing, right?

Well, maybe. Writing a new book will almost certainly make your past work sell when you market the new book. I can't tell you how many times a talk or interview about *Self-Publish and Succeed* generated sales for my previous two books. It happens all the time.

But let's not give up on your book that's collecting dust just yet.

You've put a lot of time, money, and energy into making your book a quality product, a calling card, or a tool that helps you achieve your personal, career, or business goals. It'd be a shame not to leverage your book to its full potential.

In his book *Perennial Seller*, Ryan Holiday writes, "No one can guarantee that your project will be a success, but it can be safely said that if you quit on it before your audience does, it's guaranteed to fail."[91]

If you create a really great book with a clear audience and an offer that should appeal to that audience, there's plenty you can do to get your sales numbers up, and that starts with taking a hard look at your marketing strategy. This is a process we do for our clients at Book Launchers as needed (we call it a "zero-sales audit"), and I'm going to teach you how to do it too.

Here's my step-by-step guide for how to analyze where things are going wrong with your sales numbers and how to fix them: (If you run ads, the ad data gives you some of the information you need. If not, use your own judgment.)

Step One: Metadata

First, look at your metadata. To begin, focus on your keywords. Did you pick the right ones for your book? Or maybe you did initially, but the dial has moved since then, and now they need a refresh. Maybe they aren't what buyers are searching for right now.

My favorite tool to check out keywords is Publisher Rocket, but there are other tools, like KDSPY, Keyword Surfer, and Google Keyword Planner. If you need more help, head back to chapter 9 to review how to make the most of your keywords. You can update your book description and the actual keyword boxes, but don't go wild changing everything.

I highly recommend you change one keyword or two max at a time, and then give it a few weeks to see what happens. If you change a bunch of things all at once, you won't be able to identify the change that made the impact!

---

91 Ryan Holiday, *Perennial Seller: The Art of Making and Marketing Work That Lasts* (Portfolio, 2017), 203.

Second, review the categories under which you chose to list your book. Use Publisher Rocket to see which categories your book appears in on Amazon or try the website BKLNK.com. (That is not a typo—it's just a really weird website link.)

Did your book get moved to a poor-performing or off-topic category without your knowledge? It happens! Also look at how your categories themselves sell. If you ended up in a weird category, contact KDP support to adjust the category if it's on Amazon. Alternately, if the category sells tremendously well, there may be a ton of competition that's burying your book. It may simply be that your book needs to be moved to a new category or two where it can be a bigger fish in a smaller pond.

If adjusting things here solves your problem, wonderful! If not, move along to step two.

Step Two: Amazon Ad Performance

Next, how are your Amazon ads performing? Remember, Amazon's author dashboard gives you a wealth of useful sales data. I recommend having at least 90 days' worth of ad data on hand for analysis if you're having trouble with sales and want to see if something isn't clicking (so to speak) with your ads. This allows you to get a better sense of how the ads really perform and lets you draw reliable conclusions.

First, are you getting impressions and clicks? ("Impressions" refers to the number of times your ad is displayed and hopefully viewed, whether it gets clicked on or not.) If you're getting impressions but not clicks, the first thing to look at is your book cover. How does your cover compare to others within your same categories or your desired categories? When you're comparing covers, look at the quality of the cover design and commonalities in design elements, like imagery and text. Are the images and text on your cover compelling and eye-catching? If you find that your cover doesn't stack up to its competition, it may be time for a cover redesign.

Alternately, maybe you're getting clicks but no conversions (actual sales to people who visit your book's page or who click on your ads). If this is the case, I recommend taking a hard look at your Amazon product page. First, look to see if you should make changes to the book's description. Does the description accurately sell the book and clearly lay out its hook? If not, start there.

Next, are you using a quality author bio and photo? Compare your bio and photo to those of other authors in your category if you're not sure. It's also worth looking at the book's price compared to other books in its category. If it's set too high or too low compared to the competition, that could be a problem.

Look at your book's "also bought" section. This is a good way to see who purchased your book and their reading interests. If those interests don't seem to align with your book, make sure you're targeting the right reader in your marketing. You need to teach Amazon to present your book to your ideal reader. Also be sure to double- and triple-check to make sure there are no formatting, image, link, or text errors on the book page. A typo or a broken link can be a real turnoff for some book shoppers. Read your reviews because this will often appear in the negative comments.

Adding nicer and more compelling images or encouraging readers to include video clips to the page can be helpful. Finally, look at adding endorsements or editorial reviews. This can be a big boost to your book's credibility. Having at least three endorsements or editorial reviews is a good place to start.

Of course, the other big thing to look at when auditing your book page is your reviews. The book-marketing experts at Written Word Media have this to say about the importance of reviews: "In our research, we found that the number of reviews is more important than the overall average review rating (as long as your average rating is over 3.5 stars). This means having 25 reviews with an average rating of 4.0 is better than having 5 reviews with an average rating of 5.0 stars."[92] Increasing your number of reviews is the #1 thing that converts ads to sales. That's because a high review count helps convince readers who are deciding between your book and someone else's that *yours* is the one they want to buy.

If everything covered under these first two steps seems really solid, but your book still isn't selling, it's time to look beyond your marketing data and into how *you* have been performing.

Step Three: Your Design and Product Page

Take a look at the design elements to your book. From your cover to your description to your A+ content, they should all work together as a cohesive brand and deliver the value of your book to the potential buyer.

How does your cover compare to others in your category, particularly the bestsellers? Does your book description have keywords and sell in a succinct and memorable way? Have you optimized your Amazon product page, including your Amazon Author Central page, your editorial reviews, A+ content, and more? Look at your book and the product page as a potential buyer would, and make sure it's got everything it needs to convince readers your book is for them.

Step Four: Interviews

Sometimes when an author lands a lot of media and podcasts, but their book isn't selling, we review their interviews. Often we find interviews haven't aired yet because they have been recorded months in advance of their air date. In other cases, the author failed to create curiosity or sell massive value in their interview, so even if someone watched or listened, they were unlikely to take action to connect or get the book.

---

92 Clayton Noblit, "Five Steps to Sell More Books on Amazon," Written Word Media, September 7, 2020, https://www.writtenwordmedia.com/sell-more-books-on-amazon/.

Remember your big-picture goal for your book. If you want to be a speaker, are you treating every opportunity as if booking agents for Fortune 500 companies are listening?

Are you interviewing well, being concise, telling great stories, using sound bites, and building relationships with the hosts? Are you consistently driving traffic back to your website and your email list, freebie value-add download, and/or your newsletter? Do you mention your book in interviews and clearly communicate its hook, using carefully constructed and practiced sound bites? If your answer to any of these questions is no, then it's time to change your approach and drum up some new media coverage.

At Book Launchers, we include mock interviews in our media training with our authors. This is something you can do on your own with a helpful friend, family member, or colleague. The more you practice being interviewed, the more comfortable and polished you'll be when the real interviews roll around. Check out my tips for interviews in media and podcasts back in chapter 13, if you haven't already.

In a nutshell, here are some points to hit in every interview:

- Answer the interviewer's questions succinctly, and make sure that what you're saying makes sense.
- Mention your lead magnet (that cool freebie download you offer on your website to hook readers into joining your email list)!
- Find a good place to mention your book if the interviewer doesn't bring it up (a good interviewer will), including the book's hook and your own expertise related to the book's topic.
- Mention where to find the book if folks are interested in buying it.

Nailing your interviews is a great way to drum up sales and grow your platform. Speaking of your platform ...

Step Five: Author Platform

The next thing to look at if your book isn't selling is your platform as an author. Has it grown? If it has, are you maximizing the opportunity with those new contacts to sell books, get reviews, and spread the word?

If you're not growing your platform, take a good look at the elements in your platform, starting with your website.

First up, how's your website looking? Do you have an easy-to-remember landing page (home page URL) for media interviews? Are you offering that value-add free download (or lead magnet) we've discussed? If not, it's time to add one to help drive traffic to your site. And once you have people there, you want them to sign up for your email list, so make sure the way to sign up is easily accessible. I also recommend a dedicated page for your book on your website with easy links to buy your book. Check out my tips in chapter 4 for using a universal book link. This is such a helpful tool for selling online!

And now back to that email list you've cultivated through your website. You're *using it*, right? Regularly? How consistently are you distributing content? It doesn't necessarily have to be every week, but once you decide the right frequency of newsletters and emails, stick to it! Also make sure that when you send out emails to your list you promote your book regularly, including a link to buy the book.

Finally, if you've been building one, how's your social media platform shaping up?

For starters, make sure that your book is showcased in bios, headers, or elsewhere on your pages. The most important thing here, though, is to make sure you consistently publish compelling content. I gave you some great tips, so head back to chapter 5 if you're stumped.

One of my most effective tips is to batch content so that you store up a whole bunch of goodies to post to social media once or twice a week for the next month. If you're producing video content (and you should be!), this is especially helpful because prepping to shoot video (hair, make-up, equipment setup, etc.) can suck up a lot of time. By shooting several videos at once, you maximize the value of that setup time.

Step Six: Are You Selling Your Book in the Right Place?

Finally, it's worth considering whether you're trying to sell your book in the wrong place(s). A lot of authors ask me, "Is Amazon the best place to sell my book?" The answer is maybe. But maybe not.

If your book covers a very niche topic, for instance, it's possible that your target audience doesn't buy that type of book on Amazon. You may be barking up the wrong tree if you've made Amazon your primary (or only) marketplace. Your target readers may be more likely to buy the book at a conference or receive it as a gift from a corporate sponsor who's placed a bulk order.

As an example, we've seen some of our authors at Book Launchers write books on niche topics for a specific professional audience (for instance, educators). These authors may do okay selling on Amazon, but they tend to do much better selling directly to people in their network, who sometimes buy books in bulk. In this case, sales on Amazon can grow over time through ads, but selling in bulk to managers and executives can best reach a target audience that might not think they need to learn what's in your book until it's given to them by a higher-up.

Regardless of whether your book topic is niche or broad, or somewhere in between, it's always worth considering other channels. Chapter 16 gives you a lot of great info on where to look, including live events, panels, conferences, author readings or Q&As, or speaking engagements.

Ad services other than Amazon can also be a great resource. BookBub is definitely one to look at. Niche industry magazines or websites related to your topic can also be great places to spend your ad budget.

There's No One Step That Will Solve Sales Issues

I know you want *the* answer to your book-sales issues. I wish I could tell you it was that easy.

We had a client get angry with us well after launch because his book had sold only 350 books (and almost all those sales were around launch). He didn't do anything we've talked about in this book to continue to make his book move. He believed that his book was so great it would sell itself and that we must have failed him. The reality is a lot harder to face: A book doesn't sell itself, even if it's great. Nor will doing only one thing be all it takes to make the vast majority of books reach their potential.

It's almost always a combination of strategies executed over time that result in momentum. In fact, book sales may not be the most important metric. *Self-Publish and Succeed* isn't selling thousands and thousands of copies a year, but it's helping to build Book Launchers. Just this week, three potential clients read it, and that was the reason they wanted to work with us.

That is what matters to me more than book sales—the impact the book has on Book Launchers.

For fun, I asked each person how they came to read the book. One of them got the book free at an event where we gave out books at our booth. One found my YouTube channel when searching for how to turn a book into a course, ended up watching a bunch of videos, saw that there was a book, and bought it from the video mention. The other one was searching for how to hire a ghostwriter, landed on an article on our website, and saw we had an audiobook. He downloaded and listened to it on the same day!

The fact that they bought the book or got it free doesn't matter to me as much as the fact that we had three potential authors come to work with us in one week as a result. And it wasn't any one path that got the book into their hands either. If your book isn't selling *or* getting you the results you want in your business, go back to what you aim to achieve most. What should you do with your book to get those specific results?

Do you need to do more book-specific promotions, or should you be doing more corporate outreach or local speaking engagements? Your book is a wonderful tool, and these steps I've outlined will help you diagnose where you may have issues, but sales is not the most important metric for most nonfiction authors. It's the impact you want to have and whether your book is getting you there or not.

When in doubt as to what else will help you in all your initiatives, work on growing your review count and doing something every single day to move your book into the hands of people who can advance your goals. This could be putting out consistent weekly content through email and social media and making sure to feature your book and where folks can buy it. Focus on driving readers to your website with your freebie download, and get them to sign up for your email list, where you can eventually upsell them your book if they haven't bought it already. Also try different places to sell your book to your target audience, whether that's on Amazon or a niche industry magazine or website.

From there, tracking your numbers on an ongoing basis each month is incredibly helpful. This way you can continue to see how well you leverage marketing and media opportunities and how well your overall marketing efforts work. You can do this through:

- email subscriptions and open/click-through rates,
- Google analytics,
- media or partnership inquiries,
- reviews,

- social media subscribers, and
- website traffic.

If you regularly manage and update your pages and your metadata, you're already doing some of the maintenance work needed to boost your sales and reach. Keep it up, and before you know it, you'll reach the goals you've set for your book and your business.

Remember, until you have an audience of your own, the most powerful way you can supercharge your sales, impact, platform, and income is by connecting to other people's audiences. This means you have to get out of your author shell. Building your network of companies, brands, people, and influencers who have your reader in their audiences will uncover massive opportunities over time.

Keep reading, and let's look ahead to what the future holds for you as an author.

Chapter Summary

There are six key areas to review if your book is not selling:

1. Amazon Ad performance
2. Book design
3. Interview performance (how well you leverage your media wins and other opportunities)
4. Metadata
5. Platform leveraging (whether you do enough)
6. Sales locations (the right places with the right product)

CHAPTER 20

FUTURE YOU WILL THANK YOU

WHEN I LEFT MY JOB AT REALNET CANADA YEARS AGO TO PURSUE REAL estate full-time, my coworker Connie gave me the book *Oh, the Places You'll Go!* by Dr. Seuss.[93] It seemed like a funny gift at the time, but I've reread the book so many times, I can't even count. It's full of memorable lessons and quotes that can also be applied to the experience of marketing a book.

Consider this:

"Fame you'll be famous, as famous as can be, with everyone watching you win on TV, Except when they don't because sometimes they won't."

"And will you succeed? Yes! You will, indeed! (98 and 3/4 percent guaranteed.)"

Book marketing is a long journey full of twists and turns. You won't always know where to go. You won't always see the light. You'll do things that work and many that don't.

---

93 Dr. Seuss, *Oh, The Places You'll Go* (New York: Random House, 1990).

I hope you now know that the most important aspect of marketing your book is looking beyond your sales numbers. Your book is currency. It is a tool, a vehicle to bigger and better things for you and your career, your business, and your reach as an influencer, a business, and a brand. While I hope your book sells well, and you're thrilled, all is not lost if it doesn't!

Even before you publish and market your book, the process of writing it helps you to hone your message. You can go on to repurpose that content to work for you in new ways, creating new income streams and new ways to grow your platform.

I've seen this in action with my book *Self-Publish and Succeed*, and we've seen it time and time again at Book Launchers with the success of our clients.

Look at Martin Holland, whose book, *The Profit Problem*, netted him a six-figure consulting deal from one of his readers.[94]

Education consultant Lorea Martinez's book on social-emotional learning, *Teaching with the HEART in Mind*, put her in the perfect position to reach out to her network.[95] She lined up workshops around the country, using her book as a curriculum for teachers and educators.

Or Robert Belle. After his book *Blow the Lid Off* came out, he pitched himself to TED Global Ideas to do a talk that dovetailed with the book's content.[96] His presentation has *more than two million views*.[97]

Carol Sanford, another author, has been endorsed by Tom Peters, and he's even writing the foreword for her next book, *No More Gold Stars*.[98]

---

94 Martin T. Holland, *The Profit Problem: They Say I Make Money, So Why Don't I Have Any?* (Anneal Publishing, 2020).

95 Lorea Martinez, *Teaching with the HEART in Mind: A Complete Educator's Guide to Social Emotional Learning* (Brisca Publishing, 2021).

96 Robert A. Belle, *Blow the Lid Off: Reclaim Your Stolen Creativity, Increase Your Income, and Let Your Light Shine!* (Simply You Publishing, 2020).

97 Belle, "The Emotions Behind Your Money Habits."

98 Carol Sanford, *No More Gold Stars: Regenerating Capacity to Think for Ourselves* (InterOctave, forthcoming).

That's amazing!

For these authors, their books made amazing, career-defining successes possible.

As important, many authors say that the greatest results of a book release
are the emails they get from people who thank them because their books
made a difference in their lives. You don't have to sell a million books to
make that kind of impact.

Maybe your goal as an author was to be known as a thought leader or to
build a business as a speaker, and now your book has put you on that path.
Along the way, remember that changing lives is fulfilling in a way that no
dollar figure ever is.

As you ride the emotional roller coaster that is your author life, remember
what it is you want your book to do for you. Where do you want to be in
five years? Or 10? How can your book help you get there? And what consistent actions can you take to market your book on an ongoing basis to get
that ball rolling and *keep* it rolling?

Because that is really the kicker. You're not done promoting your book *ever*.
The moment you stop putting your book out where new people can discover it through ads, promos, media appearances, social media, and more
is the moment it fades off into the distance. You may be sick of promoting
it, but everyday there is a new person (or many people) who hasn't heard of
you yet and could use your book … if only they knew about it.

If you think your book is going to sell itself, I'm here to tell you, it's not.
Some authors have big hits out of the gate, but they've worked for years
or even decades to build an audience before their book launched. Many
authors experience the true wins years after their book came out. Whether
your book sells or you're not hitting your goals yet, the missing piece is
author *action*.

Keep your big-picture goal in mind, and do something every day that moves you one step closer to achieving it.

If your most important goal is to:

- **Start a speaking career.** Use the credibility your book gives you and the content you've worked so hard to curate to land your first speaking engagements. Record them, learn from them, and pitch yourself for many more.

- **Grow a speaking career.** Send your book to every organization at which you've ever spoken, along with a nice letter about your new content. You can even let them know your rates are going up now that you have this new piece of expertise! As you negotiate contracts, boost your event fee by offering to have them buy copies of your book for attendees.

- **Build your platform.** Use your book to land media appearances, podcast interviews, and guest articles (having a link to a free download so you get email addresses), and run ads that sell your book directly to readers so you get email contact information.

- **Become a known and recognized expert in your industry.** Network with all the organizations, companies, and people who have credibility in your industry. Leverage them for endorsements, promotions, and other opportunities to get in front of their audiences. Create that know, like, and trust feeling on podcasts, video streams, and industry events. Leverage your book to do all of this, whether that involves giving the book away for free, sharing its content, or using media and awards to gain attention.

- **Sell books.** Make sure you've got your metadata on point, run e-book sales, Amazon ads, BookBub features, and Chirp submissions, and consider promotions in newsletters. Find a way to sell directly in person and online. And as you build your platform, consistently solicit reviews.

Of course, that is an overly simplified list of what we've covered in this giant book on marketing, but it's easy to see how you can find one thing to do every day to move yourself closer to your goal. If you do that every day, five days a week, you'll have done 260 things to move your marketing forward in a year. Imagine—even if that was outreach to one person a day—you will absolutely uncover some opportunities (unless you're book bombing!).

Marketing your book is something you have to keep doing. There's simply no way around it. Remember, it's your book baby, and you must nurture and care for it so it grows up big and strong.

And you don't have to do it alone! Flip to the back of this book for more information about what Book Launchers can do for you, your book, and your author platform, and how to get in touch with us. After you have posted a review of this book (hint!), please give us a call, drop us an email, or head over to our YouTube channel. I am excited to hear from you, even if it's just to tell me how something you learned in this book helped you along the way.

You worked long and hard to make your book the best possible version of itself, a calling card that opens doors for you into a future you may not have even dreamed of. Now it's up to you to position this invaluable resource of yours for maximum success. Keep driving for it. When you reach one goal, set the next one even higher.

I know you can do it.

And I can't wait to see where you go from here.

ACKNOWLEDGMENTS

THE YEAR I WROTE THIS BOOK WAS PROBABLY THE HARDEST YEAR OF MY life and business. Despite the exhausting and emotionally challenging year, I did find myself being given several gifts. One of the most precious gifts was the support of my team at Book Launchers. As the year went from rough waters to turbulent seas, they navigated a restructuring, company legal challenges, and then they ran Book Launchers for three months without me while I sorted out my immigration and work authorization issues. On top of that, they finished the book for me. I couldn't deal with the book on top of everything else, so they brought in a writer to finish the book. My team carried it through editing, design, and cover, only consulting me for the most important decisions. Without them, this book would be launching in another year—or maybe not at all.

Everyone should have a team as amazing as I do because they can get a lot done when you can't. Actually, if you're planning to write and market your own non-fiction book, you can have mine for your project. They won't run your company for you if you can't, but they can carry you through writing, editing, design, and marketing. Set up a book positioning call with us at www.booklaunchers.com/application.

I'd also like to give a really big shout out to my YouTube Besties at BookLaunchers.tv. Thank you for showing up for the livestreams, commenting the day a video is released, and just making it fun to create content. You know who you are and I do too! And I give thanks to you every single Tuesday and Friday when a new video is released.

Made in the USA
Las Vegas, NV
11 October 2023

78921205R00177